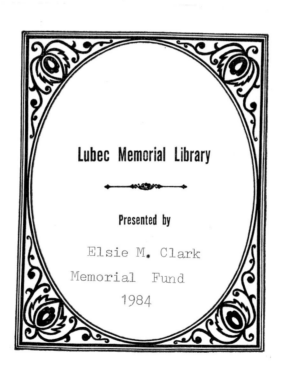

*Jack Tars*
*and Commodores*

the East Indies to take command of a Sloop of War there. —

Should I attempt to do justice, by representation
ve and good Conduct of all my Officers & Crew, during t
I should fail in the attempt; therefore suffice it to say,
of their Conduct was such as to merit my highest encom
to recommend the Officers particularly to the Notice
as also the unfortunate Seamen who were wound
of those Brave Men who fell in the Action. —

The great distance from our own
perfect Wreck we made the Enemies Frigate, forbid
attempting to take her to the United States, and not consi
to trust her into a Port of Brazils, particularly S.t Sa
will perceive by the enclosed Papers N.o 1. 2 & 3. I had
but burning her, which I did on the 31.st Ult.o af
all the Prisoners and their Baggage, which was very
having one Boat left (out of 8) and not one left
Java —

On Blowing up the Frigate Java, I proce
lace, where I have landed all the Prisoners on their Par
to England and there remain until regularly exchange
to serve in their professional Capacities in any place
manner whatever against the United States of Am
until

# Jack Tars and Commodores

## The American Navy, 1783–1815

*William M. Fowler, Jr.*

HOUGHTON MIFFLIN COMPANY

BOSTON

1984

*Also by William M. Fowler, Jr.*

William Ellery: A Rhode Island Politico
and Lord of Admiralty

Rebels Under Sail: The American
Navy During the Revolution

The American Revolution: Changing Perspectives
(edited, with Wallace Coyle)

The Baron of Beacon Hill:
A Biography of John Hancock

Copyright © 1984 by William M. Fowler, Jr.

Library of Congress Cataloging in Publication Data

Fowler, William M., date
Jack tars and commodores.

Bibliography: p.
Includes index.
1. United States.  Navy — History — 18th century.
2. United States.  Navy — History — 19th century.  3. United
States.  Navy — History — War with France, 1798–1800.
4. United States.  Navy — History — Tripolitan War, 1801–
1805.  5. United States.  Navy — History — War of 1812.
I. Title.
VA58.4.F69  1984      359'.00973      83-26500
ISBN 0-395-35314-9

Printed in the United States of America

v  10  9  8  7  6  5  4  3  2  1

*To Alison and Nathaniel*

# Contents

# *Illustrations*

*Frontispiece:* Captain William Bainbridge to the Secretary of the Navy, describing the USS *Constitution*'s victory over the HMS *Java*, 3 January 1813 (Courtesy National Archives, Washington, D.C.)

## *Following page 96*

"Battle of Tripoli," 3 August 1804, by Michele Felice Corné (Courtesy United States Naval Academy Museum)

"Blowing Up of the Fire Ship *Intrepid* in Tripoli Harbor, 1 September 1804" (Courtesy Franklin Delano Roosevelt Library, Hyde Park, New York)

Lines of the United States Frigate *Philadelphia* (Courtesy Naval Historical Center, Washington, D.C.)

"Loss of U.S. Frigate *Philadelphia*, 31 October 1803", by Charles Denoon (Courtesy Franklin Delano Roosevelt Library, Hyde Park, New York)

"Perry's Victory on Lake Erie, 10 September 1813", by T. Birch. A somewhat romanticized view of the moment when Perry transferred his command from *Lawrence* to *Niagara*. (Courtesy Franklin Delano Roosevelt Library, Hyde Park, New York)

Lines of the United States Schooner (later Brig) *Vixen* (Courtesy Naval Historical Center, Washington, D.C.)

Lines of the United States Frigates of *Constellation* class (Courtesy Naval Historical Center, Washington, D.C.)

Lines of the United States Frigates of *Constitution* class (Courtesy Naval Historical Center, Washington, D.C.)

Lines of the United States Frigate *Boston* (Courtesy Naval Historical Center, Washington, D.C.)

"Huzza for the American Navy!" (Courtesy Massachusetts Historical Society, Boston, Massachusetts)

James Lawrence by Gilbert Stuart (Courtesy Naval Photographic Center)

Frigate *Chesapeake* by Francis Muller (Courtesy Naval Photographic Center)

Joshua Barney by Charles W. Peale (Courtesy Naval Photographic Center)
John Rodgers by Gilbert Stuart (Courtesy Naval Photographic Center)

*Following page 224*

Charles Stewart. Artist unknown (Courtesy Naval Photographic Center)
"Battle of Lake Borgne" by Thomas Hornbrook (Courtesy Naval Photographic Center)
David Porter by Orlando Lagman (Courtesy Naval Photographic Center)
Frigate *Essex*. Artist unknown (Courtesy National Archives)
Lines of the United States Brig *Argus* (Courtesy Naval Historical Center, Washington, D.C.)
Lines of the United States Frigate *New York* (Courtesy Naval Historical Center, Washington, D.C.)
Lines of the United States Brig *Siren* (Courtesy Naval Historical Center, Washington, D.C.)
Sail plan of the United States Ship *Wasp* (Courtesy Naval Historical Center, Washington, D.C.)
*Wasp* and *Frolic*. Drawing and engraving by F. Kearny from a sketch by Lieutenant Claxton of the *Wasp* (Courtesy National Archives)
"Macdonough's Victory." Lithograph by Nathaniel Currier. (Courtesy Naval Photographic Center)
Isaac Chauncey by Gilbert Stuart (Courtesy Naval Photographic Center)
*Constellation* and *L'Insurgente* by William Bainbridge Hoff (Courtesy National Archives)
*United States* and *Macedonian* by Alonzo Chappel (Courtesy National Archives)

# Maps

*Preface*


After a long and hard-fought Revolution, the American republic emerged as an independent nation in 1783. It was not a
happy birth, for the nation was brought forth into a world of
hostile empires. Even our former allies had little reason to wish
us well. Beset on all sides by enemies, the new states might
easily have decided to ignore the world beyond and retreat into
the safety and solitude of landbound isolation. Those who
urged such a course, and there were many, neither understood
the nation's history nor grasped its future. America was a sea-
minded nation, and its destiny rested as much with the sea as
with the land.

Even before independence had been secured, enterprising
ship owners and bold captains were venturing to reestablish old
trading routes and create new ones. Their activities generated
both profits and trouble.

In an age when war was more common than peace, ships
flying the American flag inevitably encountered foreign entanglements in distant waters. When part of the British Empire,
the colonies had looked to King, Parliament, and most impor-
tantly the Royal Navy to protect them from the snares of adver-
saries; as an independent nation, Americans could look only to
themselves.

The nation was not found wanting. Despite the opposition of
the domestic Cassandras who saw ruin in a navy, both Congress
and the president acted to defend the republic at sea. Their

wisdom was vindicated, for in the first quarter century of the
republic's life, that navy was the chief glory of the nation.

No one sails alone, least of all a historian who for several years
has been dependent upon the largesse of others, friends and
colleagues, to aid him in his work. High on my list must be
Northeastern University. As an institution it has been most
generous. A grant from the Provost's Research and Scholarship
Fund enabled me to travel and obtain materials without which
my work would have been impossible. More than the simple
material resources, I must take note of the unwavering personal support that I have received from the university in every
quarter.

My list of indebtedness is a long one. For the second time I
was graced with a grant from the American Philosophical Society. The Department of the Navy too was most cooperative.
William S. Dudley, head of the Historical Research Branch, was
kind enough to let me share in some of his work concerning the
War of 1812. He and the staff at the Naval Historical Center
were generous, accommodating hosts during my all too brief
visit with them. Mr. Dudley, along with Commander Tyrone G.
Martin, former captain of U.S.S. *Constitution*, also took a good
deal of time to read my manuscript and make valuable suggestions.

Other institutions as well ought to be commended for doing
what they do so well — helping scholars. Among that list I
would include the Massachusetts Historical Society, the New
England Historic Genealogical Society, the Maryland Historical
Society, the Huntington Library, the New York Public Library,
the New York Historical Society, the Public Records Office, the
Library of Congress, the National Archives, the United States
Naval Academy Museum, the G. W. Blunt White Library at
Mystic Seaport, and the U.S.S. *Constitution* Museum.

In addition to those already mentioned, I owe a great deal to
several scholars and friends whose work in naval history has
guided my own. Among them I must include Christopher
McKee, David Long, and Worth Estes. To this list of friends
and colleagues I need to add my editors, David Harris and

Linda Glick, who have nudged but never nagged this tardy
author.

Anyone who can take several hundred pages of my mangled
typing and produce good copy from it deserves commendation.
I was fortunate to have three such people whose good sense
and good humor were never failing. They are Nancy Bor-
romey, Ann Marie Ciccone, and Linda Marie Leyko.

Finally there is Marilyn, wife, mother, and teacher. Somehow
she has managed to keep the family ship on an even keel while
at the same time keeping good order in her own career. Compared to that, my job was a breeze.

*Jack Tars
and Commodores*

## 1

# Troubles Abroad

While John Adams thought the ineptness of the American navy in the Revolution was enough to cause tears, others were satisfied simply to be embarrassed.[1]

Despite a few glittering moments with captains like John Paul Jones, Lambert Wickes, and John Barry, if the American navy had never existed it is hard to see how the outcome of the Revolution would have been any different. Independence was achieved at sea, but not by American ships; the great naval battles that decided the fate of America were fought by the fleets of France, Spain, and England.

The disappointing performance of the navy caused many, in and out of Congress, to question its necessity. By the end of the war, only two vessels were still in service — *General Washington*, a packet running to France, and *Alliance*, a thirty-two-gun frigate, once the pride of America, now relegated to the ignominious task of ferrying tobacco to Europe.

In peace it was impossible to justify maintaining a force that had been of only marginal use in war. Besides, Congress, which was chronically short of cash, was far more interested in finding ways to save money than to spend it. With that in mind, it had already begun to dismantle the army; the navy would follow.

On 19 March 1784 Robert Morris, the great financier to whom Congress had entrusted direction of the dwindling navy, reported that *General Washington* needed extensive repairs to fit her for sea.[2] She was, in his judgment, not worth the expense and ought to be sold. Congress agreed, and on 8 April they ordered her put up for auction.

*Alliance,* too, was in need of work. Sadly, Morris observed, "This ship is now a mere Bill of Costs and I do not think we have the Means to fit her out." Never defeated in battle, she had been commanded by both John Barry and John Paul Jones. It was an emotional issue. James Madison thought the ship ought to be kept, but he confessed that he did not know how Congress would pay. While her fate was being pondered, *Alliance* swung on her anchor in the Delaware, idle and in ill repair.[3]

Peace brought a host of problems for the new nation, not the least among them concerning foreign relations. The American nation had been born in troubled times. England was not a good loser — her troops continued to occupy American territory, and she steadfastly refused to negotiate a commercial treaty with Congress. France, America's old ally, and her neighbor Spain, whose territory stretched from the Mississippi to the Pacific, were more congenial, but nonetheless reluctant to share their spheres of influence with a competitor, and a republic at that.

Coping with challenges abroad was made even more difficult by confusion at home. On 11 June 1776, the same day that Congress appointed a committee to prepare a Declaration of Independence, it also appointed a committee "to prepare and digest the form of a confederation to be entered into between these colonies."[4] Within one month the Declaration was written and approved. It took five years to write and get approval for the Articles of Confederation. Since one of the principal causes of the Revolution had been the British government's attempt to centralize authority, it is not surprising that Americans resisted that trend when they created their own government. As America's first constitution, the Articles provided a weak central government with a high degree of decentralization in favor of the states.

War and the threat of a common enemy provided the fiber that held this fragile coalition together. In peace its weaknesses became more apparent, as the centrifugal forces of state and

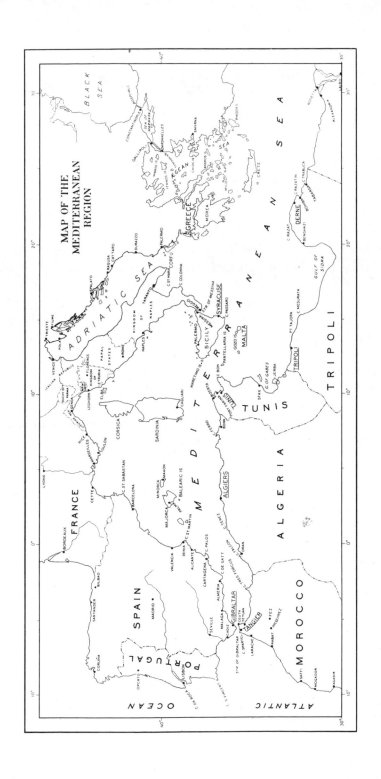

MAP OF THE
MEDITERRANEAN
REGION

regional interests took hold. Congress found itself faced with
mounting problems of finance, trade, and foreign relations
with which it had only very limited powers to deal.

As Congress lamented its impotence, disturbing news arrived. On 11 October 1784 *Betsey,* a small merchantman from
Philadelphia, was boarded and captured by a Moroccan corsair
out of Tangier. Morocco and her North African neighbors
Algeria, Tunis, and Tripoli had for generations prowled the
western Mediterranean and adjacent Atlantic, preying on merchant shipping. These Barbary States, a name taken from the
Berber tribes that inhabited the area, were ostensibly vassals of
the sultan of Turkey. In fact, however, they operated independently. They viewed the western Mediterranean as their private
preserve, and those wishing to use it had to either fight or
negotiate and pay. The latter was the preferred remedy; most
of the European powers found it cheaper to talk and pay tribute than to go to the trouble and expense of sending naval
squadrons.[5]

For a number of years, paying tribute had been British policy. As long as the American colonies were part of the empire,
their vessels and trade were protected. Independence abruptly
ended that arrangement, and American vessels were now on
their own. Morocco's seizure was the first sign of troubled times
ahead.

Fortunately for the owners and crew of *Betsey,* the emper-
or of Morocco, Sidi Mohamet, was well disposed toward the
United States. Contrary to the usual practice, he did not enslave
the crew or hold them for ransom. For reasons that are not
altogether clear, Sidi Mohamet had a genuine affection for
America. He claimed to have been the first to recognize American independence (he was actually second after France, but no
one bothered to correct him), and for some time he had been
actively seeking a treaty with the new nation. The press of other
business, coupled with congressional lethargy and indifference
to a place so far away, delayed consideration on this side of
the Atlantic. *Betsey*'s ill fortune was a reminder to tend to this
business.

Thanks to the efforts of Thomas Jefferson, the American

minister in Paris, and William Carmichael, the minister in Madrid, the Spanish government interceded on behalf of the Americans. At the same time Congress took up belatedly the issue of the treaty. While the negotiations proceeded, Sidi Mohamet refrained from any further harassment of American vessels. Early in the summer of 1786 *Betsey* and her crew were released. One year later a treaty of friendship with Morocco was ratified.[6]

Although America's brief encounter with Morocco turned out well, the threat from the Barbary powers was still quite real. Adding to the peril were the machinations of British diplomats and merchants. At Lloyds of London, the world center for marine insurance, rates on American vessels sailing to the continent were running twice as high as those charged for British ships. This difference was in part the result of wild rumors being circulated by British merchants claiming that dozens of American vessels had been captured by the Barbary corsairs. Skittish and credulous underwriters believed the tales, thus driving up the rates, which gave British shippers a decided economic advantage.

While the underwriters were hiking insurance rates, British diplomats were also hard at work conspiring to injure American trade. According to Carmichael, "the English Agent at Morocco did all in his power to render us bad office there."[7] At Algiers a similar effort was under way: the local British agent, Charles Loggie, was busily encouraging the dey to attack American ships.

The situation was perilous. Jefferson saw only two possibilities for America.

> The one to carry nothing for ourselves and thereby render ourselves invulnerable to the European states; the other (which our country will be for) is to carry as much as possible. But this will require a protecting force on the sea. Otherwise the smallest power in Europe, every one which possesses a single ship of the line may dictate to us, and enforce their demands by captures on our commerce. Some naval force then is necessary if we mean to be commercial. Can we have a better occasion of beginning one? Or find a foe more certainly within our dimensions? The motives pleading for war rather than tribute are numerous and honourable, those opposing them are mean and shortsighted.[8]

He was right, but Jefferson had no more means to conjure up warships than did Congress. John Adams, who was about to take up his new duty as minister to London, was equally angry and frustrated, but he better understood the difficulty of building a navy and the inability of Congress to accomplish the task. "I detest these barbarians as much as any Body, and my Indignation against their Piracies is as hot as that of any Body. But how can we help ourselves? . . . As to fighting of them, what can we do?"[9]

In the summer of 1785, more unpleasant news arrived. For some time Algiers and Spain had been at war. As part of their strategy against the Algerines, the Spanish navy had been blockading the Straits of Gibraltar to prevent them from attacking trade in the Atlantic. Despite Spain's best efforts, the war had been an indecisive and expensive affair. With so little to show for their labors, they decided to make peace. After the signing of a treaty, sweetened by the payment of more than a million dollars to Algiers, the Spanish navy lifted the blockade, allowing the Algerines to foray into the Atlantic. Since they were at peace with most of the European states, the Algerines were anxious to find new victims. In July they declared war on the United States.

It took several weeks for the news of the declaration to reach American ports, allowing plenty of time for a number of unsuspecting merchantmen to sail into harm's way. On 25 July the war found its first victim.

*Maria* was a small trading schooner sailing out of Boston, bound on a course for Cádiz. She was owned by William Foster and Company and most likely carrying a cargo of baccalau, dried codfish, a popular mainstay in the southern European trade. She had a crew of six, including her captain, Isaac Stephens of Charlestown. *Maria* left Boston in mid-June, and by late July she was off Cape St. Vincent on an easterly course only a day or two from port.

On the afternoon of the 25th, the lookout reported two merchantmen hove to off the starboard bow. As Stephens watched, the two merchantmen were approached by a rakish and sinister-looking vessel. She was square-rigged on the foremast but had a lateen arrangement on the main and mizzen, with a long overhang on both the bow and stern. From her appearance, there was little doubt that she was a xebec,* probably out of Algiers.

As far as Stephens knew, the United States and Algiers were at peace, thus he should have nothing to fear; nonetheless, prudence dictated crowding on as much sail as possible. The two merchantmen turned out to be Danes, with whom the Algerines had no quarrel. They quickly finished their business with them and set off in pursuit of *Maria.* If *Maria* had had a better breeze and less cargo in her hold she might have been able to escape, but that was impossible now. When hailed, Stephens had no choice but to come up into the wind and drop his sails. Within minutes a small boat was alongside, and a pack of roguish men armed with pistols and swords were coming over the gunwales. Resistance was useless. Speaking in Spanish, the leader of the boarding party asked Stephens who they were. James Cathcart, one of *Maria*'s crew, responded in Spanish, *"Americanos."* At that the Algerine leader, turning to his men, said something unintelligible to the Americans, but quite intelligible to the others, for they let out a quick shout and rushed below to examine their prize. For two hours the six captives sat on deck while the Algerines romped through the schooner, taking everything — cargo, dishes, personal belongings and anything else they could lay their hands on. When they had finished stripping *Maria,* they turned to her crew; by the time the Americans were transferred to the xebec, all they had left on were their underdrawers. At this point, Stephens needed no one to tell him that Algiers was at war with his country. After confining the prisoners below and sending a prize crew over to *Maria,* the Algerines set a course for home.[10]

Five days later off Lisbon the scene was repeated, this time with a Philadelphia vessel, *Dolphin.* She too was boarded, captured, and taken to Algiers. In less than a week the Algerines had managed to take two vessels and twenty-one crewmen, who were now prisoners of the dey.[11]

*A type of vessel found only in the Mediterranean and greatly favored by the corsairs.

In an ironic twist of fate, at the same time as *Maria* and *Dolphin* were swinging at anchor under the dey's guns, Congress was deciding on the fate of the American navy. *Alliance,* the only ship left, had not moved off her anchorage in more than a year. She was more in need of repair than ever. It was best that the ship be sold while she could still bring a price. On 5 August *Alliance* was sold at public auction for $26,000, to a syndicate headed by none other than Robert Morris.

With no navy to protect them and no money to buy a treaty or ransom the captives, Congress spent most of its time lamenting its own weakness. Near-hysterical newspaper accounts exaggerated the threat with tales about Algerine cruisers of eighteen to thirty-two guns sailing west into the Atlantic preying on American shipping. According to some reports, dozens of American ships had been taken, including *London Packet.* Under the command of one of Philadelphia's best-known mariners, Captain Thomas Truxtun, she was bound out of London for Philadelphia with Benjamin Franklin on board. After nine years abroad, the old doctor was on his way home to Philadelphia. The report of his capture stunned Americans; that America's most famous citizen should be rotting in an Algerine dungeon was more than the public could bear. According to one "eyewitness," "Poor Dr. Franklin bears this reverse of fortune with more magnanimity than I could have imagined."[12]

The account was pure fabrication. Despite the newspaper panic, Franklin was quite safe, enjoying his passage with Captain Truxtun and spending his time taking measurements of the Gulf Stream. Actually, for all of their ferocious reputation, the corsairs rarely ventured onto blue water. Their vessels were lightly built and not heavily armed, not well suited for ocean cruising or rollicking gun duels at sea. They did their best business inshore, where they could depend on the terrorizing effect of their large crews to cow an enemy. Nevertheless, whatever their force and range, they did pose a serious threat to American commerce.

In Congress, the secretary for foreign affairs, John Jay, recommended that "five forty Gun ships" be built and a "commodore" be appointed to meet "these predatory Enemies in a proper Manner." He further prodded his colleagues by telling them his advice was based "on a Presumption that the United States extend their Vision and Wishes to naval Strength and maritime Importance . . ."[13]

In this matter, as in most, Congress was moribund. Its credibility at home and abroad had ebbed to a degree that made it difficult to deal with thirteen fractious states, let alone foreign nations. Jefferson summed up the feelings of many Americans when he reflected that "my faculties are absolutely suspended between indignation and impotence."[14]

Through no efforts of its own, the United States did get a temporary respite. The Algerines had not confined their raiding to American vessels alone. They were also attacking Portuguese vessels, raising particular havoc with the trade to Brazil. In response, the Portuguese navy set up a blockade across the Straits of Gibraltar that put the genie back in the bottle. The relief was well received in America but embarrassing, since it clearly demonstrated the inability of the United States to fend for itself. In a pathetic and unsuccessful appeal to the states for money, Congress assessed the situation.

> Hence it is that our Navigation (the surest source of our Wealth and Security) is nearly Annihilated; our Commerce in every part of the Globe obstructed; The Flag of our Nation insulted, and the few Mariners who venture of the Ocean exposed to linger out their days in all the bitterness of Captivity, from a barbarous and hostile Power.[15]

If Lord Acton was right — "Power tends to corrupt and absolute power corrupts absolutely" — then the struggling American Congress must be deemed one of the most virtuous bodies ever to assemble. Yet, if they were impotent, they were not without hope. Although nascent and inchoate, there did exist a spirit of nationalism, a desire to create a more powerful America. Motivation for a more perfect union ran the gamut from nearly pure idealism to shabby greed, yet in the end the goal was the same — a stronger central government.

In May 1787 these hopes began to bear fruit. The Constitutional Convention convened in Philadelphia. With the exception of Rhode Island every state was represented, fifty-five delegates in all. Some of the luminaries from the past were absent. Jefferson was in Paris and John Adams continued in London. Others were present; George Washington sat as president of the convention and the indomitable Franklin came as a Pennsylvania delegate.

For sixteen weeks the convention debated and discussed the proposed Constitution. Their task was twofold: to create a government powerful enough to deal with national problems, yet one weak enough that it would not threaten individual liberties and state sovereignty.

One of the central issues was defense. The near-obsessive fear of a standing army guaranteed a lively debate, but in the midst of the military arguments the navy was nearly forgotten. Armies were feared for their potential threat to the republic, but few feared a navy. By their very nature, navies are extensions of power beyond the homeland, and since sailors could hardly bring their ships ashore, their influence on domestic matters was bound to be minimal. Most delegates assumed that there would be a navy, but beyond that they gave it very little thought. With practically no discussion the convention agreed that Congress had the power "to provide and maintain a navy"; and that "the President shall be Commander in Chief of the Army and Navy."

After approval in Philadelphia, the Constitution was sent to the individual states for their ratification. Out in the states the naval issue was less subdued. At the state conventions the Antifederalists, those opposed to ratification, alleged that a navy was a needless expense, designed, as was everything in the document, to enhance the power of the central government at the expense of the states. Even those who favored the Constitution were not necessarily enthusiastic about a navy, for there was a feeling that America's future lay with the land. Their faces were set with a continental gaze. The more adamant among them insisted that America ought not to have any naval force at all, for the mere existence of American ships would antagonize the European powers and lead us into conflict. Not surprisingly, such views were most often voiced by people far from the sea. These men, rooted in the land, shunned the sea and the

commerce it represented. They misunderstood their own history and extracted from their misconceptions a distorted image
of America's past and an inability to grasp her future. "How,"
exclaimed William Grayson in the Virginia convention, "will
you induce your people to go to sea? Is it not more agreeable to
follow agriculture than to encounter the dangers and hardships
of the ocean?"[16] From its very founding, America had been a
sea-minded nation. Sentiments such as Grayson's ignored the
thousands of men who for generations had gone to sea, making
America a nursery of seamen. What of the fishermen, shipbuilders, merchants, and scores of trades that owed their living to
the sea? Long before independence, the colonies had become
one of the principal seafaring regions of the world. Americans
could no more turn their backs to the sea than to the land.

Support for the navy was strongest in the north and along
the coast, a fact that gave southerners pause. Northern capital
was heavily invested in the carrying trade, which needed naval
protection. It was also true that with the north's natural advantages — good harbors, timber, and seamen — it stood to earn
substantial profits from building and maintaining a fleet. This
had certainly been the case during the Revolution. As small and
ineffective as the American squadrons were in that war, they
had nevertheless helped produce wartime prosperity in places
like Boston and Philadelphia. Building and refitting ships,
along with the sale of prizes, were lucrative activities, from
which the south had gained little in the past and stood to gain
no more in the future.

Regionalism tied to economics was a key factor in determining naval attitudes, but it was by no means the only one. Not all
southerners were naval opponents, and not all opponents were
southerners. James Madison of Virginia spoke eloquently in
support of an American navy, asserting that "Weakness will
invite insults . . . The best way to avoid danger is to be in a
capacity to withstand it."[17] Madison's sentiments contain a tinge
of nationalism. In the minds of other, less restrained Federalists, such feelings grew more ardent and became embodied in
an early version of a seapower doctrine. The model, of course,
was Great Britain. To be great a nation must be able to exert

influence beyond its borders. It must have a large commerce that it can protect and expand. This could never be accomplished by the present Confederation government, nor could it be done by the states acting individually. That arch-Federalist himself, Alexander Hamilton, spoke to the question in *The Federalist* No. 11.

> To this great national object, a *Navy*, union will contribute in various ways. Every institution will grow and flourish in proportion to the quantity and extent of the means concentrated towards its formation and support. A navy of the United States as it would embrace the resources of all, is an object far less remote than a navy of any single State or partial confederacy, which only embrace the resources of a single part. It happens indeed, that different portions of confederated America possess each some peculiar advantage for this essential establishment. The more southern states furnish in greater abundance certain kinds of naval stores — tar, pitch, and turpentine. Their wood for the construction of the ships is also of a more solid and lasting texture. The difference in the duration of the ships of which the navy might be composed, if chiefly constructed of Southern wood, would be of signal importance, wither in the view of naval strength or of national economy. Some of the Southern and of the Middle States yield a greater plenty of iron, and of better quality. Seamen must chiefly be drawn from the Northern hive. The necessity of naval protection to external or maritime commerce does not require a particular elucidation, no more than the conduciveness of that species of commerce to the prosperity of a navy.[18]

Hamilton's something-for-everyone approach assuaged the fears of many, but there still festered a strong suspicion that a navy would inevitably protect and fatten the purses of northern merchants.

Thanks to a well-orchestrated propaganda campaign, the support of men like Washington and Franklin, and the essential reasonableness of the document itself, the Constitution was approved. On 21 June 1788 New Hampshire became the ninth state to ratify, providing the necessary two thirds for the government to be formed. Elections were held and on 4 March 1789 the Federal Congress met for the first time. Seven weeks later, Washington took the oath as president. Standing by his side as vice president was the former minister to London, John Adams.

In defense policies the new administration displayed a continental bias. Naval affairs were placed under the authority of the secretary of war, Washington's old friend and former artillery commander, Henry Knox. Since America was at peace abroad and the Algerines were still cooped up in the Mediterranean, Knox's main concerns were internal. They revolved around Indians on the frontier, the creation of a regular army, and the organization of the militia.

Congress mirrored the administration's views. It was not that they were necessarily antinaval, although southern delegates still murmured about a Yankee navy; rather, they simply saw no need for one at the present. Most agreed with the sentiments of the senator from Pennsylvania, William Maclay, when he told his colleagues "that it would be time enough, half a century hence, to talk of measures for a navy."[19]

Even those who disagreed with Maclay had to admit that for the time being there was no seaborne danger comparable to the threat of the Indians. Defense was westward and landbound. Within that context, one of the major issues continued to be whether the nation ought to depend on a regular army or a civilian militia. Those who preferred professional soldiers argued that such a force could respond quicker and more effectively. The opposition raised the old specter of "standing armies" subverting the liberties of the people. Such notions were not entirely without foundation. Recent investigations have shown that while most men in the government envisioned no political use for a regular army, a few, given the right opportunity, might well have used it to intimidate and suppress dissent.[20]

Militia advocates saw in the yeoman soldier the reincarnation of Cincinnatus — a sturdy hand in the field, ready at a moment's notice to drop his plow and take up the weapons of war. It was a romantic view, but given the nature of the threat on the frontier and the relatively simple needs of the American war machine, it was a reasonable answer, at least for the time.

Invariably, on those infrequent occasions when the navy was discussed, the tone of debate reflected the greater concern over the army. Even here it was a question of regular versus militia

organization. Washington tended to favor some sort of professional army; however, that was not his view toward the navy.
He was inclined to favor a seagoing militia.

> As our people have a natural genius for Naval affairs and as our Mate-
> rials for Navigation are ample; if we give due encouragement to the
> fisheries and the carrying trade; we shall possess such a nursery of
> Seamen and such skill in maratime [sic] operations as to enable us to
> create a Navy almost in a moment.[21]

Washington should have known better. Navies, like armies, are
not created "in a moment."

"Natural genius" notwithstanding, the first Congresses did
virtually nothing about arming the United States at sea. The
lapse would be more understandable if they had at the same
time made some effort to provide support for the American
seamen still prisoners in Algiers, or to prevent others from being taken. Yet they did very little.

The only significant measure taken in regard to the prisoners
was the appointment of a special commissioner to deal with
Algiers "on the subject of Peace and ransom of our captives."[22]
For the post Washington selected none other than John Paul
Jones, a naval officer who knew far more about fighting than
negotiating. Jones, a man to whom the years had not been kind,
died shortly after his appointment.

Some writers have excused the inattention to the sufferings
of the prisoners with the explanation that America was outraged but impotent to act. James Fenimore Cooper, one of
America's first naval historians (as well as novelist), dismissed
that notion and noted pointedly

> that in the strife of parties, the struggles of opinion, and the pursuit of
> gain, the sufferings of the distant captives were overlooked or forgot-
> ten.[23]

Cooper was right. As long as the Algerines were penned up
by the Portuguese, American trade was in no real danger. The
pitiful sufferings of a handful of sailors was hardly enough to
nudge Congress to raise money for ransom or to provide protection to prevent others from sharing the same fate. As long as
there was peace and security at sea, even if it was at the suf-

france of others, Congress and the president were content to muse about a naval militia and in the meantime leave the nation without a navy. In matters of defense, the continentalists were in full control.

But peace was only a temporary condition. For the first quarter of a century of the republic's existence, war was the more normal state of affairs along the North Atlantic seaboard. Early in 1793 America's security began to unravel.

Louis XVI gained very little from helping the Americans win their revolution. His nation did have the satisfaction of seeing Britain somewhat humbled, but beyond that not much was achieved, except to increase the drain on the already overburdened French treasury and to give his people a taste of republicanism. These twin forces of finance and politics were more than enough to topple an enfeebled monarchy, and in the same year that America launched her new government, France had a revolution of her own. The French experience proved how fortunate the Americans had been. Revolutions are wondrous agents for destroying established governments, but woefully inadequate in creating new ones. History is littered with examples of chaos and instability from which new engines of despotism emerge. The storming of the Bastille on 14 July 1789 unleashed forces in France that would torment the western world for the next twenty-five years. Once set loose, the revolutionary spirit spilled across the borders of France. On 1 February 1793 France declared war on Great Britain, Spain, and Holland.

The outbreak of a major European war had grave consequences for the United States. From the moment the news arrived in the spring until Congress met in September, the administration spent a good deal of time and energy trying to remain neutral in a very unneutral world.

It was not easy. Washington proclaimed neutrality, but mere words were thin armor in the face of determined belligerents. The new French minister to the United States, Edmond Charles Genêt, contributed to the tension by setting out on a series of very unneutral acts, including arming French ships in American ports, meddling in domestic politics, and signing up soldiers for filibustering expeditions against neighboring Spanish and British territory.

Exasperated with the French, Washington fared little better with the British. As soon as the war had begun, the French government threw open her previously closed West Indies trade to all comers. By droves, American ship owners scampered to pick up their share of the lucrative business. Flying a neutral flag, the Americans were doing for the French what the British navy had made impossible for them to do for themselves. This subterfuge had a short life. Through a series of Orders in Council (June and November 1793, January 1794) the British plugged this loophole, by unilaterally invoking the Rule of 1756, which stated that trade illegal in peace is still illegal in war. Armed with this declaration, the Royal Navy quickly swept up Americans carrying French goods, confiscating vessels and cargos.

In the midst of this domestic and foreign turmoil, more bad news arrived. Thanks to the efforts of the British, in the fall of 1793 Algiers and Portugal concluded a truce. The Portuguese lifted their blockade, and once again the Algerine corsairs were in the Atlantic. Within a span of a few weeks, eleven American vessels were taken. More than one hundred seamen were prisoners, and insurance rates that had been running at 10 percent shot up to 30. David Humphreys, the American agent who had been trying to negotiate with the Algerines, reported to President Washington that "a naval force has now (to a certain degree) become indispensable."[24] Washington was receptive, and so were the members of the Third Congress, which had just assembled. The actions of the British and the French and the continuing depredations of the Algerines persuaded many that the United States must have a navy.

## 2
# "Congress Founds the Navy"

When the second session of the Third Congress assembled in December 1793, it had much to do. It had last been together in April, and since that time a good deal had happened to make this reconvening an anxious time.

As the gentlemen took their seats, it was clear that despite the platitudinous denials Congress was dividing into "parties," Federalist and Republican. The former, generally acknowledging the leadership of Alexander Hamilton, tended to favor strong central government and was attuned to northern commercial interests. Republicans were more sympathetic to states' rights and southern agrarian interests, while following the leadership of Thomas Jefferson. Federalists were likely to be pro-navy, while Republicans were less likely to be so.[1]

Washington lost no time informing Congress of the parlous state of affairs. In his annual message of 3 December, he told them bluntly: "If we desire to avoid insult, we must be able to repel it; if we desire to secure peace . . . it must be known that we are at all times ready for war." On the 4th he sent a message on the Indian troubles plaguing the frontier, followed on the 5th by a somber communication lamenting the violations of American neutrality at sea. While the president's news was being pondered, on the 8th the Philadelphia newspapers carried stories of renewed Barbary depredations. Less than a week later, Washington sent Congress a message on that issue, enclosing confidential correspondence regarding the status of the Algerine captives.[2]

The barrage of bad news focused congressional attention on the need for defense measures. After a secret debate on 2 January 1794 the House passed three resolutions: to provide money for diplomatic expenses; to provide a naval force sufficient to protect American commerce from the Algerines; and last to advise on the "Ways and Means" for providing this force. Only for the final resolution do we have a roll call vote, 46–44, an indication of how close and heated the debate must have been.[3]

Under the third resolution, nine men were appointed a select committee. Six of the committee can be identified as Federalist, only three as Republicans. In terms of naval attitudes, the makeup was even more lopsided, for of the nine only one, Nathaniel Macon, congressman from North Carolina, can be identified as an antinavy man. It took the committee less than three weeks to return a report.[4]

According to the report, six vessels would be sufficient to deal with the threat from Algiers, four frigates of forty-four guns and two smaller twenty-fours. The total cost of construction was put at $600,000, with an annual operating bill of approximately $250,000.[5] Both figures, as the congressman from Virginia, James Madison, was quick to point out, were ridiculously low.

Since frigates ordinarily rated no more than thirty-eight guns, the unusually large size of the proposed four forty-fours raised speculation that more was intended than just meeting the Algerine threat. The suspicion was not misplaced, for these vessels were superfrigates, more powerful than any other frigates afloat and able, under special conditions, to hold their own against more powerful ships of the line. The concept was not a new one. During the Revolution, Pierre Landais, a French captain in American employ, had suggested that the Congress cut down their three-decked seventy-four building at Portsmouth to a two-decked fifty-six. The plan was never carried through, but in January 1793, exactly one year prior to the select committee's report, Joshua Humphreys, the eminent

Philadelphia shipbuilder and designer, wrote to his friend Robert Morris to urge that America build such vessels on the grounds that such a ship would be "an overmatch for common double-deck ships . . ." The pronavy men on the committee could hardly have been ignorant of Humphreys' plan; however, for the sake of the passage of the current proposal, it was sufficient to note that Algiers had a forty-four and therefore America needed at least an equivalent force. To suggest that the navy might be used for anything beyond the present immediate threat would only raise the hackles of the antinaval lobby.[6]

Division in Congress tended to break on geographical lines, with the south opposed and the north in favor. Not surprisingly, overlaying the regional division, or perhaps an integral part of it, were the more philosophical issues that had surfaced in previous debates. Craig Symonds has succinctly categorized them as navalist and antinavalist positions. The former were those who saw an American navy as an instrument not just to chase pirates and protect the coasts but as a means to secure respect abroad and play a balancing role in European politics. The antinavalists thought otherwise. Some preferred an isolated agrarian America, but most felt that the future lay westward and that the nation could ill afford to waste its resources on the foreign adventurism symbolized by a powerful navy. Quite naturally, there tended to be a close correlation between the Federalists-navalists at one end of the political spectrum and the Republican-antinavalists at the other.

> The common judgment of naval historians regarding this period of United States naval policy — that Republican opponents of the navy were irresponsible ideologues — falls apart when the full meaning of the naval policy debate is appreciated. It was the Navalists, driven as they were by impractical visions of a great and powerful United States holding the balance between supplicating European power blocs, who were promoting irresponsible national programs at a time when the United States had all it could do to hold the western Indians in check.[7]

As debate waxed on, conditions abroad deteriorated. In the Mediterranean affairs grew steadily worse, and American merchants clamored for action. Traders in Baltimore petitioned for "protection of the commerce of the United States against the Algerine corsairs." In the West Indies, too, matters grew tense as the British, through an Order in Council, put a virtual halt to that thriving trade. This later threat was something of an embarrassment to the Federalist supporters of a navy, since their Anglophilia would not permit them to endorse openly a navy for possible use against Great Britain.[8]

After some narrow escapes, the final bill passed the House by a vote of 50–39 and became law on 27 March 1794. Passage did not necessarily mark a victory for the navalists in Congress. In its preamble the act stated, "Whereas, the depredations committed by the Algerine corsairs on the commerce of the United States, render it necessary that a naval force should be provided for its protection . . ." — clearly an indication that Congress had in mind only a temporary force. Even more indicative of the will of the body was Section 9, tacked on at the very end: "if a peace shall take place between the United States and the Regency of Algiers, that no farther proceedings be had under this act." Despite these limiting provisions the pronavy forces had succeeded, at least for the moment, in carrying the day.[9]

In one respect the law was vague, for it did not specify how the president was to fashion his fleet. He was authorized "to provide, by purchase or otherwise," four forty-fours and two thirty-sixes. The quickest way to "provide" was by simple purchase, as had been done so often in the Revolution, either by buying and converting merchantmen or going abroad and obtaining foreign vessels. Although Washington was charged with this decision, the man with whom the real responsibility rested was Henry Knox, secretary of war. Knox was not a navy man, his principal experience afloat having occurred on that memorable evening when he led Washington's artillery across the Delaware River to attack the Hessians at Trenton. Nevertheless, for some time he had been in consultation with others experienced in these matters, including John Barry and Joshua Humphreys. Their advice, added to his own concerns, created, in Knox's words, "an anxious solicitude that this second commencement of a navy for the United States should be worthy of the national character. That the vessels should combine such qualities of strength, durability, swiftness of sailing, and force, as to render them equal, if not superior, to any frigates belonging to any of the European powers."[10] The Revolutionary experience indicated clearly that first-class warships were built, not bought or converted from lubberly merchantmen. After the decision to build, there still remained vexing questions. Who would design them? Where would they be built? And who would build them?

To the first question the answer was obvious: Joshua Humphreys, by common consent America's best and most experienced designer. Because of a delay in appropriations, Humphreys' actual appointment as naval constructor did not come until late in June. While Humphreys is ordinarily given credit for the design of the new frigates, another designer also played a role: Josiah Fox. Fox was an English Quaker who arrived in America in 1793. In April 1794, when Fox was about to return home, Knox summoned him and asked him to stay to help with the new ships. Fox agreed, but since the billet for constructor had already been filled by Humphreys, and there was no post for an assistant, he was given the rather common title of clerk in the War Department. Within a year he was promoted to the rank of assistant naval constructor and sent off to Norfolk to supervise the construction of a forty-four there.

With two such able men intimately involved in building the first frigates, deciding which one was more responsible for the final design of the ships has become a complex and touchy issue. Partisans for both Fox and Humphreys are quick to make their respective claims. Both men did in fact prepare drafts for the ships, but since Fox was the better draftsman (not necessarily the better designer) he executed the final drawings that went out to the builders. However, as was often the case, the builders themselves made certain alterations, to say nothing of changes made at the direction of the prospective commanding officers. The credit ought to be shared, then, but in what proportion will always remain clouded.[11]

The debate over where to build these six vessels excited the twin forces of patriotism and cupidity all along the coast. Both the British example and the Revolutionary experience showed that major shipbuilding benefited from concentration. Building vessels in as few locations as possible simplified control and eased logistics; however, not since the days when the Continental Congress had launched its shipbuilding program had spoils on such a grand scale been available. Politics and economics mitigated against good naval policy. As a result, Knox decided to build the six frigates at six different locations: forty-fours at Boston, New York, Philadelphia, and Norfolk; thirty-sixes at Baltimore and Portsmouth, New Hampshire. So that he might better control the enterprise, the secretary also determined that the building would not be done by private contract, but by agents employed specifically to supervise construction. Since the government owned no yards, the actual building would be accomplished by private builders, but only under the careful scrutiny of the agent, who would secure supplies, disperse wages, and provide general supervisory control. For this he was paid a commission of 2½ percent. In addition, at each building location Knox engaged a superintendent, naval constructor, and clerk of the yard. The superintendent had general charge of the ship, and the constructor was responsible for immediate supervision. The clerk was involved with the daily maintenance of records and accounted for public property.[12] There must have been a fair amount of overlap and perhaps even conflict among these men, but that suited Knox, for in this way they provided a check on one another.

Just as sensitive as these issues was the question of who would command. The president and secretary did not lack for candidates. Before Congress created a navy, there were men clamoring for posts in it. Hoysted Hacker, famous for his exploits while in command of the sloop *Providence* during the Revolution, wrote to his friend and former naval officer, Silas Talbot, asking for his help to secure a billet. Talbot was a logical person to approach, since he was a congressman and in a position to influence the choice. What Hacker did not know was that Talbot himself was fishing for a command in the new navy.[13]

Another letter came to Washington from John Barry. Barry had last commanded *Alliance,* in the waning days of the Revolution. His war record was among the most distinguished, and his political connections were impeccable.[14]

Washington made his decision, and in early June Secretary Knox wrote to the favored six. In order of seniority, they were John Barry, Samuel Nicholson, Silas Talbot, Joshua Barney, Richard Dale, and Thomas Truxtun. Apparently, position on the list depended on date of entry into the Continental Navy and rank achieved; fitness for command played no role. Nicholson's claim to second place was undisputed. Although he did have seniority and was a member of a prominent Maryland family, his wartime record was thoroughly undistinguished. Washington and Knox might well have grimaced at appointing such a well-known mediocrity, but political realities left no choice. Silas Talbot, on the other hand, was one of the heroes of the Revolution. Unfortunately, he performed his exploits as a Continental Army officer and later in the war as a privateersman. For his service, by a resolution of the Continental Congress on 19 September 1779, Talbot was made a captain in the navy. The truth of the matter is, though, he never commanded a Continental vessel. Barney, on the other hand, was commissioned a lieutenant in the navy and never rose beyond that rank; however, he did command the Continental ship *General Washington* and was, in the ordinary use of the term, referred to as captain. A small matter, perhaps, but not to naval officers, who all subscribed to John Paul Jones's dictum, "Rank opens the door to glory." Barney protested being placed junior to Talbot, but Knox would hear none of it. Miffed, he refused to serve and went off to France to enlist in the French navy.[15] He was replaced by James Sever, a man described as having "not much experience . . . but he is supposed to possess all the requisites to form a very good Officer . . ."[16] Sever was ranked number six. Fifth on the original list was Richard Dale, who had served on board *Bonhomme Richard* during her famous encounter with *Serapis*. The last man on the captain's list was Thomas Truxtun, a well-known privateersman of the Revolution who hailed from Long Island.

As a group, the new captains were a relatively homogeneous lot. The average age was forty-four. All were veterans of the Revolution.

Appointment as commander of a building frigate carried double duty, for these officers were expected to build as well as sail. Therefore, each was ordered to undertake the duty of superintendent at the yard. Working with the constructor, agent, and clerk, he would see to the vessel's shoreside needs, from keel laying through fitting out; he did not, however, choose her name. That decision rested with the president. Timothy Pickering, Knox's replacement as secretary of war, provided Washington with a list of ten names "such as have occurred in my conversations with gentlemen on the subject." From that list the president selected *Constitution, United States, President, Constellation,* and *Congress.* The sixth frigate, *Chesapeake,* had her name assigned at a later date.[17]

| Port | Frigate | Superintendent | Naval Constructor | Naval Agent |
|------|---------|----------------|-------------------|-------------|
| Boston | *Constitution* | Samuel Nicholson | George Claghorne | Henry K. Jackson |
| New York | *President* | Silas Talbot | Forman Cheeseman | John Blagge |
| Philadelphia | *United States* | John Barry | Joshua Humphreys | Gurney and Smith |
| Norfolk | *Chesapeake* | Richard Dale | Josiah Fox | William Pennock |
| Portsmouth | *Congress* | James Sever | James Hackett | Jacob & Sheafe |
| Baltimore | *Constellation* | Thomas Truxtun | David Stodder | Samuel & Joseph Sterett |

Once the designs were in hand, the first task was to assemble men and materials. The former presented no great hurdle. American ports had an abundance of skilled workmen, although none had worked on projects of this scale. The latter was a different matter.

In ordinary circumstances, the average life span for a wooden ship was between ten and twelve years. Constant exposure to wind and water, drying and wetting, caused rot, which, even in ships well cared for, would eventually cause fatal damage. Such wear was impossible to prevent and could only be delayed by good maintenance and the use of superior materials. At least three of the new captains felt strongly that their ships ought to be built "of the most durable wood in the world" — namely, live oak.[18]

Live oak (*Quercus virginiana*) is a semi-evergreen that can be found along the American coast from Virginia to Texas.[19] It grows to a fairly large size, forty to seventy feet high and upward of twenty feet in girth. Like the conventional oak tree, it divides into large branches that often take on a tortured shape.

These misshapen limbs, with their curious curves, are perfectly designed to provide the frame pieces for wooden ships. The most attractive aspect of all about the live oak is its extraordinary hardness and durability. Its advocates predicted confidently that it "would be a great saving to the United States, as we are well satisfied (accidents excepted) that they (the frigates) will be perfectly sound a half a century hence, and it is very possible they may continue for a much longer period."[20] The drawback was distance. The stands of oak were hundreds of miles from the ship yards and in locations where cutting was anything but pleasant. To complicate matters further, the secretary decided that to save bulk, and therefore shipment costs, the timbers would be rough hewn to their desired shape at the point of cutting. In the southern coastal regions where the oak grew, the only men available were unskilled farm laborers, most of them black slaves. Skilled workmen had to be sent south from the yards.

Despite everyone's best efforts, the first cargo of live oak did not arrive until December. Malarial fevers wreaked havoc with northern workmen, who either died, deserted, or came home ill. Their work camps more resembled hospitals than work sites.

Delays and escalating costs caused concern in Congress. In mid-December 1795 the new secretary of war, Timothy Pickering, reported to the Senate that all the keels were laid and all of the frigates had a good portion of their frames in place. He expected that by midsummer the necessary timber would be delivered. All this was hardly reassuring, since it had been nearly a year and a half since authorization, and not one frigate had yet to get her bottom wet. A committee report from the House, delivered on 29 January 1796, noted that the ships "might have been built and equipped in one year, if common materials had been put together and the size of the frigates had not been extended." Even more distressing than the incessant delays were the soaring costs. Because of the increased size, the difficulty and expense of obtaining the timber, and the need for additional equipment, the report estimated it would take nearly twice as much money as originally thought to complete the project. Cost overrun is a new term for a very old problem.[21]

While Congress mulled over the frigates, they did it against a rapidly changing diplomatic background. Washington informed them "that information has been received from an agent deputed on our part to Algiers importing that the terms of the treaty with the Dey and the Regency of that country had been adjusted in such a manner as to authorize the expectation of a speedy peace and the restoration of our unfortunate fellow-citizens from a grievous captivity."[22] In private the pronavy forces gave the news a mixed review: to be sure, peace was desired, but a completed treaty meant all work on the ships must stop. On 15 February the treaty was forwarded to the Senate, where it was approved on 7 March 1796. By its terms the United States agreed to pay the dey nearly one million dollars. Half was in ransom for the captives, while the rest was sent in the form of an annual payment in naval stores and a frigate, *Crescent,* which was to be built and delivered to the dey.[23]

If Congress adhered to Section 9 of the 1794 act, this treaty struck the death knell of the navy. To thwart that possibility, a three-member pronavy committee was appointed in the Senate to rescue the frigates. They produced a bill calling for the completion of two forty-fours and one thirty-six. In an extraordinary display of largesse toward the executive, the bill also gave discretionary power to the president to complete the other three if he so desired. The House was less well disposed to either the navy or the president.

Leading the antinavy forces was a young Swiss-born immigrant from Pennsylvania who was serving his first term in Congress, Albert Gallatin. In his opposition to the Senate bill, Gallatin was launching a distinguished career in public service, a good part of which over the coming decades would be aimed at restraining or reducing naval and military expenditures. Gallatin's polestar was economy, and the idea of continuing these huge outlays for a force no longer needed (or so he thought) sent him into strong opposition.

William Loughton Smith of South Carolina ran a course exactly opposite Gallatin's. He urged total disregard for the old Section 9 and moved that all six frigates be completed. Smith's motives were both political and philosophical. As a practical matter, advocating the extreme left considerable ground in the middle for compromise. Philosophically, Smith was a navalist who believed that America must take her position in the world and that having a navy was a necessary step in that direction. After a fair amount of debate, a compromise measure passed easily in both House and Senate, providing for the continued construction of two forty-fours and one thirty-six, but with no provision for discretionary authority for the president to go beyond that number. Although the pronavy forces got less than they wished, they could take consolation in having at least salvaged half the fleet. Furthermore, unlike its predecessor in 1794, this act made no reference to a particular threat or time limit. In essence, they had succeeded in creating a small but apparently permanent navy.[24]

Although Washington presided over the creation of the navy, he did not remain in office long enough to witness its launching. The remaining months of his administration saw additional requests for money and excuses for delay arriving from the ports. By 1 January 1797 the original budget estimates had been far exceeded, and still not one of the frigates had been launched.

On 4 March 1797 a new president took office. John Adams was a friend to the navy, and had he not been called out of town to greet his wife on her arrival, he would undoubtedly have been at the Philadelphia riverfront watching the first frigate slide into the water on 10 May 1797.[25] She was a forty-four, christened *United States*.

On the other hand, perhaps it was just as well that the president was not in attendance, for as the frigate slid into the water her momentum carried her across the river and sent her aground. The damage to the ship was slight; the embarrassment great. In September the thirty-six, *Constellation*, slid into the water at Baltimore. Her captain, Thomas Truxtun, described the events as the best "launch I ever saw; the ship Cleared the ways without touching or Meeting with the Smallest accident."[26]

Unhappily, the joyous scene in Philadelphia and Baltimore

was not repeated in Boston, where the third and last of the
frigates, a forty-four, *Constitution,* made an attempt to get into
the water on 20 September. She stuck on the ways and refused
to move. Two days later a second attempt was made, with no
better results. For the next month, workmen struggled to increase the decline to the water, while applying liberal amounts
of grease on the ways. Having been twice disappointed, only a
small crowd of Bostonians gathered for the third launching, on
21 October. This time it worked, and Captain James Sever, who
had been without a command since the suspension of construction on his ship in Portsmouth, had the pleasure of christening
the new frigate with a bottle of fine Madeira.[27]

Although afloat, the frigates were still a long way from completion. As was usual with ship construction of this period, they
went into the water with only their hull and decks complete.
They would yet spend many months lying next to fitting-out
docks as riggers struggled to step masts and put in place miles
of standing and running rigging. Sails by the thousands of
square feet needed to be made and bent on; compasses had to
be installed and adjusted; skilled joiners finished the interior
work, while coopers hurried to complete hundreds of barrels
necessary to carry provisions. And all of this says nothing about
the especially nagging problem of obtaining sufficient cannon.
By the time these vessels were complete, scores of workmen
representing dozens of trades were aboard, helping to create
one of the most sophisticated, complex, and expensive products of eighteenth-century society — a warship.

Even for a moderately competent secretary of war, the
burden of overseeing the construction of these ships, in addition to the already considerable workload generated by the
army, would have been a chore. For Adams' secretary, James
McHenry, the task was overwhelming. The secretary had a
well-deserved reputation as a "bungler." Even his close political supporters, Alexander Hamilton among them, realized
McHenry's shortcomings and expressed their regret that a man
of such mediocre ability was so heavily burdened.[28]

Thus far, in its efforts to build a navy, Congress had only
concerned itself with construction. As the ships neared comple-

tion, albeit at a maddeningly slow pace, they began to confront the problems of manning and supplying them. After some debate they agreed on 1 July to a set of recommendations put forth by McHenry. Each of the forty-fours would have fifty-three commissioned, warrant, and petty officers, 245 able and ordinary seamen, and fifty-eight enlisted marines. The thirty-six would have a slightly smaller complement of forty-eight commissioned, warrant, and petty officers, 212 able and ordinary seamen, and forty-six enlisted marines.

Pay for commissioned and warrant officers was reckoned both in cash and rations, the latter being valued at twenty cents each.

> A captain, seventy-five dollars per month, and six rations per day; a lieutenant, forty dollars per month, and three rations per day; a lieutenant of marines, thirty dollars per month, and two rations per day; a chaplain, forty dollars per month and two rations per day; a sailing master, forty dollars per month, and two rations per day; a surgeon, fifty dollars per month, and two rations per day; a surgeon's mate, thirty dollars per month, and two rations per day; a purser, forty dollars per month, and two rations per day; a boatswain, twenty dollars per month, and two rations per day; a gunner, twenty dollars per month and two rations per day; a sailmaker, twenty dollars per month and two rations per day; a carpenter, twenty dollars per month and two rations per day.

Pay rates for the enlisted crews were left to the judgment of the secretary and the president. The scale established was: able seamen, eleven dollars per month; ordinary seamen, nine dollars per month; sergeant and corporal of marines, ten dollars per month; privates, nine dollars per month. Enlisted men were not allowed rations.[29]

For the commissioned and warrant officers, the pay scale compared favorably with the earnings of their peers in the civilian world. The same may not be said for the enlisted ranks, where staying ashore paid better. Of course, this does not take into account the possibility of sharing prize money, but that was a promise that could only be realized in wartime, and a chancy one at that.

To govern the men aboard ship, Congress adopted the rules

that had been drawn up in 1775 for the Continental Navy. This must have pleased the new president, since he was the original author. What was less pleasing were the steadily mounting bills. In the debate over whether to create a navy much had been made about the costs of construction, and less about the money required to keep the ships in service. There was some dismay when the secretary informed Congress and the president that to keep a forty-four in service for a year he needed:

| Pay | $ 75,009 |
|---|---|
| Provisions | 28,271 |
| Medicines, hospital supplies | 2,500 |
| Contingencies | 20,000 |
| TOTAL | $125,780 |

The bill was slightly less for a thirty-six — $105,983.[30]

Despite the cost, Adams was urgent to press forward. In March he asked Congress to convene in special session on 15 May. His purpose was to inform them of the deteriorating situation with France.[31]

Relations with France had tumbled since the halcyon days of the American Revolution. Caught between the tiger — France, powerful on land — and the shark — Great Britain, powerful at sea — the United States found itself in the uncomfortable position of being a neutral carrier, harassed by both sides. The French, reading more into the Franco-American Treaties of 1778 than the Americans would admit, employed those agreements as justification for using American ports to fit out privateers. Even more troubling, Edmond Genêt, their irrepressible minister to the United States, attempted to recruit and organize an expedition against Spanish territory from the United States. Such actions jeopardized American neutrality and strained relations. In 1794, they were brought to virtual collapse when the United States signed a treaty with Great Britain (Jay's Treaty) that the French interpreted as violating their treaties with the United States. In retaliation they refused to receive a new American minister and began to seize American vessels. Although the French were not alone in violating American rights, they were certainly in the lead.[32]

It was with this situation in mind that Adams addressed the Congress on 16 May. He told them of the conduct of the French and of the need for the nation to be ready to defend herself on land as well as at sea. Adding to the urgency of the situation, in June the secretary of state presented a report listing violations of American neutrality. Since 1 October 1796 he listed 319 incidents. One he blamed on Spain, two were the fault of Great Britain, and for the remainder he accused France.[33]

During the summer Adams dispatched three commissioners to negotiate a reopening of relations. Their lack of success and the attitude of the French exacerbated the situation. With the French showing no signs of softening their policies, in his annual address on 22 November 1797 Adams spoke harshly of them and urged Congress "to place our country in a suitable posture of defense."[34]

In March 1798 Adams asked his department heads if he ought to seek a declaration of war. He went so far as to prepare a war message, but sensing the lack of support he abandoned it. On 19 March he sent a message to Congress alluding to dispatches he had received from his envoys in Paris. He reported, "I perceive no ground of expectation that the objects of their mission can be accomplished on terms compatible with the safety, the honor, or the essential interests of the nation."[35] On 2 April the House requested to see the dispatches. Adams sent them over the following day, knowing full well they would stun the members. The letters revealed that certain French agents, referred to only as X, Y, and Z, had approached the American envoys and told them bluntly that only by public apology on the part of President Adams and the sweetener of a large bribe would relations be restored. Although they initially pledged to keep the papers confidential, the House reversed itself and voted to publish the dispatches. The Republicans, who feared war and still hoped for an amicable solution, protested, but the Federalist majorities in both House and Senate were strong enough to prevail.

Congressional and public action was predictable. One Federalist newspaper noted angrily, "To be lukewarm after read-

ing the horrid scenes is to be criminal — and the man who
does not warmly reprobate the conduct of the French must
have a soul black enough to be *fit* for *treasons stratagems* and
*spoils*."[36] The Federalists swept forward with their plans for
arming America.

On 17 April 1798 Congress enacted a law "to provide an
additional armament for the further protection of the trade of
the United States; and for other purposes." It authorized the
president to build, purchase, or hire "a number of vessels, not
exceeding twelve, nor carrying more than twenty-two guns
each to be armed, fitted out, and manned under his direction."[37]
For these purposes Congress appropriated $950,000.

Expansion of the navy was paralleled by a notable enlarge-
ment of military affairs in general. If the secretary of war had
been unable to handle his duties effectively in the somnolent
days before the French imbroglio, these added charges made it
impossible. The Federalists had no intention of allowing their
expansion program to fall into the hands of a department that
had only a part-time interest in the navy. Three days after
enlarging the navy, Congress created a separate Navy Department to administer it. Heading the department would be a
secretary with full cabinet rank.[38]

In searching for the appropriate person to fill the post,
Adams had three possibilities. He might choose a naval officer.
However, since there were so few of them, and since none had
any great amount of experience, that seemed an unlikely possibility. Another possibility might be a shipbuilder such as Joshua
Humphreys. The issue here was status. Since the secretary
would sit in the highest councils, he could never be a mere
artisan. The third type of gentleman was a shipping merchant,
a man possessed of both experience and social rank.

Adams turned first to his home state and asked George Cabot
to take the post. Cabot, in a letter declining the honor, summed
up rather well what he viewed the secretary to be:

> It is undoubtedly requisite that the officer at the head of the naval
> department should possess considerable knowledge of maritime affairs;
> but this should be elementary as well as practical, including the princi-
> ples of naval architecture and naval tactics. He should also possess skill

to arrange systematically the means of equipping, manning, and conducting the naval force with the greatest possible despatch, and with the least possible expense; and, above all, he should possess the inestimable secret of rendering it invincible by an equal force.

It is not to be expected that a man will be found possessing the ability to perform at once all the duties of an office, new and difficult; but I trust men may be found — and it seems to me indispensable that such should be found — who will, by industrious application of genius and talents, soon acquire the requisite qualifications.[39]

Adams' second choice was a Marylander, Benjamin Stoddert, who was at the time a merchant in Georgetown. Stoddert had held important posts under the Continental Congress, was well connected both in business and politics, and knew the shipping business. He did not, however, have any seagoing experience. He was an administrator, not a seaman.

Stoddert was not anxious to take the secretaryship. He was nearing fifty years of age and was more inclined to contemplate retirement than the launch of a new career. While Adams waited for his reply, McHenry was, as usual, foundering. It was all just too much for him. In near desperation, he wrote to his friend and mentor Alexander Hamilton, "Can you spare an hour or two to help me . . . ?"[40]

Fortunately for the navy, Stoddert accepted. On the same day Congress, because of the continuing French depredations, authorized the president to direct American armed vessels to "seize, take, and bring into any port of the United States" any armed vessels found "hovering" along the American coast and to retake any American vessel that might have been captured. Thus began the Quasi War with France.

## 3

# War with an Old Friend

On 19 June Stoddert took the oath as first secretary of the Navy Department. If there was a ceremony, he never mentioned it. There was little to be ceremonious about; the new department inherited a mess. McHenry was out of town and therefore unable to render assistance. Oliver Wolcott, secretary of the treasury and the person who could provide financial information, was also gone from the capital. Miffed at being left alone, Stoddert pushed ahead and immediately opened correspondence with his commanders and agents. His letters reflect an intimate involvement in numerous functions, including purchasing and transporting timber, constructing and equipping vessels, arranging contracts, and haggling with suppliers over costs of materials. A good deal of this administrative work was handled through agents at the ports. Some, such as Stephen Higginson in Boston and Jeremiah Yellott in Baltimore, were able men and greatly assisted the secretary. Others, like Tench Francis in Philadelphia, were either incompetent or lazy and gave him no end of headaches.[1]

Of course, Stoddert had also to deal with his captains. When he took office, only four were left on active duty: John Barry, Thomas Truxtun, Richard Dale, and Samuel Nicholson. In three instances — Barry, Truxtun, and Dale — Stoddert could count himself fortunate; in the fourth, Nicholson, he was cursed. Samuel Nicholson was an aged incompetent who had the confidence neither of those who served under him nor of those who commanded him. Stoddert would have loved dearly to scuttle the old man, but family and political connections made that difficult, so for the time being he endured him as commander of *Constitution*.[2]

The first navy vessel to get to sea was *Ganges*, a fast merchantman that had been bought under the provisions of the 27 April law. She carried twenty-six nine-pounders and was under the command of Richard Dale. She left Philadelphia on 24 May with orders to cruise "between the Capes of Virginia and Long-Island" and take any hostile vessel found in those waters, but only if it was found sailing within one marine league of the coast (three miles). Her departure was an occasion of some note. Secretary of War McHenry and Captain Barry both came on board to deliver Dale his orders in person and to wish him good fortune. Four days after Dale got to sea with his restrictive orders, President Adams issued new instructions to American naval officers, granting them greater latitude for taking French ships and retaking prizes.[3]

While Dale scoured the coasts with no luck, other vessels were preparing for sea. Merchants at Norfolk and other ports demanded protection. Pressed by them as well as by his own colleagues in the government, Stoddert did everything possible to push his captains to get to sea.[4] It was not easy. In Baltimore Truxtun was complaining about the difficulty of getting sufficient men. A few days later he had a more serious problem — mutiny. Not one to tolerate rebellion, incipient or actual, he summoned all hands on deck, read them the articles of war, and then ordered a marine flogged for insolence. His quick action stemmed the problem, and *Constellation* continued to prepare for sea.[5] She was scheduled to depart with the smaller *Delaware*, twenty guns, under Captain Stephen Decatur, Sr. Decatur was able to set out earlier and was told to rendezvous later with Truxtun. On her second day at sea she fell in with the ship *Alexander Hamilton*, bound from New York to Baltimore. Her captain told Decatur he had recently been plundered by a French privateer and gave him her course. Decatur set off in pursuit and soon caught up with four schooners. Not knowing which was the culprit, Decatur feigned being a merchantman, hoping to draw the Frenchman out. It worked, and after a long chase *Delaware* captured the French privateer *Croyable,* twelve guns, out of Cape François. *Croyable*'s captain expressed some surprise at being taken by an American warship, since he presumed the two nations were at peace. If he had known the situation better, he informed Decatur, he would have preferred to have been sunk. Decatur told him he regretted that it could not be so. *Croyable,* America's first prize in the Quasi War, was hauled into Philadelphia, where she was taken into the new navy and commissioned *Retaliation.*[6]

On the same day (7 July) that *Delaware* was dueling *Croyable,* Congress took further steps to sever relations with France. By unilateral declaration Congress abrogated the Franco-American treaties of 1778. Two days later they authorized naval action on all seas and on 11 July created a permanent Marine Corps, consisting "of one major, four captains, sixteen first lieutenants, twelve second lieutenants, forty-eight sergeants, forty-eight corporals, thirty-two drums and fifes, and seven hundred and twenty privates." On the 16th Congress resurrected the old building program and ordered work resumed on the three suspended frigates, *President, Congress,* and *Chesapeake.* American spirits were running at a fever pitch.[7] In some ports enthusiasm for naval armament went beyond rhetoric to construction. By an act of 30 June Congress had authorized the president to accept up to twenty-four warships from private individuals. Merchants in Newburyport, Salem, Boston, New York, Philadelphia, Baltimore, Norfolk, and Charleston rose to the occasion and by private subscription built vessels in their ports for the navy. To compensate these patriotic investors the government issued bonds bearing 6 percent interest.[8]

Stoddert was overwhelmed; with a tiny office staff, he could barely keep up with the workload. Through the fall of 1798 he continued his efforts to get his ships to sea; it was still not easy. After a short stint at sea, Nicholson took *Constitution* into Hampton Roads and remained snug at his moorings. A small squadron did manage to sail in October for the West Indies to take the war into enemy waters. Under the command of Captain

Alexander Murray, the squadron consisted of Murray's ship, *Montezuma*, twenty guns, a converted merchantman; *Norfolk*, eighteen guns, Captain Thomas Williams, built at Norfolk; and *Retaliation*, fourteen guns, under Lieutenant William Bainbridge. Murray's mission was to seize and destroy French commerce and protect American trade.[9]

This first cruise by an American squadron in foreign waters proved a small disaster. In the early hours of 20 November, off the French island of Guadeloupe, the Americans sighted two sail off to the west. Almost as soon as they gave chase they saw three other vessels in the opposite direction. *Norfolk* and *Montezuma* set out after the two in the west, leaving *Retaliation* to follow after. The three in the east seemed to be coming down on the Americans, but when Bainbridge signaled Murray that they were British, the captain felt he had nothing to fear. He held his course in pursuit of the two fleeing vessels. Bainbridge was wrong in his identification. Only too late did he realize his mistake, when the lead frigate *L'Insurgente*, forty guns, hoisted the tricolor and fired a broadside. She was accompanied by another frigate, *La Volontaire*, forty-four guns. Bainbridge wisely struck and was taken aboard *La Volontaire*. In the meantime Murray and Thomas fled with *L'Insurgente* in hot pursuit. Questioned about the strength of *Norfolk* and *Montezuma*, Bainbridge lied to his captors by exaggerating their number of guns. Unwilling to risk *L'Insurgente*, the captain of *La Volontaire* signaled her to give up the chase and return. Bainbridge had lost his own command but had helped save his two friends.[10]

Although regrettable, the loss of *Retaliation* was honorable. Such was not the case for Captain Isaac Phillips, of the U.S.S. *Baltimore*. Phillips was off Havana convoying American merchantmen when he was stopped by a British squadron under the command of Commodore James Loring. Phillips had no reason to suspect any hostile intent. Ever since the Americans had begun operations against the French, the British had been cooperative, even to the point of exchanging private signals and providing cannon. It was with considerable surprise, then, that Phillips first received a peremptory summons to appear before Loring and then, once in the commodore's cabin, was told to surrender members of his crew to a press gang. He protested but then complied. Loring took fifty-five and returned fifty, keeping five men he felt were legitimate presses. It was the kind of outrage for which the Royal Navy was well known. Ordinarily, however, they confined their impressments to merchant ships. Invading a public warship was a violation of sovereignty and could not be tolerated under any circumstances, let alone one in which the pride of the new navy was at stake. Phillips lost his command, was publicly censured by the secretary of the navy, and dismissed from the service by the president. He tried to make a creditable defense, but it was hopeless. No matter what his excuse, allowing his conduct to go unpunished would have done irreparable harm to the morale of the whole navy. So that in the future there could be no misunderstanding, on 29 December Stoddert issued instructions to commanders of all American warships that "on no pretense whatever" should they allow men to be taken from their ships as long as they "are in a capacity to repel."[11]

Despite the loss of *Retaliation,* by the end of 1798 the navy had fourteen vessels in commission and more, including several revenue cutters, on the way.[12] It was imperative that these ships be used well. From the southern states came the call to send them along their shores to protect commerce. In actual fact, despite their protestations, the southern ports had little commerce to protect.[13] Others felt that the navy ought to be used to convoy merchantmen to Europe. Stoddert fended that off by noting that those routes were not in danger and that he had too few ships to cover merchantmen bound for the Continent. The area where American merchants were taking real losses was the West Indies. By December insurance rates from New London to Tobago had risen to nearly 30 percent, causing merchants to scream with anguish. West Indian trade was vital to the economic well-being of the New England and Middle Atlantic states. The question was how to best protect that trade.[14]

After a long vacation with his family in the fall, Stoddert returned to Philadelphia ready to deal with the issue of deploying the navy. His return coincided with the arrival in Philadelphia of captains Truxtun, Dale, Decatur, and a new captain,

Thomas Tingey. They were there awaiting orders. As the secretary and his commanders reviewed the French menace and discussed ways to deal with it, certain matters became obvious. Winter and the Royal Navy had virtually eliminated any threat from the French in the Atlantic. On the other hand, problems in the West Indies were real and growing worse. Captain Alexander Murray, in command of *Montezuma,* reported 150 privateers fitting out in Guadeloupe. Murray, who according to Truxtun had the soul of a purser rather than an officer, was exaggerating; nevertheless, such a report, accompanied by stories of French mistreatment of American prisoners, made for good newspaper copy and incited demands for action. For these reasons deployment in the West Indies seemed the best strategy. Early in December, on the advice of his ad hoc staff, Stoddert ordered the creation of four squadrons in the region to defend trade and destroy the enemy.[15] Two of the squadrons were ordered to operate east of Puerto Rico, and two were sent to patrol the waters around Cuba. The whole force numbered twenty-one vessels.

The largest squadron was under John Barry. It consisted of his own frigate *United States* in company with her sister, *Constitution,* under Samuel Nicholson. Joining them were the ships *George Washington, Merrimack,* and *Portsmouth,* all of twenty-four guns. A smaller ship, *Herald,* of eighteen guns was also put under Barry's command. In addition to the naval vessels he was also assigned four revenue cutters: *Eagle, Scammel, Diligence,* and *Pickering.* The cutters were all schooner rigged and lightly armed, none having more than fourteen six-pounders. He was to cruise from St. Christopher (now St. Kitts) as far south as Cayenne and Curaçao, a distance of more than seven hundred miles. He was told to pay particular attention to the island of Guadeloupe, from which so many of the French privateers sailed. For a rendezvous Barry was ordered to use Prince Rupert Bay off the British island of Dominica.[16]

Thomas Truxtun commanded the second squadron from on board *Constellation.* His force was assigned a smaller area of operations, covering the waters between St. Christopher and Puerto Rico. In addition to *Constellation,* his force consisted of

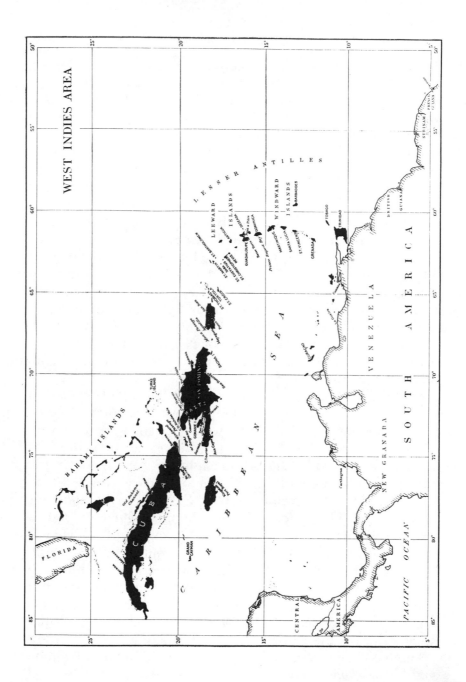

WEST INDIES AREA

the unlucky *Baltimore,* and the brigs *Richmond* and *Norfolk,* both mounting eighteen guns. St. Christopher was their rendezvous.[17]

The Windward Passage between Cuba and Haiti, through which most of the Jamaican shipping passed, was guarded by Captain Thomas Tingey, with his own command, the ship *Ganges,* twenty-four guns, accompanied by the brig *Pinckney,* eighteen guns, and the revenue cutter *South Carolina.*[18]

The last of the deployments was the smallest. Stephen Decatur, Sr., on board *Delaware* was dispatched with two revenue cutters to cruise the north coast of Cuba between Havana and Matanzas.[19]

Orders for the execution of these missions were sent to the captains in early December; however, delays in recruiting and outfitting kept the squadrons from deploying for several weeks. Port delays were in part caused by uncertainty over how much in the way of supplies these vessels ought to carry. From Stoddert's point of view, the longer the navy stayed on station the better, hence they should sail with their holds crammed. The captains disagreed. Warships so loaded down would sit low in the water and sail like tubs. One possibility was to buy from local suppliers in the West Indies, but that was expensive, to say nothing of making the fleet hostage to carnivorous merchants. Finally, the decision was made to keep the navy on station by sending supply vessels from the United States. It was a good plan, and over the course of the Quasi War the United States Navy developed a long-legged capacity.

Since their proposed mission was to protect American trade, the navy spent a good deal of its time convoying American merchantmen. Herding lubberly merchantmen was not what most naval officers wanted to do. It was dull, aggravating, and unprofitable duty. They would have preferred taking on Frenchmen in battle and dividing the spoils. Public warships were entitled to share one eighth the value of American vessels they recaptured. If they captured an enemy superior to themselves, they were to receive full value of the capture; if it was inferior, then one half would be their share.[20] Given their choice, the captains would have opted to spend their time in pursuit, but the merchants were insistent and convoying became the rule.

Stoddert's plan worked. Insurance rates came down. In the first year of operation it was estimated that American merchants saved more than eight million dollars in insurance premiums, far more than it cost to build and maintain the fleet. At the same time, the volume of American foreign trade and number of vessels engaged in it showed a healthy increase.[21]

With virtually the entire navy either in or on its way to the West Indies, Stoddert next turned his attention to a problem closer at hand — Congress. On 29 December 1798 he sent the House and Senate his first annual report. Taking the tide at its full, the secretary called for bold and expensive action: "Twelve ships of Seventy Four Guns, as many Frigates, and Twenty or Thirty Smaller Vessels." To justify such a huge outlay, he pointed out to the members, "It would not perhaps be hazarding too much to say that had we possessed this force a few years ago, we should not have lost by depredations on our trade, four times the sum necessary to have created and maintained it during the whole time the war has existed in Europe." Stoddert then proceeded to lay out a plan for building the vessels (he strongly urged against purchase) and a system of navy yards to support the fleet. Clearly, the secretary had more in mind than simply protecting American commerce in regions such as the West Indies. In fact, he was quite explicit about his intentions. His fleet would be a force not only to protect the nation and its commerce but also to annoy "the Trade of the Maritime powers . . . to insure our future peace with the Nations of Europe."[22]

Stoddert's report helped to bring forth a flood of naval legislation. The Republicans, led by Gallatin, stood in opposition, but against the surge of pronavy nationalist feeling there was little they could do.

On 9 February 1799 Congress authorized the president to instruct naval vessels to stop and examine any American ship suspected of illegal trade with the French. The 25th, an especially busy day, saw four pieces of legislation become law. First came an act fixing the pay of captains and commanders, followed by legislation implementing Stoddert's December report. It reduced his request but still left him with an impressive vote of confidence, authorizing six seventy-fours and six eighteens. On the same day, in separate legislation, $50,000 was appropriated for dockyards, $200,000 for the purchase of timberlands, and the revenue cutters were put, at the president's discretion, under the direction of the navy. For a week there was a lull, and then on 2 March another spate of laws was approved. Included were new rules and regulations for the navy, which altered and expanded the ones inherited from the Continental Navy. Another regulated the medical establishment for both the army and navy and one expanded the Marine Corps.

It was a remarkable display of support. According to Stoddert, Congress would have done even more, but it was afraid of outdistancing public opinion. But even that might change, for, as he wrote to Barry, "Public opinion is getting more and more in favor of the Navy."[23]

Success on the congressional front was matched by triumphs at sea. The navy had been able to send a very respectable force to the West Indies, and it was showing good results.

While on station in the Windward Islands off Martinique, Barry's *United States* encountered a French privateer, *L'Amour de la Patrie*. Barry set out in pursuit of the schooner. Then, perhaps because he feared being trapped on a lee shore, the Frenchman tacked toward the frigate, a course that brought him right under American guns. Barry opened up on the schooner. The third round found its mark, slamming through the hull in a hail of splinters. *L'Amour* dropped her sails and surrendered, but it was too late. An observer on board *United States* described the scene:

> In a few minutes she filled with water, upon which they hauled down their sails, and set up the most lamentable howl I ever heard; and though its said they have abolished all religion, they have not forgotten the old way of imploring the protection of the omnipotent, with gestures, professions and protestations.
>
> Our boats were immediately sent to their relief — I was in the first but when I came near, and found the crew all stript and ready for a swim, I thought it not safe to go on board, but told them the only chance for

their safety, was to run along side the ship, which they did and in a few minutes after the schooner went down. The whole of this piratical crew were saved, amounting to 60 men.[24]

On the Leeward Island station, Captain Truxtun had an even more impressive victory. On 9 February *Constellation* was running down toward the island of Nevis when at noon her lookout spotted a large vessel ten miles to the west-southwest. Truxtun bore down on the stranger. She hoisted American colors but was unable to answer the private signal for the day. Suspicious, Truxtun continued to bear down. As he drew closer, the stranger displayed the French tricolor and fired a gun to windward, signaling her hostile intentions. The Frenchman was *L'Insurgente*, forty guns and 409 men. Reputed to be one of the fastest frigates in the French navy, she might easily have used her speed and fled *Constellation,* had it not been for a sudden gale that rose up, carrying away the main topmast. As *L'Insurgente*'s crew worked furiously to clear the wreckage and prepare for battle, *Constellation* maneuvered into a "Position for every shot to do Execution." Although the American frigate mounted only thirty-eight guns, she fired a heavier weight of metal, thus evening the odds a bit.* As *Constellation* ranged up, Captain Citizen Barreault, the commander of *L'Insurgente*, hailed Truxtun and got an American broadside in reply. The battle went on for an hour and a half, with the Americans clearly getting the better of it. Gunners on *Constellation*'s quarterdeck and in her fighting tops were told to concentrate their fire on *L'Insurgente*'s top hamper. The tactic worked, and *Constellation* was able to rake her disabled enemy several times. Stunned by the volume and accuracy of American fire, *L'Insurgente*'s return fire was neither heavy nor effective. With her rigging and sails in a shambles and gore scattered across the deck, Barreault asked his lieutenants for their advice. On the simple response of his first lieutenant — "Do as you please" — Barreault surrendered with twenty-nine killed and forty-one wounded.

Truxtun could report happily that he had only one man

---

*In naval engagements the weight of the metal fired is more decisive than the number of guns employed.

killed and three wounded. The one death was not of French doing. In the heat of battle Lieutenant Andrew Sterett, in command of one of the gun divisions, took it upon himself to run through a man who was deserting his post. It was unfortunate and perhaps even unnecessary, but that did not restrain the boastful Sterett from writing home, "One fellow I was obliged to run through the body with my sword and so put an end to a coward." In his official report to the secretary Truxtun never mentioned Sterett's "deed."

Lieutenant John Rodgers was ordered on board *L'Insurgente* to take possession of the prize and bring her into port. With twelve men Rodgers went aboard and began the transfer of prisoners to *Constellation*. Darkness and high seas brought a halt to the operation, leaving Rodgers and half a dozen men to cope with a crippled ship and 173 French sailors still aboard. With pistols and cutlasses they forced the prisoners below and then stood guard over the hatches to prevent them from reaching the deck and retaking the ship. In the meantime, all *Constellation* could do was stand off as she struggled to make her own way in heavy seas. It was a long night for Rodgers and his men. Between watching their captives and handling the ship, they had all they could do. For two more nights and days they kept at their posts without rest. Finally, on 13 February, they made St. Christopher in company with *Constellation*. In recognition of his efforts, Truxtun rewarded Rodgers with command of *L'Insurgente* and ordered him to repair her damage as quickly as possible, so that she might get to sea under her new flag.[25]

From his anchorage at Basseterre Roads on St. Christopher, Truxtun dispatched his battle report to the secretary. At the same time he had also to deal with some local problems, the most important of which was exchanging prisoners. The French officer commanding on Guadeloupe, General Desfourneaux, had long been suspected, with reason, of mistreating American prisoners. With an ample supply of French prisoners, Truxtun could now open negotiations for an exchange. On his part Desfourneaux feigned outrage, asserting that since the United States and France were at peace Truxtun's behavior was incomprehensible and resembled more that of an assassin than an ally. Unmoved, the captain told the general, "I, like my Government and Countrymen in general, wish peace with France, and all the World on fair, and honorable Terms, but on any Other we disdain it, Yes Sir, we spurn the idea."[26]

Victory had its price. In addition to providing convoy escort for American merchantmen, Truxtun now had to find men to man *L'Insurgente*, renamed *Insurgente*. To do that he drew on his other ships, thereby reducing their strength. Even with this expedient, he was able to supply a crew of only a little more than one fourth the number she had sailed with under French colors.

As spring approached, Stoddert focused his attention on the American coast. He intended to bring the major portions of the fleet back to home waters. Enlistments were expiring, ships needed repair, and with the good weather on the way the coasts might need protection. His plan was to bring Barry's squadron north first, minus *Congress* and *George Washington*. Stoddert was not entirely pleased with the commodore's conduct. Barry had failed to take much offensive action and, according to the secretary, had been all too prone to keep his ships together. Truxtun, by now the darling of the navy, was expected to bring his ships home in June. By staggering their return, Stoddert hoped to reduce the load on port facilities and at the same time keep a fair number of ships at sea. Unhappily, the plan went awry. Instead of staying on station, Truxtun decided to return in May, and to his dismay Stoddert had to welcome this hero home sooner than anticipated.[27]

From the Navy Department's point of view, operations against the enemy had been quite successful. Several victories, notably that over *L'Insurgente*, coupled with the successful protection of commerce, had given the navy a grand image, which Stoddert translated adroitly into political clout in Congress. Newspapers were filled with stories of naval exploits, and the republic celebrated its heroes. Privately, some naval officers disagreed. Stephen Decatur, Sr., complained:

> Our time has been so much taken up in attending to the trade that we have had very little time, or chance of taking prizes. This is the sixth fleet we have convoyed from the Havana, amounting to 142 sail, independent of those conducted to it. We have been but four days at an anchor since we left Reedy Island in December . . .[28]

The unprofitable tedium of convoy duty was made more painful by the prevalence of debilitating fevers. Seamen coming from the north were unaccustomed to tropical ailments, and until acclimatization took place they were inordinately susceptible. During most of his tour in the Windward Islands, John Barry complained of ill health. He was not alone; the sickbays of American ships were crowded places.

The return of his ships gave Stoddert occasion to reflect on future strategy. While it undoubtedly kept insurance rates down, and thereby pleased the merchants, convoying was a passive activity that, as Decatur indicated, did not appeal to naval officers. Stoddert always listened to his captains and understood their desire for more positive action. He, too, began to evince doubts about the merit of devoting large numbers of vessels to protecting trade.

The secretary also altered his opinions on the type of vessels required for naval work. Initially, he had been delighted to receive almost anything that floated. He could now afford to be more choosy. Small vessels, such as those provided from the revenue service, were a nuisance. Their captains always over-armed them, reducing their chief assets, speed and maneuverability. Moreover, because of their limited carrying capacity, they could not be fitted or provisioned for long periods of duty. They needed frequent resupply. For these reasons, in the spring Stoddert ordered those least serviceable returned to the Treasury Department.[29]

In May, after the president had returned to his home in Braintree, Massachusetts, Stoddert wrote to him with a bold plan. During the hurricane season, when not many American ships would ordinarily be dispatched to the West Indies, why not send a few of the faster ones to ravage traffic along the French coast? Several New England merchants had recently been pressing for convoys to the Baltic and Bilbao. Stoddert had rejected the requests on the basis that the time it would take to form up convoys to Europe would give the enemy ample opportunity to prepare a warm reception. Better that a surprise raid be organized, such as the kind he now proposed. Adams offering no objection, Stoddert went ahead. He intended to employ two frigates, *United States* and *Constitution*, for the operation. The plan was a good one and might well have produced dramatic results, but delays ashore and procrastinating captains kept the ships in port too long. Late in July the secretary had to inform the president that he had abandoned the plan, since the season for West Indian deployment was fast approaching and it was too late to contemplate a European cruise.[30]

One captain was allowed to cruise eastward, however. Indeed, the orders given to Captain Alexander Murray were so vague as to permit almost anything. In command of *Insurgente,* he was told he might go virtually anywhere he wished, as long as he was off Cayenne by 20 September. Such looseness is explained by the fact that the orders were written only two days after Stoddert had officially given up the European plan; hence, they were a last-ditch effort at least to show the flag in Europe. It turned out to be a piddling and almost comic effort. Murray took no vessels and even arrived at Cayenne late.[31]

The remainder of 1799 was not an exciting time for the navy. In the face of mounting criticism about sailing delays, Stoddert struggled to get his ships to sea. For his part Adams continued to support the navy, but at the same time he also moved on the diplomatic front. Despite opposition from his own party, he endorsed sending a peace mission. Only two members of his cabinet stood with him in this act, Benjamin Stoddert and Charles Lee. In his Third Annual Address to Congress, 3 December 1799, Adams delivered a very calm and somewhat optimistic report on negotiations with the French. Nevertheless war went on.[32]

Eighteen hundred began with the United States clearly superior to the French in the West Indies. Stoddert reported cheerfully that all the vessels authorized were in the water, either on station or nearly ready to go. In addition, two frigates were being built at New York, and he anticipated they would be ready early in the summer. As for the six seventy-fours, however, the prospect was not so bright. The sheer task of bringing together the required quantity of timber strained resources to the breaking point. Assembling the vessels would, Stoddert reminded Congress, take much less time than gathering and seasoning the timber. Once it was collected, the problem of storing the timber became acute. Without proper yards in which to stockpile materials, the navy was faced with the chronic need to move supplies about. It was horrendously expensive to move these cumbersome items within the same yard, let alone transport them to another location entirely. Stoddert told Congress that the only sensible solution was to establish public navy yards. Thus far, he had managed to get only one at Washington; he wanted several more.

Strategic considerations for 1800 were unchanged from the previous year. Affecting all deployments was the absolute need, economic and political, to protect American commerce along the coast and in the West Indies. Two major exceptions to this were made. One was the dispatch of the frigate *United States* to Lisbon with a cargo of diplomats; the other, a distant mission given the new frigate *Essex*.[33] She was a thirty-six-gun vessel built at Salem, Massachusetts, under public subscription from the citizens of Essex County.[34] Under the command of Edward Preble, she left New York on 6 January in company with *Congress,* bound for Batavia in the Dutch East Indies, where she was to meet and escort home a convoy of American merchantmen. A few days out *Congress* was dismasted in a storm and forced to return home. Preble was obliged to carry on alone. He did an admirable job, and *Essex* became the first American warship to cross the Equator, double the Cape of Good Hope, and show the new flag in the East Indies. After nearly a year, she returned home in November 1800.[35]

The West Indies campaign remained much as it had been in 1799, a war against small privateers. However, in one area of the region, the island of Santo Domingo, American involvement took on some unusual complications.

Santo Domingo's history was an unhappy one. Discovered by Columbus on his first voyage, the island then had a native population estimated to be as high as one million. Within a short time, war, disease, and the Spanish had virtually wiped out the natives. Since the island's climate and soil made it a fertile agricultural area, white settlers quickly imported black slaves to labor on the plantations. By the end of the American

Revolution the island, under French control, had some half million slaves and only a few thousand white planters. Inspired in part by the rhetoric of the French Revolution, a slave rebellion broke out in 1791. From the midst of rebellion two very able leaders emerged: Benoit Joseph André Rigaud, a mulatto, and François Dominique Toussaint, a black usually known as Toussaint L'Ouverture. For nearly a decade, a shifting set of characters playing against a backdrop of international intrigue brought chaos and bloodshed to the island. France, Great Britain, and the United States, to say nothing of the islanders themselves, all had a vital stake in the future of Santo Domingo.

Toussaint, who was perhaps the cleverest player in this drama, signed a secret agreement with the British on 13 June 1799 by which he agreed to open the island's trade to Great Britain and suppress the French privateers operating from local ports. Although the United States was not an official party to the agreement, because of its friendly disposition toward Toussaint it too was given trade privileges. In return President Adams rescinded his embargo on the island and instructed American naval officers to show support for Toussaint and, whenever possible, prevent arms from reaching Rigaud's forces, who were now fighting for France. With these new instructions in hand, in July 1799 Captain Patrick Fletcher, in command of the frigate *George Washington,* left Newport to take up a station along the north shore of Santo Domingo, where *Boston, General Greene, Norfolk,* and *Herald* were already operating.

Early in October the squadron was reinforced by the arrival of *Constitution* under Silas Talbot. As senior officer, Talbot took command of the Santo Domingo squadron. It was difficult duty. Yellow fever was a constant threat, along with the usual shipboard ailments. Unlike the Leeward and Windward stations, where the enemy ventured into deep water, operations in Santo Domingo were almost entirely coastal and far more brutal. Rigaud's men lay in wait along the coast. Becalmed vessels were their favorite target. When they spotted one, they set out in rowing barges bulging with guns and armed men. They boarded the unlucky victim, murdered the crew and passengers, and took the haul ashore.

Shoal-water work was hardly the specialty of *Constitution;* for that Talbot depended upon his lighter-draft, more weatherly vessels. One such vessel was the schooner *Experiment,* twelve guns, recently launched at Baltimore. On New Year's Day 1800 *Experiment* was convoying four American merchantmen in the Bight of Leogane, at the western end of the island near the Windward Passage. About seven in the morning she and her flock were becalmed in midchannel when they spotted ten barges rowing toward them. According to *Experiment*'s captain, William Maley, "they rowed toward us with great eagerness . . . until they came within long-gun shot of the convoy, when they divided into several small squadrons, with intention to board each of the vessels."[36] What happened next is a matter of some dispute. If Maley is to be believed, *Experiment* stood by with her gunports closed, deceiving the enemy into believing that she was simply another merchantman. When the barges got within range, *Experiment* and two of the merchantmen (brig *Daniel and Mary* and schooner *Sea Flower)* opened a brisk fire with muskets and grape. The pirates were sent reeling back. An hour and a half later they returned for more. This time the barges focused on *Experiment,* hoping to knock her out and then loot the others at will. According to Maley, he let them within about 150 feet and then let loose with grape and muskets. For nearly three hours *Experiment* took heavy fire and returned the same. All this time, according to the official report, the captain was on deck directing his men. The second attack was beaten off, but not without some serious losses. A pair of barges had left the attack on *Experiment* to move against *Daniel and Mary* and the schooner *Mary.* The former was lucky and fended off the assault, but the latter was not so fortunate. When the pirates pressed the attack, *Mary*'s crew abandoned their posts, leaving her captain, William Chipman, alone on deck. The pirates murdered him and then proceeded to plunder the vessel.

After sacking *Mary,* the pirates left her a lifeless hulk and returned to shore to lick their wounds and plan a new attack. By four in the afternoon the wind had still not come up, and the Americans were lying nearly motionless. Although there was little perceptible motion, there was motion. The current slowly moved *Daniel and Mary* and the schooner *Washington* to

a point beyond range of *Experiment*. With newfound courage
the pirates rowed to the attack again. The Americans aboard
the two drifting merchantmen lost heart and abandoned ship.
Taking to the boats, they headed for *Experiment*. They climbed
on board just in time to watch their vessels being sacked.

By sunset the battle was over. *Daniel and Mary* and *Washington*
belonged to the enemy. *Sea Flower* had managed to remain safe
and *Mary* had been retaken, meaning that Maley had lost half
his convoy. In his laconic report, Maley makes much of the
point that he had no casualties other than Lieutenant Porter,
who suffered a slight wound on the arm. Whatever failures
there might have been Maley laid to the incompetence of the
marine officer on board, Lieutenant Nathan Sheridan.

In retrospect it appears Maley was a liar. While the details of
the battle are essentially correct, his account of his own role in it
is not. The wounded Lieutenant Porter was none other than
the later Commodore David Porter, and according to subsequent testimony it was he who was the real hero of the day.
When Maley saw the barges pulling toward him, he threw up
his hands and told his men to surrender. Porter and the others
kept their heads and threw the coward below. That it took some
time for the real story to emerge probably results from the fact
that the junior officers had taken over the ship — a form of
mutiny. Had that fact become known, all sides would have been
in for a long, tempestuous legal ordeal. Ironically, a few
months later Maley found himself in a similar situation and
behaved with equal cowardice. He resigned from the service in
November 1800.[37]

Talbot did not limit his squadron's activities to fending off
picaroons and escorting merchantmen. He took seriously Stoddert's admonition to render Toussaint "Friendly Offices whenever the occasion may be presented." In January he ordered
Captain Christopher Perry to cruise around the island with
*General Greene*. It was a routine assignment that turned out to be
far from ordinary when Perry reached Jacmel, a port on the
south coast, where he found Rigaud's army in possession of the
town but surrounded by Toussaint's forces. Following Stoddert's
and Talbot's policy of rendering aid, Perry patrolled the area to

prevent supplies from reaching Rigaud. Perry even went so far
as to bring his frigate close enough to shore to bombard Rigaud's forts. Pushed to starvation, Rigaud's men made a desperate effort to break through the siege lines. The breakout
failed and the entire garrison, five thousand men, surrendered.
It was a tremendous victory for Toussaint, due in no small
measure to the efforts of Captain Perry, aid that Toussaint was
quick to applaud.[38]

While Talbot was overseeing the Santo Domingo station,
Captain Truxtun returned to the Leeward Islands. He had
spent the months since his triumphant return to the United
States trying to sort out matters relating to prize money,
refitting, and, most nettlesome of all, rank. The issue had to do
with the relative rank of the three senior officers of the navy —
Barry, Truxtun, and Talbot. It was the intervention of President Adams that finally settled the matter, placing Talbot over
Truxtun.[39] Truxtun was furious. Only after being promised
that he would never have to sail under Talbot did he agree to
keep his commission. Hence Talbot's assignment to Santo
Domingo and Truxtun's posting back to the Leeward Islands.

In preparing *Constellation* for sea, Truxtun had made some
important alterations in her armament. During the engagement with *L'Insurgente* he had discovered that his ship was quite
tender — that is, she had a tendency to be overly sensitive to the
wind. In a stiff breeze the leeward gunports were likely to point
directly into the water, if not underwater, while on the windward side they would be aiming to the sky. At sea the only way
to compensate for such tenderness was to shorten sail, a course
of action that had its own unhappy consequences. The preferred method was to lower the center of gravity either by
adding ballast, which would increase displacement and reduce
speed or, in the case of a warship, make an alteration in armament. While refitting in New York, Truxtun decided to do the
latter. He replaced his main battery of twenty-four-pounders
with lighter eighteens. To compensate for the loss in metal on
the quarterdeck, he replaced the long twelves with thirty-two-
pound carronades. The carronades were shorter and lighter
guns whose virtue was the ability to fire heavy shot at short

range. Compared to her previous configuration, *Constellation*
was relatively weaker at great distances, but stronger in close.
In any case, the new arrangement reduced the weight on the
upper decks and improved the ship's sailing qualities.[40]

*Constellation* arrived at St. Christopher on 21 January 1800.
Truxtun immediately went about preparing his ship and the
others at the rendezvous for action.

> On the thirteenth, I left St. Christopher's with the *Constellation* in excel-
> lent trim for sailing, and stood to windward, in order to occupy the
> station I had allotted for myself, before the road of the enemy, at
> Guadaloupe, where I was informed a very large and heavy frigate, of
> upwards of 50 guns, was then laying.[41]

On the morning of 1 February *Constellation* was beating toward
Guadeloupe against a southeast breeze. At about seven-thirty
the lookout reported a large ship several leagues to the south
bearing westward. Truxtun was interested, but he did not
much care for chasing the stranger if it meant beating on a
course that would take him away from his intended cruising
grounds. He thought she might be a British frigate, so to entice
her he hoisted British colors, hoping that she would come up to
speak. Instead the stranger pressed on with more canvas. By
now Truxtun was convinced he had in sight the large French
frigate he had heard was lurking in the area. Indeed he had,
for the ship in question was *La Vengeance,* Captain Citizen Pitot.
The Frenchman, mounting fifty-four guns with a crew of 320
men also had on board eighty military passengers and thirty-six
American POWs. She was bound from Guadeloupe to France.

The chase lasted more than twelve hours. All that time Truxtun kept his men at general quarters. A gentleman aboard
*Constellation* described in grand terms those anxious hours.

> Oh! sir, it is not for my feeble pen to describe the ardor of Columbia's
> sons of the waves on this great and solemn occasion, seated among the
> engines of death, some at their gambols, others combing out their hair
> like Spartan sons of old, their officers and themselves congenial.[42]

In the afternoon the breeze freshened, and *Constellation* bore
down on *La Vengeance,* who thus far showed every indication of
trying to escape rather than fight. By eight in the evening they

were within hailing distance. As Truxtun prepared to call over to her, *La Vengeance* opened the dialogue with her eighteen-pounders. At that Truxtun noted in his journal:

> No parly being then necessary, I sent my principal Aid De camp Mr. Van dyke, to the different officers commanding divisions on the Main Battery, to repeat strictly my orders before given, not to throw away a single charge of powder and shot, but to take good aim, and fire directly into the Hull of the enemy, and load principally with two round shot, and now and then with a Round Shot and Stand of Grape etc. to Encourage the Men, at their Quarters, to cause or suffer no noise or confusion whatever; But to load and fire as fast as possible, when it could be done with certain effect.[43]

In better sailing trim than when she had engaged *L'Insurgente*, *Constellation* was stiff enough to come up on the weather side of *La Vengeance* without excessive heel. At close range her carronades wreaked havoc, pounding *La Vengeance*'s hull and sending a hail of grape across the decks. Truxtun had trained his crew with precision. They served their guns well with quick and accurate fire. Aboard *La Vengeance* the orders were to fire high and cripple the American's rigging. Several times Truxtun tried to maneuver into a raking position with no luck. At one point *Constellation*'s flying jib boom ran afoul of the enemy's mizzen shrouds. Fearful that American boarders would soon be swarming over the bulwarks, Pitot called for his men to prepare to repel boarders. As French marines and sailors came forward, they were met not with boarders but with "a hail of grape shot and of grenades."[44]

After more than four hours of battle, both frigates were in a sorry state. Truxtun's tactic of firing into the enemy's hull and across her decks had made a bloody mess of her crew. Pitot's decision to fire high in an effort to bring down *Constellation*'s rigging had succeeded in putting the American's ability to sail in jeopardy. At one in the morning *La Vengeance* ceased to fire and sheared off. Lieutenant Thomas Robinson, who commanded the carronades on the quarterdeck, reported that he could not bring his guns to bear. Truxtun told him it was of no consequence since the enemy was beaten and he now intended to get alongside her and finish the job. Truxtun was mistaken.

Pitot's cannon had blown away every shroud supporting Truxtun's mainmast. She was wavering. Truxtun called all available
hands to rig a jury support, but it was too late. With an unnerv-
ing crack, the mast broke off neat at the deck and went crashing
over the side, carrying with her midshipman James Jarvis, who
had refused, in spite of the danger, to leave his post in the
maintop.

In the darkness *La Vengeance*, with her men laboring at the
pumps, slipped away. Truxtun was convinced that she was so
badly shot through that nothing could save her and that she
was on her way to a watery grave. He had little time, though, to
contemplate the fate of his enemy; his own ship was in jeopardy. The hull was sound, but above decks all was in disarray. Instead of beating to windward back to St. Christopher, a
distance of 150 miles, Truxtun ordered a course for Jamaica,
seven hundred miles away but in a leeward direction.

A week later *Constellation* limped into Port Royal on the island of Jamaica. The British authorities were helpful, and the
most seriously wounded from *Constellation* were sent ashore for
care. As for the ship herself, Jamaica could not offer much in
the way of assistance. No masts of proper size were available, so
on 1 March *Constellation* set sail for home under jury rig, escorting fourteen merchantmen. On 25 March Truxtun dropped
anchor at Hampton Roads.

In all the time since the battle, Truxtun had heard nothing of
the fate of his foe. Like most of his crew, he assumed that she
had gone down. Such was not the case. With all hands either at
the pumps or plugging holes, in a display of fine seamanship
Pitot had managed to bring his ship into Curaçao.

As seems always the case in battles on land and sea, the first
casualty was truth. The after-action reports on both sides are
littered with exaggerated claims and half-truths. It is reasonably certain the *Constellation* had eighteen killed and twenty-one
wounded. Correspondingly accurate reports for *La Vengeance*
are virtually impossible to obtain, although what figures do
exist point to a casualty figure of approximately one hundred
killed and wounded. Both Truxtun and Pitot had exaggerated
each other's strength; however, in terms of weight of metal and

size of crew, *Constellation* was clearly the inferior ship. That she did so well must be credited to Truxtun's skill as a commander and the carronades on the quarterdeck. It was the first time an American warship had used these guns in battle, and their effect was noted by other commanders.

The remainder of 1800 saw no special changes in the rhythm of warfare. American and French ships continued their sparring in the Caribbean, with the Americans always getting the better of it. During the entire war the only public warship the American navy lost was *Retaliation* — and she had been originally captured from the French. The area off Santo Domingo was patrolled, and the pattern remained pretty much the same, with American warships lending help to Toussaint while battling small vessels that sortied from hidden places along the shore. Ironically, the two greatest losses for the American navy in the war were not a result of enemy action. On 8 August, U.S.S. *Insurgente* sailed from Norfolk under Captain Patrick Fletcher. She was never heard from again and presumably went down with all hands, 340 men. The other loss was U.S.S. *Pickering*, which sailed with ninety men from New Castle, Delaware, only twelve days after *Insurgente*'s departure. She too was never heard from again.

Although President Adams delighted in the American victories against the French, it was never his desire to expand the war. Indeed, it had not been his wish to begin it in the first place. As early as October 1799, against the advice of his cabinet, Adams sent a delegation to confer with the French. It had not been easy. In the spring of 1800 negotiations were stalemated, but in July the French changed their terms. The Americans were able to reach an agreement, and on 1 October a convention was signed. It took more than a year for the diplomatic details to be worked out, but for all intents and purposes the war was over at the end of 1800, when Stoddert instructed his commanders to "treat the armed vessels of France, public or private, exactly as you find they treat our trading vessels."

By every measure, the naval war with France had been an outstanding success for the United States. Occupied with greater matters in Europe, confronted with the superior British navy, and suffering morale and training difficulties arising from the purges of the revolution, the French navy was in a debilitated state. These factors help to account for their dismal showing in the face of the embryonic American fleet. Nevertheless, in several engagements their ships had fought well, and the Americans had never bought a cheap victory.

On the American side there was much of which to be proud. From an administrative point of view, Stoddert had worked wonders. With minimal staff he had overseen the purchase, construction, and dispatch of more than thirty warships, not including the revenue cutters. Thousands of men had been recruited and trained. At the same time he had helped to shepherd through Congress legislation that would shape the future of the navy. All of this could not have been accomplished had it not been for the wide support generated after the successes at sea — successes due in great measure to the determined efforts of American commanders. And while there were many who served well, none is better known or deserves more credit than Thomas Truxtun, who thrashed the French twice in important duels.

## 4
## Dancing and Wenching in the Mediterranean

Unfortunately for John Adams' political future, he was far more successful dealing with the French than with his own party. The president's determination to end the war, and his dispatch of diplomats to that purpose, had badly divided the Federalists. Feeling that he was the object of a conspiracy within his own cabinet, in May 1800 Adams demanded the resignation of his secretary of war, James McHenry, as well as that of his secretary of state, Thomas Pickering. Both were toadies of Hamilton, Adams' continuing *bête noire*, and the president had known for some time of their disloyalty.[1]

Although he had little choice, for the sake of his own political future Adams could not have picked a worse time to declare war on his Hamiltonian enemies. It was a presidential election year, and an internecine debacle in their ranks diminished Federalist hopes of retaining power.

Democratic-Republicans led by Jefferson were poised to take advantage of Federalist disarray; they were well organized and determined. After a particularly hard-fought and slanderous campaign, the results were close; Adams lost by eight electoral votes. Jefferson and his running mate, Aaron Burr, tied with seventy-three votes each, meaning that the decision had to pass the House of Representatives. It took the members of the House one week and thirty-five ballots before the majority of states cast their choice in favor of Jefferson. The new president liked to think of his victory as the "revolution of 1800," and for once most Federalists agreed that the Virginian spoke the truth. Among those most uneasy about the future under the new regime were supporters of the navy.[2]

In his inaugural address Jefferson struck a moderate stance, telling Americans, "We are all Republicans, we are all Federalists." He insisted that the hallmarks of his administration would be frugality and respect for individual rights, both of which had fared badly under the Federalists.[3]

Jefferson's actions bear witness to the sincerity of his speech. He found his Cerberus to guard the gates of the Treasury in the person of the brilliant Swiss-born congressman from Pennsylvania, Albert Gallatin. A friend to nothing that cost money, Gallatin held as his creed that the budget should balance and the debt should be paid. He and the secretary of state, James Madison, were the only people in the administration whose intellect compared in any way to the president's, which helps to explain why they were also his close and loyal friends.

Gallatin set immediately to reckoning the books. He estimated federal income at a very healthy ten million dollars a year. Against that, seven million three hundred thousand had to be set aside for debt reduction and service, leaving barely two million three hundred thousand to nondebt items. This was less than half of Adams' last budget — in 1801.

Since the expenses on the debt could not be reduced, any economies would have to come from department budgets. As the following table indicates, the largest budget belonged to the Navy Department. It therefore became a logical focus for special — and by navy partisans, unappreciated — attention.[4]

| *Federal Expenses 1801* | |
| --- | --- |
| Miscellaneous | $    230,000 |
| Foreign Intercourse | 300,000 |
| Civil List | 500,000 |
| Military | 1,780,000 |
| Naval | 2,100,000 |
| TOTAL | $4,910,000 |

Robert Smith, Jefferson's secretary of the navy, was the president's fifth choice for that position. He was reasonably capable, though not in the same intellectual league with either the president or Gallatin, and hailed from a well-connected Maryland family. His brother Samuel sat in the United States Senate. Although Smith was a faithful Jeffersonian and supported wholeheartedly the doctrine of public frugality, he did not believe that his department was in any way wasteful; like bureaucrats everywhere in every age he always wanted more. He and Gallatin did not get along, and Smith's special access to the Senate through his brother only exacerbated the tenderness between the two secretaries.[5]

In the waning days of the Adams administration, the Federalists scurried around making every attempt to graft permanently both themselves and their policies onto the new administration. The infamous "midnight appointments" were only one of several means by which they hoped to perpetuate their influence. In the matter of the navy, they realized that with both peace and Jefferson a reality, there was little they could do to preserve the fleet intact, let alone expand it. Rather than wait for their enemies to dismantle the navy, on 3 March, the day before he left office, Adams signed a bill providing for a reduction of naval armament.

It was a clever ploy. The rapid expansion of the navy during the Quasi War had brought into service several vessels of marginal or no use. Converted merchantmen and light-draft cruisers were ill suited to distant patrolling or serious battle. What was really needed were first-class frigates, and these were protected by the provisions of the law. The president was authorized to sell every vessel in the fleet, with the exception of thirteen frigates recommended by the secretary to be kept. Seven of these were scheduled for laying up, while the remaining six would be kept in active service but with only two thirds of their full crew on board.[6]

The reduction in the number of ships in service meant that correspondingly fewer men would be required. The law authorized the president to release from service all but nine captains, thirty-six lieutenants, and one hundred and fifty midshipmen. At the time there were twenty-eight captains, seven masters commandant, one hundred and ten lieutenants, and three hundred and fifty-four midshipmen on active duty. It was fortunate that the law was discretionary, for if it had been interpreted literally, the president would have been under obligation to keep only those ranks and officers specified, which would have meant a complete purge of surgeons and pursers. On the other hand, the legislation provided a convenient method to rid the service of many men who ought never to have been commissioned in the first place.

Thomas Jefferson was nothing if not complex and contradictory, and for nearly two hundred years historians have been trying to divine the motives behind his actions. Nowhere are the contradictions more apparent than in his naval policy. Despite what some unkind commentators have said, the new president was not a blind physiocrat so wedded to the land and farming that he thought all commerce a waste of time and a navy a needless expense more likely to provoke than prevent trouble. Having helped to mastermind a revolution, he was certainly no pacifist, and he did have an appreciation for the use of naval force as demonstrated in the 1780s, when he urged war on the Barbary States. At the same time, however, he was wary of the motives of those who spoke for a navy. While such a force might well be needed for protection, its existence was a constant temptation toward adventurism among those who wished the nation to play a prominent role in European affairs. The example of British history came quickly to mind. A large navy and merchant marine kept them in a near-constant state of belligerency and forced them to incur a heavy expense for maintenance and operation. Jefferson and his party wanted neither foreign entanglements nor a sea of red ink.

Yet while Jefferson held his opinions dear, he was no ideologue, and the simple fact was that America had and needed a navy. He was politician enough to recognize that and, Albert Gallatin notwithstanding, he asked Congress for large sums to support the navy and, when pressed, ordered American squadrons into battle to defend the nation's rights. His actions, though, were always predicated on the assumption that they were entirely defensive.[7]

In accordance with the law and the president's policy, the

navy was reduced. Officers were separated and frigates laid up. As vessels returned from sea duty, they were stripped and put up for sale. One of those who came home to her fate was the frigate *George Washington,* arriving in Philadelphia on 19 April 1801. She had been on a special and sad mission. While the rest of the American navy was busy smiting the French in the West Indies, she had the unhappy duty of carrying tribute to the dey of Algiers, as part of the terms by which he allowed American ships free passage. No one was particularly proud of the arrangement, least of all *George Washington*'s captain, William Bainbridge, but it was the custom, and it did keep the peace. On his arrival home, though, Bainbridge brought news of an insult that rocked the new administration.

The affair had begun innocently enough. Upon reaching Algiers, Bainbridge was met by the American consul, Richard O'Brien, who came on board accompanied by a local pilot who guided the frigate to an anchorage close under the guns of the dey's fort. The next day, 18 September, Bainbridge and O'Brien paid their respects to the dey, at which time he asked as a favor that the American ship carry his ambassador and gifts to the sultan in Constantinople. Both the captain and the consul demurred, responding as best they could that such a mission was quite outside their orders. For the next three weeks, while Bainbridge and his crew were busy offloading cargo and taking on ballast, matters with the dey remained in a somewhat uncertain state. That uncertainty was quickly resolved when on the 9th of October he told O'Brien that *George Washington* would take his entourage and gifts to Constantinople. Bainbridge was outraged, but aside from a personal display of temper he was absolutely powerless. With no other American warships to lend support, and trapped beneath the dey's guns, he could only acquiesce or be destroyed, and no one for a moment doubted that was exactly what the dey would do if his order were refused.

The Algerine ambassador did not travel light. His suite included "20 gentlemen, 100 negro Turks, 60 Turkish women . . . jewels and money." That collection of flotsam and jetsam was enough to drive Bainbridge mad, but in addition to the human cargo His Excellency insisted on bringing a menagerie of "20 Lions 3 Tigers 5 Antelopes 2 Ostriches & 20 Parrots." Bainbridge's ark got under way on 20 October, but not before another indignity was heaped upon him. The Algerines insisted that the American flag be lowered and that the Algerine flag be displayed in the place of honor at the main top. After a reasonably pleasant voyage and a friendly reception at Constantinople (*George Washington* was the first American warship to visit the sultan), Bainbridge returned to Algiers on 21 January 1801 and then set a course for Philadelphia, stopping briefly at Alicante.[8]

The news of Bainbridge's humiliation excited Philadelphia and provided ample justification for the need to be wary of Barbary intentions. Such suspicion was reinforced by news from James Leander Cathcart, American consul at Tripoli. He reported that the brig *Catherine* out of New York had been taken by the polacre* *Tripolino*. She had been boarded, stripped, and then hauled into Tripoli, where the bashaw, despite Cathcart's protests, refused to release her. Indeed, the bashaw took the opportunity to berate Cathcart publicly and demanded regular payment from the United States rather than occasional presents. If such was not forthcoming, he promised, then Tripoli would declare war. Cathcart held his tongue but not his pen, and he wrote to the secretary of state that whatever the answer he was to give, it ought to be accompanied by two frigates, or else "we will be continually exposed to the unwarrantable depredations of these Pirates whose insolence is incorrigible and who value existing treaty's no longer than they are subservient to their interests."[9]

Jefferson needed no instruction on the duplicity of the Barbary rulers. The ill fortune of *George Washington* and *Catherine* only confirmed him in his plans to deal sternly.

While he consulted with his architect friend Benjamin Latrobe to create an elaborate housing for the seven frigates to be put in mothballs, he also laid plans for the active employment of the six to be kept in active service. He had decided to divide

*A type of sailing vessel peculiar to the Mediterranean.

them into two squadrons, which would be rotated between home waters and the Mediterranean. Jefferson had qualms about a navy inasmuch as it might involve the United States in European politics; he had no misgivings about using it to chastise pariahs for whom no one felt sympathy.[10]

To command the first Mediterranean squadron Jefferson selected Thomas Truxtun. It was a rare case of merit over seniority, for Truxtun was by seniority the second-ranking officer in the navy behind Richard Dale. He was ordered to gather his vessels at Hampton Roads and provision them for a twelve-month Mediterranean cruise. Truxtun himself would command the frigate *President* and be accompanied by frigates *Philadelphia* and *Essex,* along with the schooner *Enterprize,* which had been kept in service.[11]

Truxtun's response was less than enthusiastic. As commodore, he thought he ought not to have to command his own ship. He needed a flag captain to handle *President* so that he might be freed from shipboard routine and act in the capacity of a true flag officer. In itself that was not sufficient reason to turn down command; after all, he had acted the role of commodore in the West Indies without such aid. What was more important was the promise of glory, or more correctly in this case the notable lack of it. Truxtun asked the secretary what the squadron would be expected to do. Smith's response was uninspiring:

It is . . . proper that you should know that the Object of the squadron are Instructions to our young Officers and to carry into Execution the Law fixing the Peace Establishment of the U.S. It is Conceived also that such a squadron Cruising in view of the Barbary Powers will have a tendency to prevent them seizing on our Commerce, whenever Passion or a Desire of Plunder might incite them thereto.

The Intention is to divide the Peace Establishment into 2 squadrons the second to relieve the present squadron and thus alternately to keep a force of that kind in the Mediterranean should you decline the Command after receiving my letter of 2d Inst you will still be considered as retained in service entitled to your present rank and to receive half pay agreeably to Law until your actual service shall be required I should think it more than probable that your offer to attend to the building of one of the 74's would be highly Acceptable.[12]

Smith already suspected Truxtun's response and he was not disappointed. Going to sea simply to show the flag and train men was a great letdown from the heady days in the West Indies. "Peace," Truxtun said, "can afford no field for me on the ocean."[13] The captain preferred to stay home, where he might at least expect to command a new seventy-four. Besides, it was important to stay close to Washington so that he could be in a position to lobby for higher rank should any be approved. He did agree to stay with the ships until a replacement arrived. That replacement was Captain Richard Dale, who on 22 May took command of the squadron from Truxtun.[14]

Had Truxtun known what was going on in the Mediterranean, he might well have changed his mind. When he did learn, he undoubtedly regretted his decision to sit on the beach.

Among all the nations of the world, Tripoli had one of the most unusual customs for declaring war. From late April into early May 1801, relations with the bashaw deteriorated rapidly. He had not received the tribute promised him by the United States, and as the delay continued his anger rose measurably. James Cathcart did what he could to allay the bashaw's increasing bellicosity, but it was to no avail. He would wait no longer. On 9 May the American flag was hoisted on the foretopmast stay of the bashaw's ships, where by tradition Tripolitan seamen displayed the colors of nations with whom they were at war. Cathcart saw this as the first clear sign of what was to come. The real declaration of war came on Thursday afternoon of 14 May, when a delegation of Tripolitans arrived at the American consulate with axes. Their mission was to chop down the American flagpole and thereby symbolically sever relations with the United States. They quickly accomplished their task, causing Cathcart to remark in his report to the secretary of state, "Thus ends the first act of this Tragedy, I hope the catastrophe may be happy."[15]

Unaware of events in Tripoli, Dale set sail with his squadron shortly after dawn on 2 June. Dale himself commanded *President*, Samuel Barron was aboard *Philadelphia*, William Bainbridge from Constantinople days had *Essex*, and the impetuous Lieutenant Andrew Sterett conned the schooner *Enterprize*.

Four days out, with Dale's permission, *Enterprize* parted company with the squadron and pressed ahead toward Gibraltar. She arrived at the British port on 26 June, and five days later the remainder of the squadron dropped anchor nearby. Dale's orders were to seek out the American consul, John Gavino, and with his aid secure permission from the British to use Gibraltar as a supply base. The American intention was to follow the procedure used successfully in the West Indies during the Quasi War; that is, dispatching supply vessels from the United States to a safe rendezvous and from that point resupply ships on station. For their part, the British were quite willing to accommodate the Americans. At the moment of the American arrival, the harbor was empty of any vessels of the Royal Navy. Most were at sea blockading the French and Spanish at Cádiz. To Dale's great surprise, riding at anchor were two Tripolitan warships, one a twenty-six-gun ship, *Meshuda,* commanded by Murad Reis (alias Peter Lisle), an English mercenary. The other was a smaller brig of sixteen guns. While they professed friendship for the Americans, it was obvious to Dale from the diplomatic dispatches that Tripoli's intentions were anything but peaceful; however, since he was in a neutral port, he could take no action.

Dale wasted no time in going about his business. He ordered Bainbridge to remain behind with the slow-sailing American merchantman *Grand Turk,* laden with tribute for Algiers, while he went ahead with *President* and *Enterprize* to the same destination. Barron was told to take *Philadelphia* and lay off Gibraltar in hopes that the Tripolitans would venture out and the Americans could then attack. For the time being, Murad Reis was content to swing at his mooring, disappointing Barron of a battle but at the same time depriving the Tripolitan navy of the use of two of its best ships. According to Cathcart's estimates, the enemy's entire navy was a contemptible force of seven vessels mounting 106 guns total. They were, in addition, poorly equipped and shorthanded.

> Their mode of attack is first to fire a Broadside, and then to set up a great shout in order to intimidate their enemy, they then board you if you let them, with as many Men as they can, armed with Pistols, large

and small Knives and probably a few with Blunderbussess; if you beat
them off once they seldom risk a second encounter, and three well
directed broadsides will ensure you a complete Victory.[16]

The presence of the squadron enhanced the American image among the Barbary States. Naval force was one language
they understood. On 9 July *President* and *Enterprize* dropped
anchor at Algiers. Here Dale met the American consul,
Richard O'Brien, who like his colleague Cathcart was a long-
time Barbary hater. O'Brien was delighted at the sight of
American guns, regretting only that there were not more of
them. He told Dale that while the Algerines were "growling,"
he did not think they would "bite." As for the Tripolitans, he
reported that they must either have "money or Balls without
delay." The suspicion is that O'Brien would have much preferred to deliver the latter.

On the 10th *Essex* arrived with *Grand Turk* and her cargo of
tribute. With the situation well in hand, *President* and *Enterprize*
set sail on the 11th, bound eastward to Tunis, where they arrived on the 17th. After a brief visit, principally to take on fresh
water and confer with the American consul, William Eaton,
Dale set out for Tripoli to blockade the port. By the 24th he was
patrolling off Tripoli.

There are few naval duties more burdensome than maintaining a sea blockade. The routine is boring and wearing on both
ships and men. The July heat took its toll on board the American ships off Tripoli, and the supply of fresh water so recently
taken on was quickly exhausted. The nearest fresh water was at
the British island of Malta, due north near the straits between
Sicily and North Africa. On 30 July Dale ordered Sterett to
proceed to Malta "there to take in is [*sic*] much water as you can
possibly bring back." Anxious to preserve harmony with the
British, Dale enjoined Sterett "to be particularly attentive to the
Laws and regulations of the place, and not suffer your officers
or People to get into any scrapes with the people on shore, or
elsewhere." As his mission was water, he was told that should he
encounter a Tripolitan on the way he should take him, "heave
all his Guns Over board Cut his Masts, and leave him in a
situation that he Just make out to get into some port." If he

should be fortunate enough to take a prize on the way back to the commodore, then he ought, if possible, to bring the vessel along with him.[17]

One day out on his errand Sterrett hailed a Tripolitan cruiser. Since *Enterprize* was flying British colors as a ruse, the Tripolitan allowed her to come alongside. Sterett asked the corsair the nature of his voyage. He responded that he was in search of Americans, a prey that had thus far eluded him. Sterett replied by hoisting his true colors and letting loose a broadside. That was at nine in the morning; the battle raged until noon. Cathcart's glib comment about three broadsides and a victory was off the mark.

As was their reputation, the Tripolitans made several attempts to board. Luckily, Sterett was able to cut loose their grappling hooks and thereby take advantage of his better gunnery to stand off and pound them into submission. Finally, after having feigned surrender twice to entice the Americans closer, the enemy lowered their flag a third time. This surrender was no pretense. Sterett sent a boarding party, who came back to report dreadful carnage aboard the Tripolitan. Out of a crew of eighty, twenty were dead and thirty wounded. Following Dale's orders, Sterett ordered her guns over the side and her masts cut down to the deck. The *Tripoli,* as she now revealed herself, shattered and defeated, was allowed to proceed home. Her captain, who was among the wounded, probably wished he had been kept prisoner, for upon their arriving home the dey was so furious at the shame of defeat that he ordered him mounted on an ass and paraded through the streets, "after which he received 500 bastinadoes."[18]

Sterett went on to Malta to receive the praise of the British. He had taken on an enemy of about equal strength and beaten him fairly. Most remarkable of all, the victory had cost nothing. *Enterprize* did not have a single casualty, eloquent testimony to the ineptness of Tripolitan gunners.

Sterett's victory brought a brief burst of sunshine into what otherwise was turning into a gloomy affair. On her return to the squadron *Enterprize* brought insufficient water, and Dale was forced to take *President* away from Tripoli and off to Malta to replenish her supply. *Philadelphia* continued her station at Gibraltar, while *Essex* busied herself convoying American merchantmen.

Through the good offices of Nicholas Nissen, the Danish consul, Dale was able to keep up communication with the bashaw; however, since the commodore was not empowered to negotiate a new treaty and the Tripolitans were in no mood to talk, nothing happened. They did manage to exchange prisoners occasionally.

Lack of water, spoiled provisions, and a growing sick list made Dale's position untenable. On 3 September he abandoned the blockade and set a course for Gibraltar, where he intended to rendezvous with the provision ship. *Enterprize* was sent off to collect dispatches and meet *President* at Gibraltar, where the commodore planned to give her last-minute instructions and then send her home.

At Gibraltar Dale discovered Murad Reis and his crew had abandoned their ships in the harbor and slipped back to Tripoli. Their departure ended the need to keep *Philadelphia* nearby, so Dale ordered her over to Tripoli, but only "to take a look into the Harbor" and then proceed to Syracuse for the winter. *Essex* was told that her winter station was to be near the Straits of Gibraltar. Together these two frigates were to be the entire American force in the Mediterranean as Dale himself prepared *President* for the voyage back to America.[19]

Dale's plans were set awry by an incompetent pilot. While bringing *President* out of Port Mahon, the local pilot ran her aground, removing the entire forepart of the keel. Although the frigate was not in peril, she could hardly risk a transatlantic passage, so Dale brought her into the French naval base at Toulon, where she remained from early December until the end of February 1802. From Toulon Dale managed his squadron, minus *Enterprize*, now gone home, but augmented by the frigate *Boston*, which had recently arrived in the area after depositing the new American minister to France, Robert Livingston.[20]

Although Dale's squadron might be faulted for not having done more in the Mediterranean, it did serve two very useful purposes. First, for the time being at least, the Tripolitans were cornered and their harassment of American merchantmen had ceased. Furthermore, although it is difficult to measure, it seems reasonable to assume that the mere presence of American warships gave pause to Tripoli's neighbors as they scanned about for nations to prey upon.

At home Dale's excursion helped provide a focus for the continuing debate of naval policy. As might be expected from a naval officer, in his letters to the secretary Dale urged a larger force for the Mediterranean. At minimum he thought four vessels ought to be off Tripoli, not including a bomb ship, which he recommended be built "to heave a few shells in the Town now and then."[21]

In his first annual message to Congress, Jefferson alluded to the situation in the Mediterranean. He described the steps already taken and gave handsome praise to Sterett's gallantry. True to Republican beliefs about limited government and his role as president, he told them that the American force was authorized only to undertake defensive measures and that it was up to Congress to determine whether they wished more vigorous offensive actions taken. For his part, Jefferson hinted strongly that force was much in order.[22]

The president's sentiments were echoed and amplified by Secretary Smith, who was already hard at work fitting out a relief squadron for Dale. The plan was to send a force of approximately the same size as Dale's to keep the pressure on the Tripolitans. Making up the force were the frigates *Chesapeake*, *Adams*, and *Constellation*, along with the plucky *Enterprize*. Secretary Smith offered command of *Chesapeake* to Truxtun, who would also, because of his seniority, be commodore. Perhaps recalling the previous unpleasantness, Smith promised Truxtun that a junior captain would be appointed to command the frigate so that he might be free to handle the greater command and enjoy the dignity of the commodore's office. Hugh Campbell would be flag captain. The order to command *Adams* went to Edward Preble. Alexander Murray got *Constellation* and Sterett retained *Enterprize*.[23]

Truxtun went dutifully to Norfolk, where he was startled to

see the ill condition of his flagship. She had sat unattended at
the dock for nearly a year and had only one officer on board.
He did what he could, but after a month of effort he still lacked
a full crew. Given his prior experience with the Navy Department, Truxtun began to have his doubts about Smith's willing-
ness to live up to his promises. On 23 February the secretary
delivered devastating news that confirmed Truxtun's worst
fears: Hugh Campbell was not available to go on board
*Chesapeake,* and there would be no replacement. Truxtun, always sensitive to real or imagined slights, was furious. He told
Smith that

> The officers destined for this ship are all young and very inexperienced
> and though in due time may be clever they are deficient at present and
> the task for me on the intended service would be too severe without
> some aid and I have had heretofore much trouble in organizing a
> squadron and at the same time attending all the duty in detail on board
> my own ship.

Unless his conditions were met, he would resign.[24]

Smith and Truxtun were a bad mix. The captain was inordinately sensitive; the secretary, callously blunt. Smith wrote,
"The condition Sir, is impossible." He read Truxtun's message
"as absolute" and therefore could do nothing but accept his
resignation. In his place he immediately appointed Richard
Valentine Morris, who was instructed to repair to Norfolk as
soon as possible. Thomas Truxtun would never command
again.[25]

Morris' orders provided for considerably more latitude than
that granted to Dale. On 6 February Congress had recognized,
but not declared, a state of war with Tripoli, thus making it
possible to remove some of the fetters. According to the new
rules, the president could instruct his officers "to subdue, seize
and make prize of all vessels, goods and effects, belonging to
the Dey of Tripoli" and to take any other measures "as the state
of war will justify." Although Morris was told very few specifics,
other than that he was expected to protect trade, it was quite
clear that the secretary expected vigorous action.[26]

Rather than wait at Norfolk for all the squadron's ships to
assemble, Smith decided to send them across as soon as they

were ready. On 14 March *Constellation* left New York, arriving at Gibraltar on 28 April to find *Enterprize* already there. On 27 April *Chesapeake* set sail from Hampton Roads and arrived in Gibraltar on 25 May. The last of the squadron to arrive was *Adams* on 21 July. She had a new captain. Edward Preble's chronic bad health had made it impossible for him to command. In his place went the now available Hugh Campbell.[27]

While awaiting the arrival of his squadron, Morris went about his business. High on the list of priorities was his social life. He had brought his wife with him, referred to by Henry Wadsworth, the poet Longfellow's uncle and midshipman aboard *Chesapeake*, as the Commodoress. Wadsworth thought her "not beautiful or even handsome but she looks very well in a veil." Mrs. Morris brought in tow their young son, Gerard, and a black maid, "Sal."[28]

Also accompanying Morris was another idler, James Leander Cathcart, the ex-consul at Tripoli, who was instructed to begin peace negotiations with the bashaw. However, the terms were to be strictly on the basis of status quo ante bellum and not a cent to be paid in tribute. On these grounds, it is difficult to imagine that either the secretary of state or Cathcart held out much hope for success.

Morris' squadron behaved more like a touring company than a naval force. Although their object was to blockade Tripoli, not one of the new squadron even got there until July. First off the port was *Constellation*, Captain Alexander Murray, who upon arrival found a Swedish squadron already in place since that nation was having some difficulty with the bashaw. For two months the American frigate jockeyed offshore. *Constellation* was too large for the job; the combination of her deep draft and the timidity of her captain kept her so far to sea that she was well over the horizon, hardly ideal for blockading a port. Murray's ineffectuality was testified to by an American merchant captain, Andrew Morris, late of the brig *Franklin* out of Philadelphia. Morris had taken on an assorted cargo at Marseille, and it was only after "assurances . . . from all quarters" that the Tripolitans were safely bottled up by the Americans that he decided to venture toward Gibraltar and the Atlantic. It was a fatal experience. The Tripolitans, with their swift, shallow-draft vessels, had no trouble at all evading the lumbering Americans, and only a few days out *Franklin* found herself boarded and on her way to Tripoli. Angry at being captured, Morris was furious at what happened next. *Franklin,* with her corsair escort, sailed to Tripoli harbor in broad daylight, in full view of *Constellation,* which made absolutely no attempt to intercept. Murray, according to Midshipman Wadsworth, was an "old woman."[29]

For all his faults, at least Murray was close to the hardships of blockade duty. Richard Morris, on the other hand, had yet to leave Gibraltar. His excuse for remaining at anchor was that he had to watch the Tripolitan vessel that Murad Reis had abandoned, and if that was not sufficient, he also explained his presence as necessary due to the heightened tension between the United States and Morocco.

The commodore's excuses ceased to be relevant when on 21 July the frigate *Adams,* Captain Hugh Campbell, arrived to reinforce him. Clearly, there was no need to keep two frigates, *Adams* and *Chesapeake,* along with *Enterprize* at Gibraltar. On 17 August Morris left his snug harbor with a convoy bound to Malta via Leghorn. Little did he know that at the same time Murray was leaving Tripoli and also setting out for Malta. Tripoli was now completely uncovered.

No one was more frustrated at the seeming inability of the Americans to bring results than the three consuls Eaton, Cathcart, and O'Brien. In a curious reversal of roles, it was the diplomats who urged action and the naval officers who preached patience. The consuls, especially Eaton, would hear nothing of pacific measures. What particularly incensed them was the conduct of the naval officers. When at Gibraltar, they seemed to relish nothing more than drinking. When they left that safe anchorage, all they wanted to do was traipse about from one port to another, taking in the sights and having a general good time. Aside from a few sporadic exchanges of gunfire with the Tripolitans, the only gunpowder expended was in dueling, a habit to which the young high-spirited and hot-tempered officers seemed unhappily addicted. In exasperation Eaton asked, "What have they done but dance and wench?"[30]

From Leghorn Morris sailed for Malta, with a brief stopover at Palermo. Among those on board was Cathcart, whom Morris had promised to deliver to Algiers. After some repairs, thanks to the help of the British, *Chesapeake* sailed to Syracuse. From there it was back to Malta. On 29 January 1803 Morris finally set out for Tripoli in company with two recent arrivals, *John Adams,* Captain John Rodgers, and *New York,* Captain James Barron. Winter gales and a shortage of provisions soon canceled that plan, and after a stormy passage Morris' squadron took refuge in Tunis Bay.

At Tunis the cruise, which thus far had simply been a dismal failure, turned into opera buffa. The bey of Tunis was in a foul mood. A Tunisian vessel, *Paulina,* had been captured by *Enterprize.* He was not pleased and had been haranguing Eaton demanding her return. In addition, by his reckoning the United States owed him a fair sum of money. In his correspondence with Morris, Eaton suggested the mood of the bey and warned the commodore to tread softly, but upon arrival Morris went ashore anyway, taking with him his lieutenant John Rodgers and Cathcart. Eaton detested Morris and made little attempt to hide his feelings. Morris reciprocated, and neither listened to the advice of the other. After a long meeting with Eaton, Morris decided against the consul's recommendations to present himself to the bey. The meeting was a heated one, climaxed by some unpardonable behavior on the part of the commodore. Instead of politely waiting for the bey to dismiss him, Morris stood abruptly, turned his back, and walked out of the chamber. By the time the three Americans were back at the dock, three hundred armed Tunisians had gathered to block their passage. Much to their chagrin Morris, Rodgers, and Cathcart were placed under arrest. For several days the Americans remained under confinement, with Eaton trying to negotiate their release. Morris refused to budge on any issue. Freedom finally came only after the commodore made amends to the bey. Morris paid him twenty-three thousand dollars and gave up the American claim to *Paulina.* On 13 March Morris was at sea again on his way to Algiers, leaving Rodgers behind to negotiate the final details of the settlement. As for Eaton, the bey declared him persona non grata, ending his career as consul at Tunis. However, rather than sail with an officer he detested, Eaton elected to stay and sail with Rodgers. Eaton, Cathcart, and Rodgers all shared the same opinion of Morris — a very low one.[31]

Morris continued to Algiers, arriving on the 19th. Here he found the situation little better than at Tunis; however, this time he had the good sense not to go ashore. The Algerines refused to receive Cathcart. Morris refused to dally and sailed the next day, leaving Richard O'Brien, the incumbent consul, to settle matters and taking with him a much annoyed Cathcart.

At anchor in Gibraltar, Morris could only reflect on the worsening climate in the Mediterranean. Eaton, never an optimist, summed up the situation in his diary. He wrote:

> I fear that all the United States has tried to accomplish in Barbary has been in vain. Unless something drastic is done to reverse the decline in our fortunes, and I know not what it might be, the United States soon will be forced to abandon the entire Mediterranean Sea.[32]

In that frame of mind, William Eaton returned to the United States ready to make his report. Morris could not have been comfortable at that thought.

One of the perennial problems encountered with long deployments overseas was the need to replace crews. Ordinarily men were recruited for a period of one year, which began when the vessel departed for service. Since *Constellation* was the first of Morris' squadron to arrive in the Mediterranean, she was the first to go home, arriving in Washington 15 March. The next to leave was *Chesapeake,* which made home on 1 June. When she departed Gibraltar on 5 April, Morris moved his command to the frigate *New York.* It was now one year since he had arrived in the Mediterranean, and all Morris had to show for his presence was a long list of port calls, some angry Barbary leaders, and an American consular corps that despised him.

Morris was not unaware of his failings. Indeed, in a curious way he admitted to them by not even corresponding with Secretary Smith. For four months he never so much as sent a note regarding his activities. What could he say?

In the spring of 1803 Morris decided to make another attempt at Tripoli. In company with *Enterprize,* commanded by Isaac Hull, *New York* left Gibraltar late in April on her way to Malta, where he planned to rendezvous with *John Adams,* then doing convoy duty in the area. Together the squadron would move on to Tripoli where, if all went according to plan, they would be joined by *Adams.*

On 25 April, en route to Malta, *New York* was sailing to the south of Sardinia when disaster struck. The log book tells the tale:

April 25th. At 8 A.M. we were alarmed by an explosion of powder in the cockpit: Beat to Quarters and discover'd that the accident had happen'd in the Gunners Store Room situated in the Cockpit and not far from the Powder Magazine: The consternation among the people was great, but soon ranks were form'd and those in the Cockpit supplied with water, wet blankets, swabs etc. and the fire was extinguish'd in one hour and a half: The Boats were hoisted out on the first alarm, and the signal of distress made. Found very considerable damage done. The Gunners Stores almost entirely consum'd Pursers Slops, Marine Clothing, and Hospital Stores receiv'd considerable damage, amount not yet ascertain'd. But the greatest misfortune is the injury done to those in the cockpit at the moment of explosion: a number of whom are so shockingly burn that their lives are despair'd of . . . It appears from the Gunner's Account that early in the morning as is usual he had directed John Staines gunners mate to return the signal lanterns to the Store Room and that he (the Gunner) going into the Store Room soon after to see everything in its proper place, found that Staines had left a candle there which he extinguished and came on deck to reprimand his mate for such carelessness: not yet satisfied that all was safe he returned to the Store Room to examine it and by removing some sheep skins he observed some sparks of fire which fell out of them into a Bucket that contain'd some damaged powder prepar'd for smoking the birth deck,* from them it communicated to the Powder Horns hanging up in the Store Room and by the explosion of them and the damaged powder to the bulk head of the Marine store burst and it communicated to about 37 dozen blank cartridges therein.[33]

*They were used for fumigation.

Although the door to the main magazine was blown open, by some miracle the flames did not get inside. Had they reached that far, *New York* and her crew would have ended their careers in the air over Sardinia. Fourteen men died, many of them in an agonizing manner from the effects of burns. Six days later *New York* limped into Malta to await the rest of the squadron.

Because of the need to repair *New York* as well as recopper *Enterprize*'s bottom, Morris did not sail until 20 May. While he and Hull supervised repairs, John Rodgers was patrolling at sea. On the afternoon of 12 May off Tripoli he spotted a sail obviously trying to evade the blockade. He went in pursuit, and by sunset *John Adams* was alongside the stranger, which proved to be no stranger at all. She was Murad Reis's old flagship, *Meshuda,* the one that had been holed up in Gibraltar for the last two years. Through a convoluted and specious exchange of papers, she had become Moroccan and was now on her way to Tripoli as a peaceful merchantman carrying "provisions and necessities." Upon examination, her cargo in fact turned out to be "Guns Cutlashes Hemp and other contraband articles." Rodgers took the ship in company and brought her into Malta.[34]

At nine in the morning of 22 May, Morris' squadron — *New York, John Adams,* and *Enterprize* — made Tripoli. Six days later they were joined by *Adams.* With this force at his disposal, the commodore had a real opportunity to do harm to the bashaw.

Without waiting for the Americans to come within range, the batteries from Tripoli opened fire. They did no damage. While the crew was watching the Tripolitan cannonballs fall harmlessly into the sea, *John Adams* signaled — strange sail to the west. Morris ordered *Enterprize* to pursue. Hull obeyed and sailed parallel to the coast, drawing some ineffective fire. The quarry turned out to be a felucca, a type of small swift vessel favored by the Tripolitans. Rather than face *Enterprize,* the felucca beached herself and the crew went over the side to scurry ashore. *Enterprize* stood off while the commodore came up. Some, including Midshipman Wadsworth, hoped Morris would allow them to land and burn the boat. The commodore wavered and then said no, arguing that risking his men to destroy such a piddling prize made no sense. Despite some

grumbling from the more adventuresome on board, Morris'
decision was a sound one.

What followed was several days of desultory cannonading,
producing little effect on either side. Then on 1 June *Enterprize*
came alongside *New York* to report that several feluccas, apparently carrying grain, were beached about thirty-five miles west
of the city. Morris decided to investigate. He ordered Lieutenant David Porter and Wadsworth to take ten men from *New
York* and *Enterprize* ashore to reconnoiter. The two boats rowed
close enough to the feluccas to hear the men talking. They laid
offshore about a quarter of a mile and landed on a small island
where, much to the delight of his companions, Wadsworth
raised his hands to heaven and in a mock ceremony claimed the
land for the United States. At midnight they returned to the
ships and Porter made his report.

Porter's reconnaissance persuaded Morris to make a landing
in force. At dawn nine boats, two of them filled to the gunwales
with combustibles, ferried fifty men to shore. Resistance was
light, and the Americans easily set fire to the boats. From protected positions the Tripolitans fired, but with little effect. Just
out of range a group of horsemen pranced about. One bold
soldier rode forward to within range of American muskets.
According to Wadsworth, he "bit the dust."

By ten in the morning the men were back on board. This first
landing on the shores of Tripoli was "good sport." Casualties
were light: five men wounded, one of them David Porter.
Enemy casualties were never confirmed, but the evidence is
clear that they were heavier than the Americans'. As for the
purpose of the mission — destruction of the feluccas — less can
be said. As soon as the landing party withdrew, the Tripolitans
raced down to the beach and put the fires out, saving the boats
and most of their cargo.[35]

Despite the bluster, the bashaw was unimpressed with the
Americans. Nicholas Nissen wrote to his friend Cathcart, whom
Morris had deliberately left behind at Leghorn, that the
bashaw's price for peace was half a million dollars. Thus far,
according to Nissen, the blockade had been useless, and the
American bargaining position was a poor one indeed. Nissen

was quite correct. After being guaranteed safe-conduct Morris went ashore to negotiate. The bashaw had whittled his demands down to two hundred thousand dollars in cash, plus twenty thousand a year and reparations for all damage done by the Americans. Morris offered five thousand cash and ten thousand in ten years if relations remained amicable. The gap was unbridgeable, and on 10 June Morris left Tripoli for Malta, leaving *John Adams, Adams,* and *Enterprize* to maintain the blockade.

Watching the harbor on the evening of 21 June, Rodgers noticed some unusual activity. Suspecting that some of the bashaw's cruisers were going to break for sea, he ordered *Enterprize* and *Adams* to draw closer. The next morning Hull informed Rodgers that a large enemy cruiser was at anchor close to shore. *John Adams* made for her, and as she did Tripolitan gunboats put off from shore to aid the cruiser. Meanwhile, on the beach Tripolitan infantry and cavalry were going through their ineffectual ritual of great movement and threatening gestures. Rodgers drew alongside at pointblank range and for forty-five minutes pounded the Tripolitan until her crew went over the side "in the most Confused and precipitate manner." By this time, Rodgers' worries were less with the enemy and more with the shoal water. The leadsman was signaling a quarter less five fathoms, and in places the bottom could actually be seen. Rodgers wore ship* and headed for deeper water while lowering the small boats to send over a prize crew. Before the Americans had a chance to take possession, the cruiser blew up, sending her masts and rigging arching into the air. Four days after the battle, Rodgers received orders from Morris to abandon Tripoli and bring his squadron to Malta, thus giving the Tripolitans free rein to sortie and raid American shipping.[36]

Morris' early departure from Tripoli brought him back to Malta only five days late for the birth of his son. A few unkind people suggested that this is why the commodore had left his station. While Morris and his wife were celebrating the addition

---

*The process of bringing a ship onto another tack by bringing the wind around the stern. The other method of changing direction is tacking, which would bring the wind across the bow.

to their family, back in Washington the commodore's professional career was coming to an end. After hearing all the rumors about long port calls, drinking, dueling, and wenching, to say nothing of the failures at Tripoli, Secretary Smith decided to summon Morris home to answer for his conduct. On 21 June orders were sent, instructing him to return on board *Adams. New York* and the remainder of the squadron were to be turned over to Rodgers, who would remain in command until the relief force under Edward Preble arrived from the United States.[37]

## 5

# Preble Takes Charge

Edward Preble was as hard and sharp as the Maine coast from which he came. Born in 1761 at Falmouth (later Portland), Preble first went to sea in 1778, as a seaman aboard the privateer *Hope*. Two years later he was serving in the Massachusetts State Navy as an acting midshipman on the frigate *Protector,* commanded by John Foster Williams. In the postwar years he turned to the merchant service and within a short time was commanding vessels on coastal and transatlantic routes. But the humdrum rhythm of mercantile voyaging was not to his liking, and as soon as Congress founded the navy Preble was at the door seeking a commission; however, it was not until 1798, with the onset of the Quasi War, that he got his appointment — as lieutenant on board *Constitution.* A variety of circumstances kept Preble from his first post, and by the time he went on active duty it was not on board *Constitution* but rather to command the brig *Pickering.* Preble acquitted himself well, and his obvious talents won him promotion to captain in 1799. With the rank came a greater command — the frigate *Essex,* which he had the honor of commanding when she became the first American warship to double the Cape of Good Hope and show the flag in the Indian Ocean.[1]

Unfortunately, Preble paid a high price for his East Indian voyage. The long stay at sea contributed to a bad case of ulcers, which was to plague him for the rest of his life. Upon return to the States he went home to Portland to recover and to marry.

In April 1801, en route to Washington, Preble received new orders from the Navy Department. He was ordered back to *Essex* to prepare her for sea — a preliminary for the Dale expedition. He declined — his ulcers were still too painful to allow him to command. Nine months later he was offered *Adams.* Thinking himself recovered, he accepted and proceeded, only to discover that he was still not strong enough to take the deck. For a second time he retired to Maine, hoping to recover.[2]

While Preble was resting on the shores of Casco Bay, Secretary Smith was busy planning ways to bring the Tripolitans to heel. The experiences of both Dale and Morris indicated clearly the need for smaller vessels able to sail snug to the coast and pursue the corsairs into shoal water. In February 1803 Congress and the president approved the construction of four small warships, not to exceed sixteen guns, specifically designated for duty in the Mediterranean. One of the four, the brig *Argus,* was to be built in Boston. Preble, who by now was quite well enough to travel, was given the task of supervising her construction, and for that purpose he went down to Boston. *Argus* was not the only reason the captain was in town. Although the records are not clear, it appears that Preble knew something greater was in store for him. On the captain's last visit to Washington, he had met with Smith and had dined with Jefferson. Undoubtedly, both the secretary and the president had shared with him their misgivings about the situation in the Mediterranean and their desire to send another squadron in the spring, of which *Argus* would be a part.

They told Preble that Richard Dale was again slated to be commodore. Dale, however, had his own agenda. He wanted to be an admiral. However much Smith might sympathize, such an appointment was politically impossible, and he told Dale so. In a huff the would-be admiral resigned. Smith then turned his attention to the old warhorse John Barry. But Barry's seagoing days were over: he was ill and in less than a year would be dead.[3]

The elimination of Dale and Barry left Preble as the most logical candidate for commodore, and although it would be several months before he received official word of his appointment, he could not have been unaware of what was coming. In April, when he arrived in Boston to supervise *Argus,* he had every reason to believe that *Constitution,* then lying in ordinary* across the river in Charlestown, would soon be his flagship, from which he would command the new Mediterranean squadron.

Preble was not disappointed. On 14 May Smith dispatched orders assigning him to the frigate and enjoining him to prepare her to sail "at the shortest possible period." He was also told to use his own discretion in deciding whether the ship needed heaving down.†[4] Smith, however, made no mention of his appointment as commodore.

On the day after receiving his orders Preble and Nathaniel Haraden, *Constitution*'s sailing master and the man who had been her caretaker while in ordinary, were peering into all the frigate's innards. Once through with the inside inspection, Preble ordered the carpenters to make ready a caulking stage alongside the hull so that he might scrutinize the copper bottom. Moving along the hull poking, prodding, and lifting, Preble and Haraden found cause enough to heave down *Constitution.* The job began on 28 May.

> The tide being at maximum high, on 28 May *Constitution* was kedged cautiously through a narrow channel to a position off May's (Union) Wharf, where she was anchored fore and aft. It was a 10½-hour job, but only one of the many laborious processes to be accomplished in this herculean process. All the gun deck ports had to be planked up and caulked to ensure the hull's watertight integrity while careened. Guns and ballast — and filled water casks — had to be distributed to assist in the evolution. Gigantic blocks about five feet tall had to be attached individually to the mainmast and foremast, and their two mates to adjacent positions on the wharf. A 140-fathom purchase fall of 10-inch rope was rove through each pair of ship and shore blocks, and led to its own capstan. These would be used to heave her over when the time came. The rudder was unslung and secured to the wharf. Braces were rigged against the fore and main masts on the side toward which the ship would be careened and complementary stays rigged to 18-inch wooden outriggers on the outboard side. Relieving tackles also were

---

*The historical equivalent of putting a ship in mothballs.
†The process of cleaning the ship's bottom.

rigged under the hull to prevent her from capsizing and also to be used if necessary in righting her.

The stage was set by 10 June, when all hands heaved 'round and the heavy frigate was made slowly to roll her port side out of the water. The carpenters then manned their stages and began stripping off the old copper sheets. With them off, seams were caulked with oakum and payed over with a mixture of tallow, tar and turpentine; then sheathing paper was laid on and new sheets of copper tacked on. At the end of each day, the ship was righted. By Friday, 17 June, this daily routine had gotten the entire port side of the hull resheathed. Preble and his toilers spent the weekend winding ship and rerigging her in order to do the starboard side. This time, the process went more quickly; at 5 P.M. on 25 June, the last sheet was tacked home, the carpenters hauled off their stages, giving nine cheers, and the caulkers and seamen responded in kind.[5]

Between heaving down *Constitution* and watching *Argus* take shape on the ways, Preble was a busy man. His job would have been made easier had the navy enjoyed proper facilities. Heaving down was an expensive, cumbersome, time-consuming, and dangerous task. For ships the size of *Constitution,* a far easier method was simply to bring them into a dry dock, but there was none in North America and would be none for three more decades. It was difficult enough to get Congress and the president to build ships; it was virtually impossible to get them to maintain them.

While Preble moved about the Boston waterfront he received another order from the secretary, confirming his position as commodore. Smith informed him that the president, having the "highest degree of confidence" in him, had "determined to commit the command" of the Mediterranean squadron to him. It would consist of *Constitution* and her sister frigate, *Philadelphia,* along with the four vessels authorized in February: *Argus* and *Siren,* sixteen guns each, and schooners *Nautilus* and *Vixen,* each twelve. In addition *Enterprize* would be kept in the Mediterranean and put under Preble's orders.

It was an imposing force, and one designed for the mission — blockading and chastising Tripoli. To some degree the preponderance of small vessels made it less powerful than Preble might have wished. Like all naval officers, he always wanted bigger ships. Nevertheless, since his brigs and schooners carried carronades, they had a far more powerful, if short-ranged, punch than comparable vessels.[6]

As Preble prepared for sea he gave some thought to strategy. He proposed to the secretary that he be allowed to purchase three or four small vessels of Tripolitan rig. He planned to use them to infiltrate the harbor and coasts, perhaps even as decoys to lure an unsuspecting enemy within range. It was a good plan and Smith recognized it as such, but at the same time it cost money and to some degree went beyond current congressional authorization, since it called for the addition of vessels to the squadron. However, Smith was a clever enough bureaucrat to find an answer. Preble was told that if the proposed negotiations between the newly appointed consul, Tobias Lear, and the bashaw broke down, then he was authorized to charter one or more small vessels for the purposes he intended; however, to cut costs he would have to man the boats out of the crews already on board his squadron.[7]

Despite Preble's best efforts, the initial projections for getting *Constitution* to sea were not fulfilled. Two months after he took command, she was still moored off Long Wharf, taking on ballast. Aside from the problems of repair and outfitting, Preble was having considerable difficulty recruiting a crew. To pare expenses, the secretary had actually reduced wages and ordered crews signed on for two years. Neither move worked as an inducement to serve, especially in the face of the higher wages paid in the merchant service. Preble was not alone in his woes. Charles Stewart, commander of *Siren,* then building at Philadelphia, also lamented the difficulty of obtaining men. Eventually, Preble and his captains filled their complements, but only by relying heavily upon foreign seamen, who saw service in the American navy as preferable to shipping aboard British and European vessels.

On 20 July Preble opened his sailing orders from the secretary. The squadron commands were assigned: William Bainbridge was to command *Philadelphia*; *Siren* was Charles Stewart; Isaac Hull was appointed to *Argus.* However, since Hull was in the Mediterranean commanding *Enterprize,* the new brig would be taken out by Stephen Decatur, Jr., who would exchange commands with Hull once on station. John Smith was named captain of *Vixen*, and *Nautilus* was given over to Richard Somers.[8]

As was the custom of the department, the orders were rather detailed. The secretary was concerned that the Tripolitans be restrained and punished, but that in accomplishing that Preble was not to harm or in any way antagonize other powers in the region. As had been the case with Dale and Morris, Gibraltar was designated as the principal supply base, although given the considerable distance from there to Tripoli, Preble received permission to create additional depots at Malta and elsewhere as needed. The message to Preble was clear — the government was determined to bring Tripoli to terms and was prepared to keep a force on station until that end was accomplished. An even clearer indication of Smith's recognition that this might well be a lengthy process was his order to the commodore to establish a permanent shoreside hospital to care for American seamen.

*Vixen* was the first member of the squadron to get to sea. She sailed from Baltimore on 2 August. Preble was ready for sea on the 9th, but adverse winds kept him in the harbor until the 14th. Once at sea, the voyage was a pleasant and fast one. The commodore and Tobias Lear, the consul-designate to Algiers, who was on board, had considerable time to discuss the diplomatic and naval strategies to be employed against the Barbary States and in particular the Tripolitans. On 6 September, off Cape St. Vincent, *Constitution* hailed a stranger that turned out to be the Moroccan warship *Maimona*. A Moroccan vessel in the Atlantic gave cause for some concern, but a careful examination of her papers established her legitimacy. Unknown to Preble, only a week before off Cape de Gata (approximately six hundred miles east on the southeast coast of Spain), *Philadelphia*, which had sailed before *Constitution*, had also stopped a Moroccan vessel, but with a different result.

When Bainbridge summoned the Moroccan to send an officer over to *Philadelphia*, he did not identify himself as an American. The Moroccan turned out to be the emperor's ship,

*Mirboka,* with another vessel in tow — the American brig *Celia,* recently captured. Unaware of Bainbridge's true identity, the Moroccan admitted to taking *Celia,* at which point Bainbridge revealed himself and the fact that *Mirboka* was now his prize.[9]

After parting company with *Maimona,* Preble continued his approach to Gibraltar. Light breezes and hazy weather made progress maddeningly slow and the commodore more irritable than usual. In the twilight of Wednesday 14 September *Constitution*'s lookout announced a strange sail, apparently a large warship.[10] In poor visibility she could not be identified. As they drew close Preble beat to quarters,* fearing the worst, and hailed the stranger to ask her identity. "What ship is that?" he called. The call back was far from satisfactory. "What ship is that?" the stranger replied. "This is the United States frigate *Constitution.* What ship is that?" Again, out of the mist, "What ship is that?" Obviously the stranger was delaying, but for what purpose? The most likely answer would be that she was trying to maneuver into a good position for delivering an unannounced broadside. Preble would have none of it. He hailed the stranger once more. "I am now going to hail you for the last time. If a proper answer is not returned, I will fire a shot into you." This brought a more substantive response: "If you fire a shot, I will return a broadside." By this time Preble's own notoriously short fuse was lit. "What ship is that?" he called back.

"This is His Britannic Majesty's ship *Donegal,* eighty-four guns, Sir Richard Strachan, an English commodore. Send your boat on board."

Such presumption was too much for Preble, who hollered back, "This is the United States ship *Constitution,* forty-four guns, Edward Preble, an American commodore, who will be damned before he sends his boat on board any vessel." He then shouted down the deck to his gun captains, "Blow your matches, boys." Silence followed, and after several very tense minutes a small boat appeared alongside *Constitution.* A boarding ladder was dropped, and an English officer climbed onto

---

*The summons to prepare for combat.

the deck. His captain, George Elliot, of His Majesty's frigate *Maidstone,* offered his compliments. The officer explained that Captain Elliot had misrepresented himself and his ship because of his uncertainty as to *Constitution*'s nationality. He was, as Preble had suspected, buying time while his men went to their guns.

Elliot's response satisfied Preble. Preble's response impressed his men. The commodore's irascible and unbending manner had done little on the voyage to endear him to his officers and men. This incident, though, showed his mettle, and while many might never grow to feel affection for the man, they would always speak proudly of having served with him and the honor of being one of Preble's Boys.

On the 12th *Constitution* finally came into the Straits of Gibraltar. Preble headed first for Tangier. He hove to in the harbor, raised his colors, and fired a gun, the signal for the consul to send out a boat. He then waited but no boat appeared, a clear indication of trouble. Being alone and uncertain, Preble decided to sail across the Straits to Gibraltar. He arrived in the afternoon.

At Gibraltar Preble was brought up to date on the Moroccan situation by Bainbridge and the local American consul, John Gavino. Although the sultan's attitude was not clear, matters did not bode well. The next morning *Vixen* arrived, and in the afternoon *New York* dropped anchor. She was still under the command of Richard Morris, who had already received his orders to return home. The plan was for him to leave *New York* for John Rodgers and take *Adams* home. For his part, Rodgers was ordered to remain as commodore of a two-frigate squadron composed of *New York* and *John Adams.*

On Wednesday 14 September, *Adams* and *John Adams* arrived. When he entered the bay, Rodgers was not pleased to see the commodore's pendant flying from *Constitution.* He was senior to Preble, though junior in age, and felt that he had been usurped. He let his feelings be known to Bainbridge, who reported them to Preble. Preble was sure of his position and had no intention of yielding anything to Rodgers; however, from a practical point of view he had to be conciliatory. With

two of his squadron not yet arrived, *Siren* and *Argus,* Preble
needed Rodgers' help, especially in light of Moroccan behavior.
As soon as he heard of Rodgers' prickliness, he wrote a kind
note expressing his high regard for him and his wish to do
nothing to impinge upon his rights. Rodgers responded by
asking permission to call upon Preble so that they might effect a
common policy against Morocco. It was not a happy marriage,
but it would at least provide a temporary union of the squadrons.[11]

The situation was not good. Tripoli was actively at war
against the United States; Tunis had expelled the American
consul; and Morocco was making belligerent sounds. The only
Barbary State that showed the least good will toward the United
States was Algiers. All this forced Preble to conclude that force
was the only answer. He did not mince words, and less than two
weeks after his arrival he told Smith his feelings.

> I suspect the demands of the Barbary Powers will increase, and will be
> of such a nature as to make it imprudent for our Government to comply
> with, all of them excepting Algiers appear to have a disposition to
> quarrel with us unless we tamely accede to any propositions they choose
> to make, I believe a firm and decided conduct in the first instance
> towards those of them who make war against us would have a good
> effect.
>     The Moors are a deep designing artfull treacherous sett of Villains
> and nothing will keep them so quiet as a respectable naval force near
> them.[12]

With a fair-sized force at his disposal, Preble spoke with authority. The emperor was willing to listen. Through his
intermediaries he informed the commodore that the activities
of his ships had only been in retribution for Rodgers' seizure of
*Meshuda.* After several days of discussion with the emperor and
his representatives, the Americans, including Lear, James
Simpson, the American consul at Tangier, and Preble, finally
reached agreement. On 11 October the Moroccans ratified the
old treaty of 1786, ending the threat of hostilities. Three days
later, *Constitution* left Tangier firing a thirteen-gun salute. The
honor was returned by the Moroccan fort.

Back in Gibraltar Preble faced a problem of a different sort.

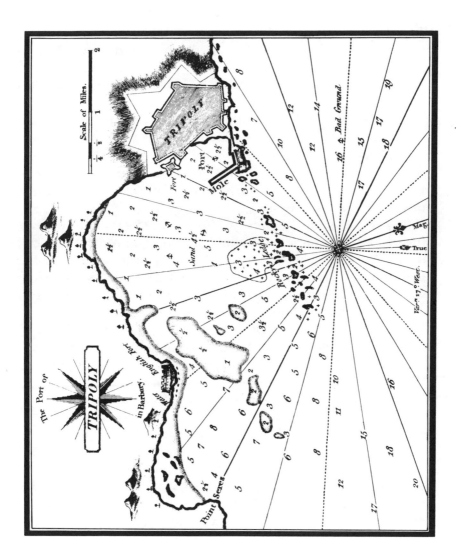

The Port of

TRIPOLY

in Barbary.

While he was across the Straits, three American seamen had
deserted *Siren,* then at anchor in the bay, and gone aboard
H.M.S. *Medusa,* lying nearby. The American commander,
Charles Stewart, asked his British counterpart, John Gore, to
return the men. Gore replied that one of the men mentioned
was not aboard and that the other two were British subjects and
therefore could not be surrendered. There followed a rather
testy exchange of letters, by which each accused the other of
luring away and harboring deserters. As soon as Preble returned, he jumped into the fray and went to Gore's superior,
but with no greater results.

Matters were little better onshore. American and British
officers had a "misunderstanding" in a private room at a local
tavern. At all levels relations with the British seemed to be
deteriorating. Preble's peremptory demands did not sit well
with the proud British, especially in their own port, while their
conduct was hardly that of a gracious host.[13]

By 19 October the American squadron at anchor in Gibraltar
included *New York, John Adams, Siren, Constitution, Enterprize,*
and *Nautilus. Philadelphia* and *Vixen* were off Tripoli. *Argus* was
still en route from the States.

With Morocco under control, Preble could now face east and
move against Tripoli without fear of trouble breaking out in
the Straits behind him. Initially, he decided to move his ships to
a forward base at Valetta on Malta. However, since that too was
a British possession, he was having second thoughts. He was
increasingly suspicious of British actions, and there was no indication that the officers on Malta would be any better disposed
toward Americans than those at Gibraltar. For this reason, he
ordered the squadron to Syracuse on Sicily, a place of far less
comfort than Malta and farther removed from Tripoli, but
serviceable nonetheless.

On 12 November, invoking his authority as commodore, Preble declared Tripoli in a state of blockade, warning both the
Tripolitans and anyone else who might venture into those waters that they did so at risk of capture. On the 13th he ordered
*Constitution, Argus,* and *Nautilus* under way to join *Philadelphia*
and *Vixen* at Tripoli. Lack of wind delayed the departure by a

day, but finally on the 14th Preble was on his way to deliver personally the bad news to Tripoli. Four days out, the squadron had the Barbary Coast in sight and laid a course for Algiers in order to set Tobias Lear and his suite ashore. After a brief stay in that port, Preble made sail on the 22nd. On the 24th, off the south coast of Sardinia, *Constitution* spoke to the British frigate *Amazon*. She bore news of an American disaster.

*Philadelphia* and *Vixen* had reached Tripoli on 7 October. Considering the mission, they were a well-matched pair. *Vixen* handled the inshore work, while *Philadelphia* worked the waters offshore and provided a powerful backup, should her small consort flush any large quarry.[14]

Tripoli harbor is a shallow indention along the coast, approximately six miles wide at the broadest and not more than four miles in depth. Its hard sand bottom provides a poor holding ground, and with an average sounding of less than three fathoms it is a difficult place to bring a large ship. The land mass protects the area from easterly and westerly gales. To the north, shelter is provided from heavy seas by a long rocky ledge that begins on the west side of the harbor and continues in a southeasterly direction for nearly two miles. To enter the harbor a vessel must either pass around the eastern tip of the ledge and then navigate through some tricky waters up to the town or take the more customary route through a narrow passage in the ledge on the western end, barely two hundred yards wide.[15]

Once inside the harbor, the mole and fortress were off to the west or starboard side of an entering vessel. The mole itself was about half a mile long and ran in a southeasterly direction. Behind it was a snug little harbor where the dey's vessels could ordinarily be found.

In sum, Tripoli harbor was a tight and shallow place with little room for maneuver and not much water under the keel. Captain William Bainbridge was fully aware (or should have been) of these hazards.

On 22 October Bainbridge ordered *Vixen* to pursue two corsairs reportedly operating off Lampedusa, an island one hundred and fifty miles to the north. *Vixen*'s departure left *Philadelphia* alone to cover the port. At nine in the morning on the last day of October *Philadelphia*'s lookout spotted a sail, almost certainly Tripolitan, bearing west, hugging the coast in an obvious attempt to avoid Bainbridge and make port. *Philadelphia* gave chase and the stranger hoisted Tripolitan colors. By eleven the Americans were close enough to open fire. The wind was from the east, and *Philadelphia* was making a good eight knots. Running before the wind, cannons echoing, and an enemy about to be taken — all on board were drawn into the excitement, which must have been a welcome relief from the boredom of blockade. Bainbridge knew the waters were shallow; indeed, he had three leadsmen heaving from the chains and calling out the depth. By eleven-thirty Bainbridge realized that his quarry was safe, that there was nothing he could do to intercept her. He came around and was beating back out to open water when he suddenly felt his ship shudder and grind to a stop. She was hard aground on a sloping ledge. The terse account forwarded to the secretary cannot possibly convey the emotion of the captain or the frantic activity of the crew as they struggled to free *Philadelphia*.

> Immediately lowered down a Boat from the Stern, sounded and found the greatest depth of water a stern, laid all sails aback, loosed top Gall^t Sails and set a heavy press of Canvass on the Ship, blowing fresh to get her off, cast Three Anchors away from the Bows, started the Water in the hold, hove overboard the Guns except some abaft, to defend the ship against the Gun Boats, which were then firing on us, found all this ineffectual, then made the last resort of lightning her forward by Cutting away the Fore Mast, which carried the Main Top Gall^t mast with it, but labour and enterprise was in Vain; for our fate was directfully fixed.[16]

From the shore the Tripolitans rejoiced at *Philadelphia*'s distress, and within minutes the frigate found herself taking fire from gunboats. Able to maneuver so as to avoid *Philadelphia*'s batteries, the gunboats kept up a brisk fire from their eighteen- and twenty-four-pounders. By four in the afternoon Bainbridge was desperate. He called a council of war. With the consent of his officers he ordered the flag struck. Some attempt was made to scuttle, but since the ship was already sitting on the bottom, all that accomplished was to give her a severe list. The only other option was to blow her up, but, as Bainbridge wisely acknowledged, "I thought such conduct would not stand acquitted before God or Man, and I never presumed to think I had the liberty of putting to death the lives of 306 Souls because they were placed under my command . . ."[17]

As the Tripolitans came over the gunwales Bainbridge and his men were uncertain about their fate. For the captain there might well have been a sense of déjà vu. Almost five years before (20 November 1798), Captain William Bainbridge had surrendered *Retaliation* to the French. He was the first, and perhaps the only, American naval officer to surrender two commands to an enemy.

The first order of business was looting the ship. Once that had been accomplished, the Americans (307 of them) were taken ashore. From one perspective at least, the prisoners might take comfort. However capricious and ferocious the corsairs appeared, for the most part they were not murderers. Killing the Americans would have made no sense; they preferred to do business. The government in Washington would never ransom corpses, but it might well pay dearly for live sailors. The Tripolitans were businessmen.

For the next nineteen months and three days the Americans were prisoners of the bashaw. Their conditions varied according to the mood of the Tripolitans, which in turn was, for the most part, determined by the actions of Commodore Preble. Despite what many Americans wished to think about the barbarity of the Tripolitans, and contrary to some of the hysterical accounts appearing in the public press, there is no evidence to suggest that in their long captivity the Americans were ever tortured. What deprivation they did endure was probably not much worse than what the bashaw's subjects thought was part of everyday life. The statistics support this conclusion. Five Americans died, all of them seamen. Enlisted men and officers were kept separate, with the latter receiving better treatment, a fact accounting for their lower mortality. To the embarrassment of Bainbridge and the men of *Philadelphia,* five of their company "went Turk" — that is, converted to Islam and swore fealty to the bashaw.[18]

In accounting for the relatively benign treatment accorded the Americans, one additional factor must be mentioned: the continuing and never faltering efforts of the Danish consul, Nicholas Charles Nissen. He was always there, interceding with the bashaw on behalf of the prisoners, advancing money for food and clothing and forwarding correspondence (sometimes secretly) between the prisoners and the outside world. For his humanitarianism, Nissen received official thanks in the form of a congressional resolution requesting the president to make known to Consul Nissen "the high sense entertained by Congress of his disinterested and benevolent attentions manifested to Captain Bainbridge, his officers, and crew, during the time of their captivity in Tripoli."[19]

On hearing the sad news, Preble forgot his quarrel with the British and bore up for Malta, where he hoped to get more recent and complete intelligence. He arrived on Sunday afternoon 27 November. Rather than take time to enter the harbor and anchor, he sent lieutenant John Dent ashore in the jolly boat while *Constitution* stood outside. Dent was gone four hours, and when he returned at four-thirty in the afternoon he brought official confirmation, including a letter from Bainbridge himself, of *Philadelphia*'s fate. Preble wasted no time. He ordered a course laid for Syracuse, where he planned to rendezvous with his squadron and plot strategy.

The commodore was in a difficult situation. In enemy hands *Philadelphia* was a serious threat to his safety. He had only two choices: destroy her or retake her. Speed was of the essence; the longer *Philadelphia* remained in Tripolitan hands, the more likely they would be able to refloat her and get to sea. *Philadelphia*'s capture created other problems as well. Thanks to able diplomacy and Preble's presence, American prestige, as witnessed by the settlement at Tangier, had been on the rise in the Barbary world. The untoward business at Tripoli was most damaging to this image, and the ineptness it revealed might well tempt some to test American strength and resolve. As for Tripoli, not only did they have possession of a fine frigate, far superior to anything they ever could have purchased or built themselves, they also had 307 Americans. In terms of bargain-

"Battle of Tripoli, 3 August 1804," by Michele Felice Corné

"Blowing Up of the Fire Ship *Intrepid* in Tripoli Harbor, 1 September 1804"

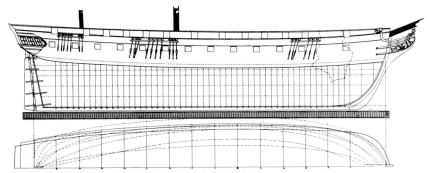

Lines of the United States Frigate *Philadelphia*

"Loss of U.S. Frigate *Philadelphia*, 31 October 1803," by Charles Denoon

"Perry's Victory on Lake Erie, 10 September 1813," by Thomas Birch.
A somewhat romanticized view of the moment when Perry transferred
his command from *Lawrence* to *Niagara*.

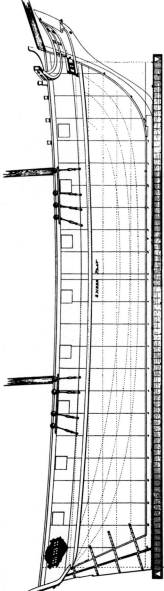

Lines of the United States Schooner (later Brig) *Vixen*

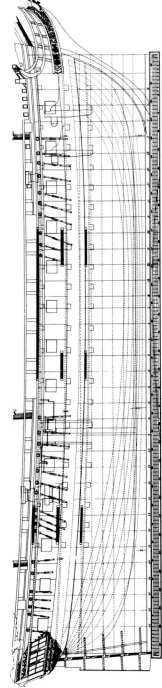

Lines of the United States Frigates of *Constellation* class

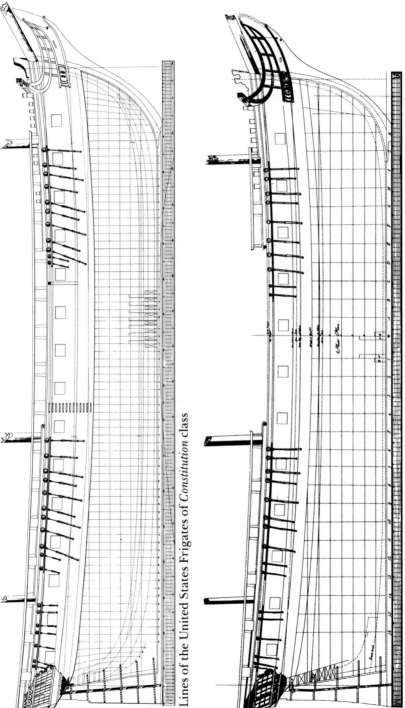

Lines of the United States Frigates of *Constitution* class

Lines of the United States Frigate *Boston*

# Huzza for the American Navy!

John Bull stung to agony by the Wasp and Hornet.

James Lawrence by Gilbert Stuart

Frigate *Chesapeake* by Francis Muller

Joshua Barney by Charles W. Peale

John Rodgers by Gilbert Stuart

ing, the bashaw had the upper hand. With that kind of lever-
age, any attempt by Preble to negotiate was bound to be
difficult.

At Syracuse the squadron received a generous welcome.
Marcello de Gregorio, the governor of the island, then part of
the Kingdom of the Two Sicilies, wined and dined the Americans, offering the use of land facilities to store provisions and
refit their ships. His kindness was not without reason. For generations Sicily had been a favorite target of the corsairs. The
presence of the Americans would ward off attacks and provide
a modicum of protection that the impotent Neapolitan navy
had thus far been incapable of providing.

Preble remained for nearly three weeks. He used the days to
refit his ships, especially *Constitution*, for winter cruising off
Tripoli. He also spent considerable time dealing with logistics.
Already his vessels were in need of new spars, duck, and cord-
age. Several anchors had been lost, and they too needed replacement. As for provisions, much of what had been sent out
in store ships had, upon inspection, been discovered to be rot-
ten. Some supplies could be obtained locally but most could
not, at least not at reasonable prices, so Preble was faced with
the necessity of resupply from home.

In addition to stores, the commodore also requested ships.
He asked the secretary to send him three additional frigates,
two to replace *Philadelphia* and one to patrol off Gibraltar.

On 17 December *Constitution* and *Enterprize* left Syracuse,
bound for the coast of Tripoli. It was risky. Northerly winds
made winter cruising dangerous, and if anything should happen to *Constitution* there would be little to prevent the Tripolitans from breaking out and ravaging American commerce.
Nevertheless, under the circumstances Preble felt it essential to
demonstrate American power.

Six days out they fetched up on the coast. The same day
*Constitution* sighted a small vessel beating offshore. As a ruse,
Preble flew English colors. The stranger was taken in, ran down
toward *Constitution*, and was intercepted by *Enterprize*. Her
name was *Mastico*, and she was a small ketch-rigged vessel. On
board the Americans found a number of Tripolitan officers, as

well as a fair amount of correspondence, all of it in Arabic. A
closer search turned up some arms and personal belongings
from officers aboard *Philadelphia*. Satisfied that he had just
cause for suspicion, Preble put a prize crew aboard and ordered *Mastico* into Syracuse, where he could continue his inquiry. In the meantime *Constitution* and *Enterprize* prowled the
coast.

Severe weather changed Preble's plans. In the face of strong
northerlies, it was simply too dangerous trying to hold station
off a lee shore. On 29 December *Constitution* and *Enterprize* were
back in Syracuse.

Since it was clear that little could be accomplished for the
season, Preble left *Constitution* in charge of Lieutenant Dent and
sailed off for Malta, where the winter could be easier and the
company certainly more interesting. Before he left, Preble
wrote to the prisoners, charging them to "behave like Americans" and promising that "the time of your liberation is not far
distant." He also took the time to write Cathcart at Leghorn,
asking him to inquire about procuring small gunboats. Preble
was laying plans for the spring offensive.[20]

At Valetta Preble found the company most congenial. Apparently the troubles at Gibraltar were purely the product of
the local commanders and did not reflect any policy on the part
of the Royal Navy. The American commodore paid his respects
to the governor, Sir Alexander John Ball, and to Rear Admiral
Sir Richard Bickerton, second in command to Lord Nelson in
the Mediterranean. The British graciously returned the com-
pliment. The admiral went even further. He told Preble that
he could bring *Constitution* into Malta at any time and enlist
Maltese seamen and pilots to serve aboard.

Among the items Preble had brought with him to Malta were
the papers seized on *Mastico*. Unable to find anyone in Syracuse
to do the translation, he hoped for better luck in Malta. The
business went very slowly. As it turned out, the delay worked to
his advantage, for while the translators were laboring, Preble
was approached by emissaries from Hamet Karamanli, brother
of the bashaw and, according to him, the rightful ruler of
Tripoli. Would Preble help him regain his throne? Preble was
sympathetic and provided all the encouragement he could;

however, the decision to help or not would have to come from Washington.

Karamanli's men were not the only Tripolitans seeking an audience with Preble. Representatives of the bashaw also presented themselves to discuss peace terms. Their offer was unacceptable and was refused.

On Wednesday 25 January Preble was back in Syracuse on board *Constitution*. The first order of business was to decide *Mastico*'s fate. In three days her quarantine would end and once again she would be able to sail. Preble wasted no time; all the evidence indicated she was Tripolitan, and therefore on the 28th he declared her a lawful prize. Her cargo was set ashore and seven of her crew, Greek Christians, volunteered for *Constitution*'s crew.

Preble's decision pleased his men: each would share in the prize. But the commodore had more in mind than just lining pockets; *Mastico* had a special role to play. For more than a month he had thought about virtually nothing but *Philadelphia*. Bringing her free was impossible; she must be destroyed. But how?

The answer came from Lieutenant Stephen Decatur, commander of *Enterprize*. He too had been giving a great deal of thought to the problem, and he now proposed to the commodore a plan. No American vessel could ever hope to gain the harbor of Tripoli, but *Mastico*, with her Tripolitan rig and appearance, might well be able to penetrate without raising suspicion. Why not send her in with Americans hidden below, come up to *Philadelphia*, board, and burn her?

Like most good plans it was simple. It was also extremely dangerous. Whether Preble had considered such a scheme before Decatur came forward is not certain; however, since the lieutenant was the first to suggest it, he should have the honor of command. Preble renamed the ketch *Intrepid* and ordered her brought over to the mole to be equipped for a cruise. Only Preble, Decatur, and a few other officers knew her mission, but as considerable quantities of arms and combustibles were brought aboard, sailors in the squadron must have had a fair idea of *Intrepid*'s destination.

It took only a few days to ready *Intrepid*, and on 3 February, in company with Stewart's *Siren,* Decatur left Syracuse. Most of the men, all volunteers, came from *Enterprize.* Several of them, including James Lawrence, Joseph Bainbridge, and Thomas Macdonough, would later go on to become well-known commanders in their own right. *Constitution* provided three men, among them Midshipman Charles Morris.

Next to Decatur, the most important man aboard was the pilot, Salvadore Catalano. A Sicilian from Palermo, Catalano was well acquainted with the waters of Tripoli harbor; in fact, he had been in the harbor on the day *Philadelphia* was captured and had witnessed the sad spectacle. No friend to the Tripolitans, he had volunteered his invaluable services, not the least of which was his ability to speak Arabic.

*Intrepid* and *Siren* arrived off Tripoli on the 7th. The weather was terrible, and for nine days the two vessels jogged offshore waiting for a favorable wind. Finally, on the evening of the 16th, a light northeast wind came up. The plan called for Stewart to stay off the mouth of the harbor in a position to cover the retreat. *Intrepid* would sail into Tripoli, come up to *Philadelphia,* and board. Most of the men were to stay hidden below. Catalano would take the helm and respond to any challenges.

About seven in the evening *Intrepid* entered the harbor. The wind was light, and it took nearly two and a half hours to cover the distance to *Philadelphia.* As they drew within hailing distance, the watch on the frigate challenged. Catalano responded in Arabic that they were from Malta and had lost their anchor in the recent gale. Might they have permission to tie up alongside the frigate until they could safely proceed in daylight? Ralph Izard, a midshipman from *Constitution* on board *Intrepid,* described to his mother what happened next.

> They gave us a hawser to make fast to her by and we then hauled up along side of her and 50 of our men and officers boarded her instantly. The Tripolitans on board of her were dreadfully alarmed when they found who we were. Poor fellows! About 20 of them were cut to pieces and the rest jumped overboard. We set fire to her and in less than 15 minutes from the time we first boarded her the flames were bursting out of her ports. It is astonishing that not one of our men was the least

hurt. But it is a miracle that our little vessel escaped the flames, lying within two feet of them and to leeward also![21]

Escape was a bit hazardous. The Tripolitan gunners from shore and aboard vessels in the harbor opened up on the Americans. With all sail set and sweeps out, *Intrepid* pulled out for dear life. As they neared the edge of the harbor they were met by boats from *Siren*. Lines were passed, and *Intrepid* was taken under tow. About midnight *Intrepid* and *Siren* were back together, with Stewart and Decatur rejoicing at the awesome but sad sight of *Philadelphia* lighting up the southern sky.

"Business or Enterprise, have you completed, that you were sent on?" was the signal hoisted on *Constitution* as soon as Preble saw *Siren* entering Syracuse harbor. The reply brought jubilation. As the victors passed by *Constitution*, *Vixen*, and *Enterprize*, three cheers went up. Decatur came on board to make his report.

Having humbled the Tripolitans and regained American honor (Admiral Nelson reportedly referred to Decatur's triumph as "the most bold and daring act of the age"),[22] Preble could relax for a while. He dispatched his vessels to carry letters to the consuls and to patrol off Tripoli, but it was still winter, so there was little else to do. He wrote to the secretary, again urging him to send more ships to protect what he thought was a commerce "immensely valuable" to the United States, made especially so by the continuing war between France and England, which left Americans in a perfect position to garner neutral trade.[23]

Preble's comments point up his dual roles as sailor and diplomat. Like his predecessors and successors on this distant station, Edward Preble bore both olive branch and mailed fist. Although not an official emissary, he was by default the chief negotiator in a situation fraught with difficulty. Diplomats win fame by bringing peace, naval officers seek victory. The two are not always compatible, and not infrequently Preble was faced with a dilemma over which course to follow. He was most always a naval officer first.

For the most part, Preble abided a rather strong dislike for

American diplomats, and he had an especially visceral reaction to the horde of incompetent foreign nationals who served as vice consuls at the various ports. Thus, prepared to be at least suspicious of diplomats, he must have been thoroughly aghast when Robert R. Livingston, the American minister to France, informed him that he had persuaded the French to use their offices to effect an end to hostilities. The person designated to accomplish this feat was Bonaventure Beaussier, French consul at Tripoli. Livingston asked the commodore to deliver dispatches outlining this plan to Beaussier.

About 20 March Preble sailed to Tripoli. He made the harbor on the 26th. He had expected to find both *Siren* and *Nautilus* on blockade duty; to his surprise, the only vessel in sight was *Siren*. *Nautilus* had been forced to seek refuge to repair damages from a collision with *Siren*. After receiving that report, Preble immediately sent a message ashore to Beaussier, inviting him aboard for dinner. The consul came on the 28th. Judging from Preble's diary, it was one of those occasions that begin well and then deteriorate. By dessert it was clear to the commodore that the consul was pro-Tripoli and would be of little help. Preble was more than ever convinced that force was the answer.

Preble left Tripoli, sailed to Tunis for a show of force, and then returned to Syracuse via Malta. He remained at Syracuse twelve days, allowing time for the crew to take on fresh provisions. During the stay a bit of unpleasantness developed, as a result of the local governor's refusal to return an American deserter. When Decatur, now back in command of *Enterprize,* from which the sailor had deserted, boarded a Maltese coaster and took the man by force, the governor retaliated by holding Lieutenant Richard Somers and eight men in the city. Preble demanded their release and to demonstrate his resolve ordered the squadron to clear for action. In the morning the Americans were released.

Under way again on 25 April, *Constitution* made the now common brief visit to Malta and Tunis, then proceeded northwesterly around the tip of Sicily, stopping at Palermo. The visit to Palermo lasted only a few hours, and by early evening the frigate was bound for Naples. A good deal rested on this visit to

Naples. Preble was convinced that passive blockade of Tripoli would never bring the bashaw to terms. Only by direct and violent action could he hope to persuade the Tripolitans to negotiate on a reasonable basis. To accomplish that he needed shallow-draft gunboats able to sail close enough to shore to deliver effective fire. He also needed mortar or bomb ketches equipped with large-bore mortars capable of throwing shot in a high arc over the walls of the town. Such vessels were common in the Mediterranean, but for political reasons difficult to obtain. None of the littoral nations would lend boats to Preble for fear of antagonizing their neighbors. The exception was the Kingdom of the Two Sicilies, which in either hot or cold form had been carrying on a war with the Tripolitans for years. They also had the advantage, at least from an American perspective, of being a virtual dependency of the British, with whom Preble had developed a very close working relationship.

*Constitution* dropped anchor on 9 May, and Preble went immediately to see General Sir John Acton, the British prime minister of the Kingdom of the Two Sicilies. He was sympathetic, but told the commodore to put his request in writing and he would place it before the king. The following day Preble returned to have dinner with Acton and presented him with a letter asking for the loan of "eight Gun and two Mortar-Boats prepared for Sea with a sufficient stock of Powder, Shot Shells, Muskets Sabres etc." Also included in Preble's request was the loan of two "floating batteries" and "eight long Brass Cannon 24 or 32 pounders . . ." With unwonted speed, His Majesty embraced "very willingly this Opportunity of favoring the Government of the United States" and agreed to provide Preble everything he wished, reducing only the number of gunboats from eight to six, and the long guns also from eight to six.[24]

Preble loaded stores and cannon quickly. By the 20th *Constitution* was on her way to Messina, where the gunboats and bomb ketches were waiting. Since the king had said nothing about the floating batteries, Preble must have assumed they would not be forthcoming, so the long guns that had originally been intended for them now found their way into *Constitution*'s battery, making her more formidable than ever.

Preble arrived at Messina on 26 May. The next day he visited with the Neapolitan commander, Admiral Maresciallo Marchese Espluger, who told him the gunboats were available immediately but that it would take at least three weeks to prepare the bomb ketches. Also at Messina was the schooner *Nautilus,* undergoing recoppering and topside refitting. Preble decided not to wait for either the ketches or *Nautilus.* He signed on ninety-six Neapolitan seamen to man the gunboats and detached most of the crew from *Nautilus* to augment his squadron. Among those taken off *Nautilus* was her commander, Lieutenant Richard Somers, who now became the commanding officer of the gunboat flotilla. At ten in the morning on Wednesday 30 May, *Constitution* with her six gunboats scurrying close behind set sail. A two-day sail brought them to Syracuse, where they met *Enterprize* and *Intrepid.*

Ordering Somers to remain behind at Syracuse, Preble decided to sail to Malta and Tripoli, probably to gain intelligence for his upcoming campaign. En route the frigate had a close encounter with the shore, as the lieutenant in charge of the watch placed too much faith in the local pilot. Having survived that, Preble stayed at Malta only three days, long enough to take Richard O'Brien aboard and head for Tripoli. At Tripoli O'Brien went ashore to test the diplomatic climate; he found no change. For his part Preble spent the time listening to the reports of his captains on blockade duty. He was back in Syracuse on 25 June.

On 12 July Preble was ready. From Messina he sent the following message to any American warship arriving in the Mediterranean.

> I sail tomorrow morning for Tripoli with the Enterprize Nautilus, 6 Gun and two bomb Vessels, the Syren Argus Vixen and Scourge are now blockading that Port — I shall attack the Town and Harbor immediately after my arrival and hope to succeed in bringing the Bashaw to an honorable peace — I have long been expecting a re-inforcement to the Squadron and have been extremely anxious for an arrival from the U.S. to know if my expectations have been well founded. Having no vessel in the Squadron excepting this ship whose cannon can make any Impression on the Bashaw's Walls I expect we may suffer much. Of course you will see the necessity of sailing immediately to our assistance after your arrival here without waiting to land anything you may have brought out for the Squadron.[25]

Little did Preble know that at the very moment he was writing his reinforcements were on their way. The frigates *President*, *Essex*, and *Constellation* were already halfway across the Atlantic bound for Gilbraltar.

At dawn on Friday the 13th (no one seemed to notice that irony) *Constitution* and her escorts made their way out of Syracuse. It was an impressive sight — *Constitution* in the van, followed by *Nautilus*, *Enterprize*, six gunboats (numbered one through six), and two bomb ketches. It was the largest American naval force to face Tripoli yet. Despite what he wrote, Preble was confident of victory.

## 6

# "To the Shores of Tripoli"

Not surprisingly, the gunboats sailed like slugs. They could barely make headway, and in the first thirteen hours at sea they averaged less than two knots. Flat bottomed and heavy, they were even difficult to row. Finally, Preble had no choice but to pass them a line, and soon all of the small boats were under tow. They made Malta on 16 July and were off Tripoli by the 25th. As Preble later reported to the secretary, "Our squadron now consisted of the *Constitution,* three brigs, three schooners, two bombs and six gunboats, our whole number of men one thousand and sixty."[1]

At first glance the Tripolitans would seem to have had tremendous odds on their side. The town was thick-walled and had one hundred and fifteen large cannon. On the water they had nineteen gunboats, two galleys, two schooners, and a brig all drawn up in line of battle. To man the battlements and vessels, the bashaw had assembled in the neighborhood of twenty-five thousand men. Numbers alone, however, do not win battles. The Tripolitans were neither disciplined nor well led; the Americans were both. Preble's main problem was getting close enough that the town and fort would fall within range of his guns without being clobbered by return fire.

After some problems with the weather, the Americans were in position to attack on 3 August. With a fair east wind Preble moved to within two to three miles of the batteries. At that point he noticed that the Tripolitan vessels had divided into two divisions and were advancing out beyond the rocks. It was a foolish move on the part of the enemy, since they were risking their fleet by removing it out of supporting range of the shore batteries in the face of a superior enemy.

Quick to take advantage, Preble signaled his captains to come within hailing distance. He ordered the gunboats divided into two divisions of three each, one led by Stephen Decatur and the other by Richard Somers. The plan was for the gunboats to engage the enemy directly, backed up by the brigs and schooners. At the same time, the bombs were to move close enough to be able to lob their shells onto the town. Mindful of *Philadelphia*'s fate, *Constitution* would remain offshore, ready to engage if the situation required.

The squadron moved into position, and at two-thirty Preble signaled a general engagement. The fight was brief and furious. Command and control became an immediate problem for the Americans. Preble observed the battle from *Constitution* and communicated to his subordinates by means of signal flags. Unfortunately, the gunboat commanders had apparently failed to assign anyone to observe the flagship. To compound the problem, Somers, in command of the first division, was so far to leeward in gunboat No. 1 that, despite his best efforts, he could not come up to his other two boats, Nos. 2 and 3, in time to lead them into battle. Instead, they attached themselves to Decatur's command.[2]

Decatur's division bore down on two Tripolitans under sail just outside the rocks. They quickly came about and scurried for safety closer in. Decatur then turned his attention to the remaining enemy boats anchored to leeward. Altogether, excluding the two boats that had already fled, the Tripolitans had sixteen vessels drawn up on an east-west line outside the rocks. Five on the eastern end of the line were grouped together to defend the western passage, while the other eleven were on line in front of the molehead battery. Within the harbor were three or four other Tripolitans, whose assignment was to block any American penetration of the harbor.

By approximately three in the afternoon Decatur had closed to within a few feet of the five boats in the western passage, all the while delivering a murderous fire of canister and grape. Like the two before them, these five also withdrew in haste. With a favoring breeze, Decatur continued on a westerly course that quickly brought him up to the remaining eleven. Unlike their comrades, these elected to stand and fight, a reasonable decision since they had superior numbers. With him Decatur now had his own gunboat, plus No. 2, under the command of his brother James; Joseph Bainbridge, William's brother, came along in No. 5, and John Trippe in No. 6. Somers was still busy elsewhere. Number 3, with Joshua Blake, was unengaged and standing offshore.[3]

Decatur was determined to beat the Tripolitans at their own game. He grappled and boarded the first Tripolitan, going over the gunwales onto the enemy's deck with his good friend Midshipman Thomas Macdonough at his side, along with twenty other men. In ten minutes of bloody work they cleared the decks and took a prize. Decatur gave her over to Lieutenant Thorn, returned to his own boat, and took the Tripolitan under tow. As they were clearing the battle area, gunboat No. 2 came close aboard to deliver sad news. Stephen's brother James, commanding gunboat No. 2 had been mortally wounded, treacherously as it turned out. His boat had been hotly engaged with an enemy who had struck its flag. When young Decatur came aboard the Tripolitan captain shot him in the head. In the ensuing confusion, the enemy gunboat escaped while No. 2, now under the command of Midshipman Brown, made her own retreat.

By all accounts, Stephen Decatur became a near madman when given the news. Although he could muster only eleven men, the remainder of his crew being on board the prize, he cast off from Thorn and went in pursuit of his brother's murderer. To his dying day Decatur was convinced that he found the right man. In the fog of battle that certainty is questionable; nevertheless, Decatur caught up with the presumed culprit and boarded. He hacked his way to the captain and there in Olympian battle the two commanders met. The Tripolitan lunged at Decatur with a boarding pike. He parried the thrust but snapped the blade of his cutlass. A second lunge found its target, wounding Decatur in the arm. With amazing strength the lieutenant wrenched the pike away from the Tripolitan and then, like dazed fighters, the two commanders grasped one another and fell to the deck. The Arab attempted a blow at Decatur's head, only to have it blocked by an American seaman, Daniel Frazier, who used his own body to protect his captain.[4] With his right hand the Tripolitan took a small yataghan* from his sash and prepared to drive it home. At that moment Decatur found his pistol, cocked, and fired, taking the life out of his enemy. With their leader dead the crew surrendered, giving Decatur his second prize of the day.

While Decatur was subduing his quarry, Sailing Master John Trippe on No. 6 was doing his part as well, engaging an enemy on Decatur's leeward side. As he drew close, the stern of his boat pressed against the Tripolitan. Trippe hastily called boarders away and, along with ten others, leaped across. As they gained the enemy's deck, they looked back at a shocking sight. Awkward in the water, like all the gunboats, No. 6 was falling off. The midshipman left in command could not bring her up. Trippe and his party were all alone. Against odds of at least three to one, the Americans fought savagely, as did the Tripolitans. Wounded eleven times, Trippe finally fell to the deck, but the Americans triumphed, giving them their third catch of the day.

Although Somers was never able to engage enemy gunboats, he did move close enough to fire on the molehead battery. The return fire was heavy, and he was having difficulty extricating himself with his barely maneuverable No. 1 when a lucky shot from one of the bomb ketches fell into the battery, wrecking several guns and gracing Somers with a chance to retreat.

Within the harbor the Tripolitans had watched their rout with consternation. By late afternoon reinforcements were sailing out. *Constitution* and the other large vessels delivered a heavy fire, discouraging any attempt to cut off the American gunboats. At four-thirty Preble signaled to all vessels, "Join company as soon as possible."

Despite the gallantry of his men, Preble was disappointed,

*A long knife or short saber without a crosspiece.

for the action in fact had accomplished very little.[5] The capture of three small boats was hardly sufficient cause for celebration. The Americans withdrew and spent the evening to the north of Tripoli, repairing damage, shifting prisoners, and reprovisioning. At nine the next morning a sail was sighted coming out of the harbor. It was the French privateer *La Rusé*. She was escorted to *Constitution* and persuaded to return to Tripoli with a message. The offer of fifty thousand dollars' ransom still stood, Preble announced, but only until the arrival of additional American frigates, at which time he would not pay one cent. The bashaw was as stubborn as the commodore, and through Monsieur Beaussier he flatly refused the American offer. Preble decided to attack again.

The plan for the second attack owes much to Preble's junior officers, especially Charles Stewart. Stewart argued against another frontal assault and proposed instead to bombard the town from a small bay just to the west. The position was close enough that the bombs could lob their shells into the town from an area that, according to intelligence reports, was undefended. It had the further attraction of being far enough away from the main batteries that should the enemy sortie to drive off the attackers, they would have to expose themselves and so risk having their retreat cut off by the American schooners and brigs.

On the morning of 7 August the American squadron began to move. Light winds kept *Constitution* at anchor (she was the only one in the squadron that could not be maneuvered by sweeps), but the other vessels broke out the sweeps and pulled for their positions. Unhappily, the Americans failed to reconnoiter properly, and as a result they got two surprises. The first was a strong westerly inshore current against which they had great difficulty rowing; the second was that, contrary to reports, the Tripolitans had fortified the bay area. As soon as they got within range, the Americans had a hot time of it. One of the gunboats most immediately involved with the new battery was No. 9. Suddenly, in the midst of the battle, she blew up with a tremendous roar. When smoke cleared, all that could be seen was her forward section, slowly settling in the water with her crew still manning the bow gun. They tried for one more shot, but just as the gunner was placing the match to the hole she slid under the water, with her crew giving a defiant three cheers. Ten men died in the explosion.

As evening approached, the wind began to shift onshore. Preble ordered disengagement, and the American squadron withdrew toward the northeast. An evaluation of the day's bombardment did not give the commodore much pleasure. His men had been able to silence several enemy guns, but that was only a temporary accomplishment, for in due time they would be back in operation. The bomb vessels and gunboats did manage to come within range of the town and had delivered fire onto the buildings. However, even that was of limited value. Tripoli was a place of mud and stone, hardly flammable, although collapsible with a direct hit. The truth is, Preble's bombardment was not doing great physical damage to the town. It was embarrassing to the bashaw, but little else.

During the battle a strange sail had been sighted. *Argus,* sent to investigate, came back with the news that it was the frigate *John Adams,* Master Commandant Isaac Chauncey in command. Chauncey came aboard *Constitution* to deliver devastating news. He handed Preble a letter from Secretary Smith dated 22 May, informing him that Samuel Barron would succeed him as Mediterranean commander. In his private journal Preble recorded his sharp reaction: "How much my feelings are lacerated by this supercedure at the moment of Victory cannot be described and can be felt only by an Officer placed in my mortifying situation."[6]

For Preble time was running out. He desperately wanted the laurels of victory, but to garner them he had to finish his business before Barron arrived and before the fall weather made keeping station offshore too difficult. He kept up his correspondence with the bashaw and increased the offer to $120,000. At the same time, to keep the pressure on, he launched a third and then a fourth attack, but they accomplished little. Nicholas Nissen, who was certainly in a position to know, wrote that except for the first attack, on 3 August, all the others were of "absolutely no consequence."[7]

As a last resort, early in September, with Barron still not on the scene, Preble decided to gamble. *Intrepid* (formerly *Mastico)* had just joined the squadron. Preble made her into an "infernal," a floating powder keg. Five tons of black powder, fifty nine-inch shells, one hundred thirteen-inch mortar shells, and a large quantity of combustibles were all stowed aboard. The scheme was to slip quietly into the harbor, come up close to the fortress, light the fuse, and blow it up. As wild as it seems, volunteers to man *Intrepid* were not lacking. Perhaps seeing in this venture their chance to imitate Decatur's *Philadelphia* exploit, Lieutenant Richard Somers of *Nautilus* and Midshipman Henry Wadsworth of *Constitution* came forward, joined later by Acting Lieutenant Joseph Israel. Those three officers, in company with ten enlisted men, were charged with the task. On 1 September *Intrepid* moved toward the harbor. They were only four hundred yards outside, and still undetected, when the wind took an unkind direction and forced them to withdraw. The next day the squadron made a fifth attack on the port, and the following evening *Intrepid* was ready to try again. She was escorted by *Argus, Vixen,* and *Nautilus.* A few hundred yards outside the western passage, the escorts came about and left *Intrepid* to proceed on her own. She passed under the walls of the fortress. Two alarm guns were sounded. For the next ten minutes all was silent, when suddenly a huge explosion took place. Somehow, perhaps deliberately to avoid capture, *Intrepid* blew up prematurely. All hands were lost.[8]

The loss of *Intrepid,* frustration at not being able to bring the bashaw to terms, poor weather, and the imminent arrival of Barron cast a gloom on Edward Preble. For these reasons, on the morning of 6 September, he had a conference with his senior officers and announced his decision to end offensive operations. That evening *John Adams, Siren, Enterprize,* and *Nautilus* sailed for Sicily with gunboats in tow. *Constitution, Argus,* and *Vixen* remained to keep up the blockade. At noon on the 9th *Argus* signaled strange sail to the northeast. Barron had arrived.

It did not necessarily follow from Barron's arrival that Preble would leave; indeed, it was Secretary Smith's expectation that Preble would remain to aid in the reduction of Tripoli. That might have been, but when Preble learned that in addition to Barron, John Rodgers would also be present, he decided to leave. There was no way he would allow himself to be third in command, especially under John Rodgers, for whom he still harbored resentment over his conduct at Gibraltar.

From the 9th through the 13th Preble and Barron patrolled and conferred off the coast of Tripoli. Barron had brought with him William Eaton, the consul who had previously proposed to Preble the scheme of cooperating with the bashaw's brother, Hamet Karamanli. Hitherto Preble had been cool to the idea, but he now seemed more receptive. Perhaps months of frustration had induced him to try anything.

Barron, Preble, and Eaton agreed on a plan. On 13 September Barron summoned Lieutenant Isaac Hull, captain of *Argus*, and delivered two sets of orders, one written and the other verbal. The written orders instructed Hull to proceed to Malta, refit, and then sail to Smyrna and provide escort for any American vessels returning down the Mediterranean. Those were only a "disguise," for in the verbal orders his real mission was explained — "to proceed with Mr. Eaton to Alexandria in search of Homet [*sic*] Bashaw, the rival brother and legitimate sovereign of the reigning Bashaw of Tripoli; and to convey him and his suite to Derne or such other place on the coast as may be determined the most proper for cooperating with the naval force under my command against the common enemy: or, if more agreeable to him, to bring him to me before Tripoli."[9]

The same day Hull received his orders, Preble left the coast of Tripoli bound for Malta en route home. Nothing, however, was ever easy in the Mediterranean. Barron grew ill with a liver ailment and became virtually incapacitated. He remained ashore at Syracuse. Since he could not command at sea, he asked John Rodgers to "hoist the Broad pendant on board *Constitution*."[10] Barron, however, did not surrender overall command; from his sickbed he continued to direct the movements of the squadron. Since the season was too dangerous for a close blockade he directed Rodgers to take *Constitution* to Lisbon in the hope of finding men to fill up his complement, by that time nearly eighty men short.

John Rodgers was an unpleasant man. Noadiah Morris, one

of Preble's Boys and no friend to Rodgers, once described him as an officer whose "reputation as a fighting man has originated, I believe, in his black looks, his insufferable arrogance, and the frequent and unmerited assaults he has made on poor and inoffensive citizens."[11] One man who would testify to the absolute accuracy of this statement was the American consul at Lisbon, William Jarvis. He had the unenviable task for six weeks of dealing with Rodgers. The captain seemed incapable of understanding why all of Lisbon, and especially Jarvis, did not move mountains to suit him. In a heated, lengthy, and sometimes silly exchange of letters, the diplomat and the officer assailed one another. Rodgers did get his men, mostly foreigners, and finally, to the relief of everyone, he left Lisbon on 9 February 1805 and headed back for the Mediterranean to report to Barron.[12]

*Constitution* entered the harbor at Valetta on the afternoon of 23 February. Rodgers went ashore and found that Barron had moved his headquarters here from Syracuse. The change had been made apparently because of a general dissatisfaction among the officers with life on Sicily, where by all accounts accommodations were primitive and the social life nil. At Malta the society was far more refined, although for Barron it mattered little, since his health was still poor and left him in confinement.

Compared to the heady days of Preble's command, life with Barron was dull. To be sure, the weather prevented close operations against Tripoli, but the commodore's indisposition also contributed to a lethargic spirit. Adding to the miasma was a bit of internecine warfare among Barron, Rodgers, and the senior American diplomat, Tobias Lear.

While the senior American commanders were preoccupied with their own business, William Eaton was busy in Egypt. It is difficult to know just how seriously Barron, Rodgers, and Lear took this man. Barron probably expected more than Rodgers, while Lear thought the entire scheme preposterous. Nevertheless, not a person to be put off, Eaton pushed ahead.

When Bainbridge, who at this point knew more about Tripolitan attitudes and capabilities than any other American, heard about the scheme with Hamet, he was nonplused. He told Lear, "Whoever has advised such a measure must be entirely ignorant of the power of the present ruler and of the disposition of his Subjects who always detest the miserable exile . . ." According to the captain, Hamet was effeminate and pusillanimous, hardly a rock upon which to found a revolution.[13]

*Argus* arrived at Alexandria on 26 November. The resident English consul came on board, along with a "number of Turks."[14] From their conversation Eaton learned that Hamet was probably in Cairo. He also discovered how dangerous life was in Egypt. Although Egypt was nominally under the rule of Turkey, the invasion of the French and their subsequent defeat had left a good deal of doubt regarding who was actually in charge.[15]

As the officer responsible for the safety of this party, Hull had no intention of allowing Eaton to proceed upriver without proper escort. Eaton loaded silver and guns, each indispensable for dealing with Hamet, into a barge flying both the American and British flags. Accompanying him from *Argus* were Marine Lieutenant Presley Neville O'Bannon; naval lieutenant Joshua Blake; Midshipmen George Mann and Eli Danielson; an Englishman, Richard Farquhar; a Turk, Seid Selim; Eaton's servant, Ali; and six other servants.[16]

It is difficult to fathom the intrigue, plotting, and cast of characters that followed Eaton in Egypt. For months the local authorities, vassals of the sultan, did a diplomatic dance while under their noses an expedition was being put together to overthrow the bashaw of Tripoli, another vassal of the sultan. In the center of this sandstorm was William Eaton, who began to style himself "general" as he went about his business attired in flowing Arab robes.

Hull's reaction to all this was muted. He expected Eaton to make the necessary arrangements with Hamet, help him to recruit and arm his mercenaries, and then join him on *Argus.* Once on board *Argus,* according to the plan, Hull and Eaton would sail to the town of Derne, rendezvous with Hamet, and help him to take Derne. From that point, if all went well, the

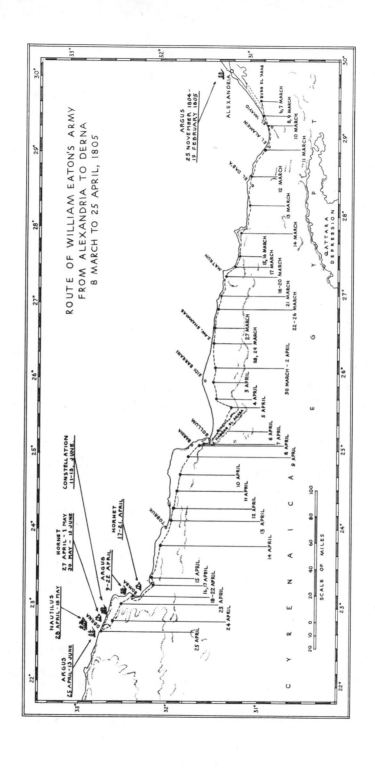

ROUTE OF WILLIAM EATON'S ARMY
FROM ALEXANDRIA TO DERNA
8 MARCH TO 25 APRIL, 1805

force would march on to Tripoli and there, sometime in April or May, meet up with Barron's force and together reduce the town.

Hull's understanding of the plan was correct, with only one exception — Eaton would march with Hamet. On 19 February Hull left Alexandria for Malta, carrying dispatches to Barron from both Hamet and Eaton requesting that reinforcements meet them at the port of Bomba, a few miles to the east of Derne. In addition to Eaton, Hull also left behind Lieutenant O'Bannon, Midshipman Pascal Paoli Peck, and seven enlisted marines. Four days later, Eaton concluded a formal agreement with Hamet, pledging to aid him in regaining his throne. In return Eaton extracted two unusual concessions. One made him "commander in chief" and the other assigned to the United States all the tribute due to Tripoli from Denmark, Sweden, and the Bavarian Republic, as a method of compensating the Americans for their expense. Clearly, at least in Eaton's mind, the question of principle in paying tribute was not whether, but only to whom.

On 6 March Eaton's expedition commenced its march across the desert "with about 300 well mounted Arabs, 70 Christians recruited at Alexandria, and 105 camels."[17] Relations between the Christians and Moslems soon deteriorated under the pressures of the campaign. To compound matters, food ran short and rations were reduced to rice and water. Midshipman Peck noted the situation.

> Water was growing more and more scarce every day, and the Arabs becoming more troublesome. They seemed determined not to proceed to Bomba until news came of the arrival of our vessels, never once supposing they would arrive, but remained under an idea that we wished to get possession of some strong hold in their country, and reduce them to Christianity. They said it was impossible for a christian and mussulman to have the same interest. Our provisions were drawing to an end, and our christian soldiers on the point of mutinying. Our prospects were now gloomy indeed, when, on the 10th of April at the time when we had discovered a mutiny, a courier arrived with news of our vessels being off Bomba.[18]

The vessels referred to were *Argus, Hornet,* and *Nautilus.* The

first two had been ordered to the coast on 23 March and arrived early in April. However, not finding Eaton, who was still
on the march, they stood offshore. On 15 April, Eaton finally
made contact with *Argus* and two days later with *Hornet.* The
timely arrival of the Americans breathed new life into Eaton
and his men as they prepared for the push on Derne.

Although still too ill to resume command at sea — Lear had
even despaired of his life — Barron continued to exercise overall authority. It was in that capacity that he had decided to
continue his support of Eaton; he had sent *Argus* and *Hornet*
for that purpose. He had also planned to send the frigate *Congress,* laden with artillery borrowed at Messina, but he had second thoughts on that scheme. Considering the uncharted waters and dangerous shores that would have to be navigated to
provide close support for the land operations, Barron decided
to send the smaller *Nautilus* instead. She arrived off Derne on
26 April, the day after Eaton and his band had taken up position outside of the city.

On 27 April *Argus* and *Hornet* came into sight. The entire
American force, land and sea, was now in place for the attack.
Eaton delivered his ultimatum to the governor of the city. The
reply was succinct: "My head or yours."[19]

At two in the afternoon of 28 April, the attack commenced.
The American vessels concentrated their fire on the fort, while
Eaton with one division and Hamet with the other attacked on
the landward side. At approximately three-thirty in the afternoon, from the deck of *Argus,* Isaac Hull had the thrill of
seeing "Lieutenant O'Bannon, and Mr. Mann Midshipman of
the *Argus,* with a few brave fellows with them, enter the fort,
haul down the enemy's flag, and plant the American Ensign on
the Walls of the Battery . . ."[20] The marines had indeed arrived
on "the shores of Tripoli."

Routed, the Tripolitans fled toward the town, leaving their
cannon behind them fully loaded and primed. O'Bannon and
his men wasted no time in turning the guns and using them to
deliver a hot fire at the fleeing enemy. Caught on all sides, the
enemy surrendered, and by four in the afternoon Eaton had
full possession of the town. The Tripolitans were not whipped

completely, though, and the Americans prepared for a counterattack.

Although Eaton was busy congratulating himself on his victory, the war was far from over. In his report to Barron after
the fall of Derne, Hull made note of all the difficulties Eaton
had been forced to overcome thus far and suggested that if
they should now push on to Tripoli, even more obstacles were
in their way.[21] Derne could be held without much difficulty, but
to move beyond its walls would require a large reinforcement
of men and material; certainly more than Barron could or
would be willing to provide.

On 18 May Barron wrote a very revealing letter to Lear.
Since both men were in Malta at the time, and close by one
another, it seems unusual that Barron would have taken the
time to dictate such a long communication. In fact, it is less a
letter than a memo of understanding, for it represents the combined opinions of both Lear and Barron and was probably
written more for posterity than for any other reason. In it
Barron expressed his pessimism that anything worthwhile was
likely to come out of the Eaton expedition. Further, he noted
that at least three of his frigates were in no condition to weather
another winter in the Mediterranean and must return home
for repairs. Barron knew that despite his advantages over the
bashaw, there was no way for him to force a release of the
prisoners. The choice was simple — make peace on conditions
not entirely in favor of the Americans or prosecute this war of
honor at the expense of 307 Americans and an unknown
number of future casualties. Barron knew the answer and so
did Lear.[22]

On 19 May Barron wrote to Eaton that Hamet was "un-
worthy of further support" and that he was dispatching Lear
on the frigate *Essex* to Tripoli for the purpose of concluding a
peace. Three days later Barron wrote his second in command,
John Rodgers, then on board *Constitution* off Tripoli, that he
was too ill to continue as commodore and that Rodgers must
now take charge. In one curious line Barron did hold back
from complete abdication: he told Rodgers that should his
health improve, he reserved the right to resume command.

*Essex* joined the squadron off Tripoli on 26 May. Lear himself delivered Barron's letter to Rodgers. That same afternoon *Essex* moved in toward the harbor and signaled for a parley. The bashaw made a swift response, and negotiations were under way. The Spanish consul represented the bashaw and came on board to discuss terms with Lear. Lear's first offer was $60,000 in cash for the release of Bainbridge and his men, followed by a treaty. The bashaw refused. Nicholas Nissen then came back into the picture as a go-between. Time was of the essence. Lear knew that Rodgers was not pleased at the prospect of paying tribute and would prefer battering the bashaw into submission. Even though that was manifestly impossible, the commodore seemed willing to try. He did not get the chance. With his brother the pretender at Derne with a force whose size had been greatly exaggerated to him, the bashaw had no stomach for more war. He consented to Lear's offer, but with a condition. A secret proviso was written into the treaty, which no one aside from those intimate with the negotiations (Rodgers was not among that group) knew about. For some time the bashaw had been holding Hamet's wife and children at Tripoli. By all rights, once the war was over and Hamet withdrew, the bashaw was under obligation to release his hostages. However, he feared that if he did he would have no rein on Hamet and that the brotherly conflict might immediately begin again. Lear, who had little regard for Eaton and despised Hamet, was quite willing to pay any price for peace as long as it was with someone else's coin. The deal was struck; Bainbridge and his men were freed, but not the Karamanli family, and peace was proclaimed.[23]

The only real loser in all of this was Hamet Karamanli. His family was returned to him eventually, but he was still destitute. After considerable lobbying, out of a sense of guilt and shame for having abandoned an ally, Congress voted in 1806 to pay him a lump sum of $2,400 and a pension of $200 per month for life.

Almost as soon as he was freed, Bainbridge asked quite rightly for a court of inquiry. A court was convened on board *President,* 29 June. James Barron sat as president, joined by captains Hugh Campbell and Stephen Decatur. After a brief review of the circumstances surrounding the loss of *Philadel-phia,* the board "unanimously agreed that no blame could be attached to Captain Bainbridge or his Officers for the loss of said ship."[24]

With the situation in Tripoli under control, Rodgers turned his attention to Tunis, where the local bey was making troublesome sounds. The commodore (Rodgers now held the post in the clear since Barron was on his way home on board *President*) decided to make a show of force for the benefit of the Tunisians. He dispatched *Congress* and *Vixen* to take up positions immediately and await the arrival of the remainder of the squadron.

At the rendezvous in Syracuse, Rodgers was assembling an imposing force. It included the frigates *Constitution, Constellation, Essex,* and *John Adams,* along with the brigs *Argus* and *Siren,* the schooners *Nautilus* and *Enterprize,* and the bomb vessel *Hornet.* Also joining in the expedition were several small newcomers to the Mediterranean and the United States Navy — gunboats, nos. 2, 3, 4, 5, 6, 8, 9, and 10. Unlike the Neapolitan boats borrowed by Preble, these were American built and had been sailed across the Atlantic by their crews.

On Wednesday 31 July the American squadron sailed boldly into Tunis Bay and took up a line athwart the entrance. Fresh from their "victory" against Tripoli, the Americans were not to be trifled with. *Nautilus* was sent in with a message — direct, brazen, and to the point. The bey was given thirty-six hours to respond, after which Rodgers would begin operations. The commodore was spoiling for a fight. If he could not have it at Tripoli, then he would have it at Tunis. The bey, however, had other ideas. Although he told Lear, who had come ashore to negotiate, that he viewed Rodgers' insolence as nothing less than a declaration of war, his actions belied his speeches. The talks went on — interminably, it seemed to Rodgers. There was the occasional ritual exchange of cannon fire, but all of this was more in the nature of theater than of war. By 14 August the bey agreed to return to a peaceful relationship with the United States. To underscore his intention, he announced that he would send a minister to Washington.[25]

For the next three weeks Rodgers remained at anchor, conducting the business of the squadron. During this time several of his vessels departed, and finally on 5 September the commodore himself left, bound north for Syracuse. For the remainder of the fall and into the early winter, Rodgers remained in the waters near Sicily, making occasional voyages to nearby ports to show the flag and train his crew.

On 28 November Rodgers received an unwelcome request from the secretary. Anticipating success against Tripoli, Secretary Smith had dispatched orders on 5 August to Barron (now Rodgers) to send back to the United States the gunboats and any other units of his squadron that could be spared. Although Smith was vague about precisely what could be "spared," it seems certain that he, most likely at the nudging of Jefferson and Gallatin, hoped that the expensive American presence in the Mediterranean could be reduced.

It flies in the face of logic to believe that a commander would willingly reduce his force so long as there is the slightest evidence of a threat. Rodgers saw dangers everywhere, and on 29 December he replied to the secretary's request (not order) that he consider rotating his units as soon as the Tunisian minister returned from the United States with a firm treaty in hand. Since the minister was not due back until late spring at the earliest, Rodgers had plenty of time to find work for his ships.

Despite Rodgers' objection, frugality won out. On 12 October Smith sent him another letter.

> If we should not be at war with Tunis, or any other of the Barbary Powers, it is the command of the President that the frigates *Constellation*, *Congress*, *Essex*, and *John Adams*, and three of the five small vessels of war under your command, be immediately ordered home, and you will without any unnecessary delay order them to the Eastern Branch.[26]

Rodgers' reply to this *order*, as it now was framed, was to state that since the secretary was ignorant of the situation at Tunis, he would ignore this recall and await instructions after the government in Washington could be more fully informed. With a slight extension of this logic, Rodgers could conceivably stay on station for as long as he pleased, with as many vessels as he pleased. Such behavior could not be tolerated, and on 22 March Secretary Smith ordered Rodgers home. The order was sent in a calculated manner. In one of his summer letters of 1805, full of the usual bombast, Rodgers had told Smith that when peace finally arrived he would like permission to return home. In the context of the letter the request is almost fatuous; nevertheless, from his perspective Smith had determined that despite the commodore's opinions, peace had been achieved. He took Rodgers at his word and ordered him home.

Captain John Dent of the brig *Hornet* delivered the news to Rodgers at the Syracuse anchorage. Also in the dispatches were several newspapers quoting Eaton, who immediately upon his return to the States had launched a verbal attack on everyone connected with the Tripolitan "sellout." Whatever reluctance Rodgers had about leaving his command was erased instantly when he learned his character was in question. He turned command of the squadron and *Constitution* over to Captain Hugh Campbell while he went aboard *Essex* and headed for home.

Rodgers' departure was accompanied by a dismantling of the squadron, so that by spring the only American warships left on the Mediterranean station were *Constitution, Enterprize,* and *Hornet.* It was a far cry from the force made available to Preble and Barron, but given the tranquility of the time it was adequate to protect American interests. It was the intention of the secretary to keep such a small force in the area on a more or less permanent basis. That plan went awry when on 22 June 1807 off the Chesapeake capes H.M.S. *Leopard* fired on the American frigate *Chesapeake.* The ensuing crisis demanded that all American warships return home immediately. For the first time in several years, there would be no American naval presence in the Mediterranean.

For six years the United States had maintained a naval squadron in the Mediterranean. Beginning with Dale in the summer of 1801 and continuing through Campbell's departure, American warships had been present, protecting American interests and warring on the Tripolitans. Was it worth it?

Wars are not ordinarily judged on the basis of cost-accounting methods, but since this enterprise was begun, conducted, and justified on the grounds of the need to protect a valuable commerce, it seems only fair to look at it from a cost-benefit perspective.

The figures below represent the actual expenditures of the navy from its founding through 1805.[27]

| 1798 | $   570,314.24 |
| 1799 | 2,848,187.26 |
| 1800 | 3,385,340.48 |
| 1801 | 2,117,420.74 |
| 1802 | 946,213.24 |
| 1803 | 1,107,925.32 |
| 1804 | 1,246,502.74 |
| 1805 | 1,409,949.67 |

The large figures for 1799, 1800, and 1801 are the result of significant expenditures for ship construction. While it is impossible to determine what the expenses of a normal year might have been, 1802 seems a reasonable guess. Indeed, even that year might be too high, since without the troubles in Tripoli naval expenditures would probably have continued on a downward spiral. Nevertheless, using 1802 as a benchmark, it would seem that the three years of war cost nearly one million dollars. That figure is conservative. It does not, for example, reflect the cost of losing *Philadelphia*, or the expense of pensions to be paid at a later date. Clearly, it would have been much cheaper in almost every way to have paid the tribute. Why then, in the midst of Republican austerity, did the government not pay the Tripolitans and their neighbors?

One answer is honor. For generations, misinformed Americans have been quoting John Marshall's "Millions for Defense, Not one cent for Tribute" as an example of the pain Americans felt at paying bribes. The fact of the matter is, Marshall was talking about the XYZ affair, which was a clear case of extortion. The Barbary situation was far less clear. For two hundred years the European nations had been paying tribute, arguing only over the amount, not the principle. Honor became an issue for Americans only after the war broke out; it did not cause it.

War came because it was thrust upon the United States.

Tripoli declared war on the United States, not the other way around. The war continued, however, because it was popular, even more popular than cutting the budget. That popularity grew from American victories at sea; not even the loss of *Philadelphia* could diminish the enthusiasm. On the contrary, her loss resulted in greater resolve and a personalizing of the conflict, which now became not just a trade war, but a glorious effort to free fellow Americans. Furthermore, the war really cost very little. Aside from the financial burden, which, despite Gallatin's penny-pinching grousing, the nation could afford, the war made no great demands on Americans. In the midst of war commerce grew in the Mediterranean, and the casualty lists were always small. At the end of the war, under the leadership of Lieutenant David Porter, the officers in the Mediterranean contributed to a fund for the erection of a monument to the six officers killed in the battles of Tripoli — hardly an overwhelming number.[28] Nations more often tire of wars not because they cost money, but because they take a painful toll in lives and property. In the latter regard the Barbary wars were a bargain.

# 7
## Men at Sea

In the years between its founding and the conclusion of the War of 1812, 2,881 men took commissions in the officer corps of the U.S. Navy, and many times that number enlisted as seamen. On board their ships they lived in a world described by Herman Melville as an "oaken box." It was here that "the sons of adversity meet the children of calamity, and here the children of calamity meet the offspring of sin."[1] For Melville, who had himself sailed in a man-of-war, the navy was "the asylum for the perverse, the home of the unfortunate."

Melville's biases toward the navy are well known, but some of his strictures smack of truth, especially those dealing with the common seaman who slung his hammock between decks, ate with his mess mates, and surrendered himself to the discipline of the ship. The image of the jolly Jack Tar dancing a hornpipe or whiling away his off-duty hours attending to the seamen's arts and crafts obscures the reality of men battling endless days of boredom, tedium, death, and disease.

The natural perils of the sea, combined with the unnatural perils of combat, the long periods away from home, and the harsh discipline, made it difficult to persuade American boys to sign on board a warship. In the Royal Navy, where conditions were even harsher, impressment served as an effective means to supply manpower. Much as some American officers might have wanted to resort to that practice, they were prevented by both law and custom. American seamen were "volunteers," al-

though undoubtedly there were times when seamen were induced to "volunteer."

The scope of the problem was considerable, for navies are
huge consumers of manpower. A forty-four-gun frigate required at least 400 men; a thirty-gun frigate, 340 men; thirty-
two-gun vessel, 260 men; twenty-four guns, 180 men; eighteen
guns, 140 men; and schooners, 70 men. In 1805 there were
actually more men on duty in the American navy than in the
army, and for several years between 1801 and 1812 the numbers in the two services were nearly equal.[2]

Filling the ship's complement was a task assigned to the captain. He was given broad instructions, such as those issued to
Thomas Truxtun in March 1798.

> You will cause such of the Sea Officers as may appear best calculated for
> the Business, to open Houses of Rendezvous in proper Places & to exert
> Themselves to engage One hundred & thirty able Seamen at the follow-
> ing Terms of Service and Rules of Wages — The Seamen to engage for
> twelve Months unless sooner discharged. The pay of the able Seamen to
> be fifteen Dollars per Month and Three Dollars Bounty — The Ordi-
> nary Seamen, Ten Dollars per Month and Two Dollars Bounty. —
>
> You will instruct the Officers at each Rendezvous to engage none
> other than healthy robust and well organized Men, and to reject those
> who may be scorbutic or consumptively affected.
>
> You will direct the Surgeon, or a Mate to attend at those Places to
> examine each Sailor and Marine, and to certify to the recruiting
> Officer, that they are well organized, healthy, robust, and free from
> scorbutic and consumptive Affections, before he engages Them or pays
> them any Bounty. If Bounty or Wages is paid to any without such a
> Certificate, it will be at the risk of the Officer paying it. The Officer of
> each Rendezvous shall make out on every Saturday, a Return of the
> Number of Seamen recruited within the Week, stating therein the
> Number delivered over to the Ship, and transmit the same to the Cap-
> tain, and a Duplicate to the Secretary for the Department of War.* —
>
> You will also transmit to the Secretary for the Department of War, a
> weekly return, exhibiting the Number of Marines, able and ordinary
> Seamen on board the Ship, and the Incidents that have taken place
> respecting Them or any of them, as also the Progress that has been
> made for preparing her for sea. —

*These orders were sent on 16 March 1798. The Navy Department was created
on 30 April 1798.

The commanding Officer at each Rendezvous, on the desertion of a Seaman, besides the usual Exertions and Means to be employed on such Occasions to recover and apprehend him will transmit as soon as possible, a Description of him to the Secretary of War. —[3]

At the "Rendezvous," usually a busy street corner, crowded tavern, or some public meeting place, a drum roll would sound and the officer would begin his pitch. A good tale or two, promises of glory and excitement, and during war prize money, drew men around. As a final enticement sailors might be offered money in advance, although this bait was usually avoided since the temptation to desert with the cash was more than some men could resist. In some cases unusual measures might be needed. William Laughton, commander of a gunboat at Alexandria, Virginia, was having so much trouble finding men that he finally resorted to paying the fine of a seaman who had been jailed for fighting so that he could get him out of jail and on board his boat.

Pay in the American service was slightly less than in the merchant service. In peacetime, when there was no hope for prize money, seamen were more likely to look for a berth aboard a merchantman than a warship. Although this made naval recruiting more difficult, fewer seamen were needed in peace when there were far fewer naval ships. During the War of 1812 the Royal Navy drove American merchantmen off the seas, thereby releasing thousands of sailors for other ventures, but that was small comfort to the navy as it found itself in fierce competition with privateers, whose promise of a short and lucrative voyage far outweighed any appeals to patriotism.

At first men were signed for one year, commencing when their ship left port. For those who failed to read the fine print, it often came as a shock that their enlistment did not begin when they signed on but only when they had upped anchor and were at sea. To avoid such problems, captains were warned to enlist men only when the ship was ready to leave. One year was a reasonable enlistment when the navy was in home waters or sailing nearby in the Caribbean. Operations in distant waters, however, presented different problems. Shipping men home from the Mediterranean after one year was cumbersome and inefficient, so in February 1802, when Congress authorized action against Tripoli, it tacked on to that legislation a section allowing seamen to sign on for two years.[4] To some degree that change made life a bit easier for commanders; on the other hand, longer enlistments are never a boon to recruiters. To further complicate matters, in June 1803, when Preble was preparing *Constitution* for the Mediterranean, the secretary, as an economy measure, ordered him to cut the pay of new seamen by two dollars per month.[5]

Who were these men? Where did they come from? We really do not know much about the thousands of enlisted men who served in the navy. A recent study by Ira Dye on merchant seamen from the Philadelphia area for the periods 1796–1803 and 1812–15 sheds some light. Although care needs to be taken when equating merchant and naval seamen, it would seem likely that they have a good deal in common.[6] Dye found the peak of age distribution at twenty-two to twenty-three years old, accounting for 19 percent of the total sample. There was a concentration in the late teens and late twenties, with decreasing numbers in their thirties and almost none over forty. Clearly, seafaring for the common sailor was a young man's business. Dye found that most sailed only a few years, with few ever staying in the business more than fifteen years. The myth of the old salt is just that — a myth. Nearly half of the seamen studied came from urban areas (49.5 percent), compared with a total contemporary urban population in America of only 5 percent. Nearly 18 percent were black, almost certainly freemen. In the country as a whole, the free black population accounted for only 2.5 percent of the total. The question of blacks serving in the navy is an interesting one. By act of Congress they were barred from service in the Marine Corps but were not, at least by law, excluded from the navy. Some captains — Edward Preble, for example — did order their recruiters "not to Ship Black Men," and on another occasion the secretary instructed Samuel Nicholson not to admit "Negroes or Mulattoes." But with the demand for sailors so high and the supply of experienced black seamen so great, such instructions were frequently winked at and many blacks served aboard American men-of-war.[8] Perhaps as many as 25 percent of Oliver Hazard Perry's men on Lake Erie were black. Other references to blacks or mulattoes serving on American ships appear in the records, but thus far not enough work has been done to come to any firm conclusions about actual numbers.

Enlisted ranks in the navy, as in the army, had their own hierarchy. At the head were the petty (from the French *petit*, small) officers, who were appointed by the captains. First among them, and perhaps the most unpopular man on board, was the master-at-arms. He was the ship's police officer, overseeing discipline, guarding against smuggled liquor and acting as the eyes and ears of the captain.

Boatswain's mates (pronounced bo'sun) were responsible for assisting the boatswain in maintaining sails, rigging, anchors, and the like. They were the maintenance men who saw to the day-to-day operation of the ship.

Ranked above the enlisted men, but below commissioned officers, were the warrant officers, who received their "warrants" from the president. Generally they were veterans with particular specialties — boatswain, gunner, sailmaker, and carpenter. Also appointed by warrant were the purser and the sailing master. The former was in charge of reckoning the ship's accounts, while the latter's main duty was navigation and seeing to proper trim for the vessel.

In terms of nationality, the men aboard ship were a mixed lot. Evidence suggests that a fair number of Englishmen signed up, preferring service in the republic's navy to the harsher treatment they could expect on board the vessels of His Majesty. Frenchmen, too, could be found amongst a ship's company, along with a smattering of other nationalities. In 1803, when Preble, writing from Boston, complained "I do not believe that I have twenty native American Sailors on board," he was echoing a common complaint.[9]

While the navy suffered chronic problems securing enough men to fill out the enlisted ranks, it had no difficulty finding commissioned officers. Here the only problem was quality. At the first whisper that a navy was in the offing, the politicking for commissions began, and it never stopped. At the birth of the service officers, most with Revolutionary experience, had been plucked out of the merchant trades and put on the quarterdeck of a warship. That practice gradually disappeared as the service matured and brought its own men up through the ranks. Like officers of the Royal Navy, upon whom they modeled themselves, the American officers were a relatively homogeneous group. Most came from middle- and upper-class families, where one could expect to find "gentlemen."

At the lowest rung of the officer's career ladder were the midshipmen, senior only, according to some, "to the ship's cat."[10] These teenagers — and some even younger — were on board to learn seamanship and command. With the establishment of Annapolis still nearly half a century away, apprenticeship at sea was the best way to launch a naval career. Most of the "boys" came to their post through political influence. It was a hard school, and not surprisingly attrition was high, although those who did manage to stay often climbed to high rank and fame.

A midshipman's duties usually came down to almost anything the captain thought he ought to do. Since they were potential officers and gentlemen, midshipmen were quartered separately from the enlisted men and outranked them. Still, if they were not part of the seamen's world, neither were they yet ready to be taken into that "band of brothers" on the quarterdeck. Caught between the two the midshipman spent his time standing watch, listening to the schoolmaster/chaplain lecture, practicing navigation, or running errands for the officers.

Luckiest among the midshipmen were those with the opportunity to serve under able tutors. David Porter had the good fortune to serve under both Thomas Truxtun and John Rodgers. Of all the captains in the republic's navy, none took more care to educate his officers than Thomas Truxtun. To a junior officer recently posted to *Constellation* he wrote:

> it is the duty of every one and more particularly Officers, to Support Sturdily the Constitution and Government under which we derive our Commissions, and in a regular Service Such as we are engaged in, no Officer must attempt to offer an opinion to me on the duty to be performed, without its being previously asked, but on the Contrary,

Carry all orders into execution without hesitation or demur. Such examples will act as a Stimulus to Officers of an inferior grade, as well as
others, and introduce that sort of Subordination, which can only insure
a happy and well govern'd Ship . . . an Officer in Carrying on duty
agreeable to his Station or otherwise, Shou'd be Civil and polite to every
one, and particularly so to Strangers for Civility does not interfer with
discipline; So that the detestable and ruinous practice to Subordination
in being too familiar with Petty Officers etc. is not practised . . . While an
Officer is diligent in doing his duty and Causing others to do theirs, and
in preventing Sculking and Loitering about, he is at the same time
never to lose sight of that humanity and Care that is due to those who
may be really Sick, or otherwise Stand in need of his assistance and
attention.[11]

If the midshipman acquitted himself well and to the satisfaction of his captain, he could expect to be commissioned a
lieutenant. The timing of the promotion depended on the
availability of berths, which in turn was a function of the number and size of vessels in service. On a large frigate there might
be as many as six lieutenants. The most senior, or first lieutenant, functioned as the ship's executive officer and oversaw all of
the day-to-day operations. Immediately under him were the
junior lieutenants, each of whom had responsibility for a certain number of the crew, called a division, as well as for a
specific section of the ship during battle.

Senior to all those aboard was the captain, who was, in the
words of David Porter:

The little tyrant, who struts his few fathoms of scoured plank, dare not
unbend, lest he should lose that appearance of respect from his in-
feriors which their fears inspire. He has therefore, no society, no smiles,
no courtesies for or from any one. Wrapped up in his notions of his
own dignity, and the means of preserving it, he shuts himself up from
all around him. He stands alone, without the friendship or sympathy of
one on board; a solitary being in the midst of the ocean.[12]

He had absolute control and absolute responsibility.

The midshipmen, lieutenants, and captain were line officers,
generalists who dealt with the overall operation of the vessel
both as a sailing ship and, when necessary, as an instrument of
war. In addition, on board the major warships were two non-
combatant officers, the surgeon and the chaplain.

Seeing to the physical well-being of the crew was the job of the surgeon. He inspected the men as they came on board and helped fight the sailor's real enemy — disease. With the aid of his mates he tended the men in the sickbay, visiting them at least twice a day, according to regulations. In times of battle he moved his operations below to the cockpit, a dark, dank compartment deep in the bowels of the ship, which was likely to become a bedlam of blood, gore, and screaming men. For those seriously wounded, the prognosis was grim. The best estimate is that one third of those wounded died. By contrast, the figure of those dying from wounds in modern war ranges from 2 to 4 percent.[13]

Traumatic wounds in battle accounted for only a fraction of the surgeon's business. He spent most of his time trying to cure disease rather than tending wounds. In this regard he worked from the generally held assumption that illness proceeded from an improper balance of the "humors" in the body; therefore, his treatments aimed at restoring the proper proportions among the humors. If the illnesses on board ship were basically routine, so were the methods of treatment. Medicinals or "drugs" were designed to *counteract* the patient's symptoms chiefly by *purging* the body of whatever was thought to have caused the disease. The following chart indicates some of the common medicinals, how they were classified, their function, and an example of a disease or illness the medicinal might actually have been used for.

The last of the specialist officers was the chaplain. He was "to read prayers at stated periods" and "perform all funeral ceremonies." In addition, he was the ship's schoolmaster, charged with teaching "the midshipmen and volunteers, in writing, arithmetic, and navigation, and in whatsoever may contribute to render them proficients."[14]

Officers and enlisted men both proudly called themselves sailors. Another group of men on board, however, did everything they could to disassociate themselves from being thought of as shiphandlers — the marines. On the larger vessels, the marine contingent numbered about 10 percent of the total crew. It was usually commanded by an officer at the rank of

## Treatment of Common Illnesses

| Medicinal | Class | Function | Illness |
|---|---|---|---|
| *Castor Oil* (Ricini) *Chinese Rhubarb* (Rhei) *Jalap* Calomel | Cathartics (strong laxatives) | To move bowels, in order to rid body of disease-producing materials; used more than any other drug class | All disorders, especially of the gastrointestinal tract |
| *Laudanum* *Paregoric* (both contain opium) | Narcotic | To slow bowel movement and relieve pain | Severe diarrhea and pain |
| *Peruvian Bark* (contained quinine) | Astringent | To combat fever and dry, or heal, diseased tissue | Intermittent fever, and almost all other fevers as well |
| *Acidulated wine* | Tonic | To give the body strength and tone | Consumption |
| *Ipecac* | Emetic | To induce vomiting | Any severe illness |
| *Cantharides* (Spanish Flies) | Epispastic | To raise a blister on the skin, to facilitate loss of disease-producing material | Any severe illness |
| *Pearl Barley* | Refrigerant | To cool fevers or reduce inflammation | Any fever |
| *Antimony* *Mercurial Ointments* | Diaphoretic Escharotic | To increase sweating To heal sores | Any fever Venereal disease |

lieutenant or captain,* assisted by one or two sergeants and corporals. Although they were part of the ship's company and therefore under the authority of the captain, the marines did not participate in the ship's operation. In the words of Marine Captain Daniel Carmick, on board *Constitution*, "I permit them [marines] to do no kind of work that will Tar their Clothes."[15] Indeed, they did not. Marines stood sentry at the captain's cabin, guarded the magazine, were present when the grog ration was being dispensed, and when necessary acted as an honor guard for the ship and captain. From the perspective of a seaman looking up while holystoning the deck on his knees or looking down as he was furling sail in a raging gale, these seagoing soldiers had it easy. Friction led to sparks, and finally in August 1801 the secretary found it necessary to send a circular letter defining the two worlds and laying down certain rules of conduct "to correct any erroneous opinions."[16] The circular helped but did not cure the problem — no one has ever been able to do that.

Life on board ship had a temporal rhythm all its own, marked by the sounding of the bell and the change of watches. Since a ship's business, especially at sea, went on around the clock, it had been necessary, at some remote point in history, to divide the crew in a way that would allow for safe navigation and a reasonable amount of rest. Each day was divided into seven watches, five of four hours each and two of two hours. The two-hour watches ran from 1600 (4 P.M.) to 1800 hours (6 P.M.) and 1800 to 2000 hours (8 P.M.). These short or "dog" watches were set so that the crew, who were ordinarily divided into two groups or watches themselves (starboard and larboard), would not end up serving the same hours every day.

Within each watch particular assignments were made. By tradition, the more experienced seamen were either sent forward to handle the complex set of lines controlling the sails on the foremast and the foresails, or they might be assigned aloft as fore, main, or mizzen topmen. The rest of the watch went to

*In the Marine Corps the officer ranks are comparable to those of the army. A marine captain was the equivalent of an army captain, not a naval captain.

other stations, most of which had to do with cleaning and maintaining the ship. Endless hours were spent holystoning decks, whitewashing ceiling planking, scrubbing brightwork, tending rigging, repairing small boats, and dozens of other chores. Occasionally, the day might be enlivened by the call to general quarters and perhaps a bit of gunnery practice and a few moments at repelling boarders. It might also be interrupted by the melancholy command, "All hands muster to witness punishment."

Meals were timed for the change of watch; that is, the men going on duty ate their meals shortly before their watch began, while those coming off ate as they were relieved. Breakfast was at about eight, lunch at noon, and dinner at four. The timing was for the convenience of the ship and not the men; witness the fact that between the last meal of the day and the first of the next as many as sixteen hours might pass.

While the commissioned and warrant officers ate in their own areas, at tables, and with service, the crew were divided into "messes" of eight to ten men each and ate on the deck, picnic style, out of communal pots. Breakfast, the least formal meal of the day, usually consisted of tea along with bread or hardtack, a biscuitlike substance well deserving of the description "hard." Breakfast, like all meals, was followed with a ration of grog.* Toward the end of breakfast, and other meals as well, smoking was permitted, but only in the area of the cook's galley.

Lunch was the main meal of the day. On a rotating basis each mess elected a "mess cook," whose job it was to go to the galley, bring back the hot food, and then clean the area, paying careful attention to preserving the leftovers, which would be served for the final meal of the day. The menu was hardly exciting, but it was plentiful and healthful — if the food had not spoiled, which was often the case.

---

*In 1740 the British admiral Edward Vernon, with an aim to reduce the drunkenness in his fleet, ordered that the sailor's ration of one pint of rum per day be diluted by adding a quart of water. Vernon's nickname in the fleet was "Old Grogham," from the material of which his boat cloak was made. Hence the watered rum became known as grog.

the ration shall consist of, as follows: Sunday, one pound of bread, one pound and a half of beef, and half pint of rice: Monday, one pound of bread, one pound of pork, half a pint of peas or beans, and four ounces of cheese: Tuesday, one pound of bread, one pound and a half of beef, and one pound of potatoes, or turnips and pudding: Wednesday, one pound of bread, two ounces of butter, or in lieu thereof, six ounces of molasses, four ounces of cheese, and half a pint of rice: Thursday, one pound of bread, one pound of pork, and a half a pint of peas or beans: Friday, one pound of bread, one pound of salt fish, two ounces of butter, or one gill of oil, and one pound of potatoes: Saturday, one pound of bread, one pound of pork, half a pint of peas or beans, and four ounces of cheese: and there shall also be allowed one half pint of distilled spirits per day, to each ration.[17]

Added to the structured hierarchy and carefully measured days were a plethora of rules and regulations. Some came from the Congress and president, others from the secretary. The captains could legislate behavior themselves, of course. It was a world in which "forms, measured forms are everything." Not infrequently these forms were violated.*

Despite all the formal rules, punishment for misbehavior depended very much on the attitude of the commander. In the case of officers, physical punishment could not be inflicted. If the commander thought the officer was a person of worth, he might try a private dressing-down and perhaps confinement to quarters. If, on the other hand, he saw the accused as not worthy to hold a commission, then more formal and public procedures might be tried.

In the case of enlisted men there were far fewer restraints. For the most serious crimes, such as desertion in battle or treason, hanging was prescribed. For most offenses among enlisted men, however, flogging was the favorite punishment. It was simple, direct, and public. Regulations forbade the captain from ordering more than twelve lashes on his own authority. If the offense required more, he was obliged to summon a court-martial. However, appearance did not always match reality. Clever commanders, Preble being among the most prominent, soon found a way to administer far more than the routine

*See Appendix.

twelve and still remain legal. What he did was to take a major offense and dissect it into smaller components that fell within the twelve-lash rule. Thomas Ayscough, a seaman aboard *Constitution*, fell victim to Preble's cleverness when on 23 November 1804 he was given forty-eight lashes, in increments of twelve, for four different offenses. Ayscough, no favorite of the captain's to begin with, was found drunk. Instead of pressing the one charge of drunkenness, which would have required a court-martial, Preble had the man brought forward on four lesser counts that he as captain could deal with. Ayscough was found guilty on all four and punished accordingly.[18]

Drunkenness was the most common offense in the navy, followed by neglect of duty, a nebulous term that covered a wide area, and then theft and desertion.

Without question, punishment was quick and brutal. But in a society that tolerated slavery and gave the master almost absolute rights over his slave, a society whose ordinary family law gave the father near-absolute power over his children, the authority of the ship's captain ought not to be seen as an aberration. Nor should it be left unsaid that the men aboard were hardly the pick of society. There was some truth to the sentiments expressed by Truxtun, that when a young officer comes aboard a man-of-war for the first time, he is apt to have far too rosy a view of those who serve under him.

These are partly occasioned by the nature of the sea service and partly by the mistaken prejudices of people in general respecting naval discipline and the genius of sailors and their officers. No character, in their opinion, is more excellent than that of the common sailor, whom they generally suppose to be treated with great severity by his officers, drawing a comparison between them not very advantageous to the latter. The midshipman usually comes aboard tinctured with these prejudices, especially if his education has been amongst the higher rank of people . . . Blinded by these prepossessions, he is thrown off his guard and very soon surprised to find, amongst these honest sailors, a crew of abandoned miscreants, ripe for any mischief or villainy. Perhaps after a little observation, many of them will appear to him equally destitute of gratitude, shame or justice, and only deterred from the commission of any crimes by the terror of severe punishment. He will discover that the pernicious example of a few of the vilest in a ship of war is too often apt

## Sample Daily Routine, U.S.S. Constitution

| | Morning Watch 4–8 A.M. | Forenoon Watch 8–12 Noon | Afternoon Watch 12–4 P.M. | First Dog Watch 4–6 P.M. | Second Dog Watch 6–8 P.M. | Evening Watch 8–12 P.M. | Midnight Watch 12–4 A.M. |
|---|---|---|---|---|---|---|---|
| Sailing Master | Up at dawn Check weather Review previous night's log | Check ship's trim Instruct midshipmen | Supervise cleaning hold | Confer with captain on night orders | On call | On call | On call |
| *(meals)* | | Breakfast Grog | Dinner | Grog | Supper | | |
| Surgeon's Mate | Up at dawn | Hold sick call Fumigate berthdeck | Inspect provisions | Check patients in sickbay and hammocks | On call | On call | On call |
| *(meals)* | | Breakfast Grog | Dinner | Grog | Supper | | |
| Marine Officer | Up at dawn Check captain's sentry | Conduct small arms training | Supervise cleaning of equipment | Supervise cleaning of equipment | Check captain's sentry | On call | On call |
| *(meals)* | | Breakfast Grog | Dinner | Grog | Supper | | |
| Able-bodied Seaman | Up at dawn Stow hammock Pump bilge | On watch: 2 hours in rigging, 2 hours on deck | Gun drills and gun cleaning | On watch: 1 hour in rigging, 1 hour on deck | Sleep | On watch: 2 hours in rigging, 2 hours on deck | Sleep |
| *(meals)* | | Breakfast | Dinner | Grog | Supper | | |

to poison the principles of the greatest number, especially if the reins of discipline are too much relaxed, so as to foster that idleness and dissipation which engender sloth, diseases and an utter profligacy of manners.[19]

Despite the unpleasantness associated with naval service, men did go to sea, and more than that, they served well. The men serving in the new republic's navy acquitted themselves in a fine manner. To be sure, not everyone was entirely happy to be on board, but whatever discontent there might have been was never deep or widespread enough to cause the kind of violent mutinies suffered by the Royal Navy at Spithead and the Nore in 1797. Indeed, while many British deserters joined the American ranks, the reverse seems hardly ever to have been the case.

# 8

## Toward War

On 29 April 1962 President John F. Kennedy hosted a dinner honoring Nobel Prize winners of the Western Hemisphere. In his welcoming remarks he said, "I think this is the most extraordinary collection of talent, of human knowledge, that has ever been gathered together at the White House, with the possible exception of when Thomas Jefferson dined alone."[1]

Kennedy was right, and contrary to what some have suggested, Jefferson was neither insouciant nor naïve in matters maritime and naval. Indeed, in retrospect Jefferson's naval policies had triumphed in the Mediterranean. The problem now was to devise policy that fitted the needs of peace. It was a storm in which the president found himself driven between the Scylla of Gallatin's parsimony and the Charybdis of Smith's navalism.

Traditionally, when peace broke out, governments put their ships up in "ordinary," that is, stripped them of equipment and laid them up at a dock with a caretaker on board. This was the practice of the British navy, as well as the other major European powers. However, the procedure was expensive and British experience indicated that the total cost of maintaining ships in wet storage for twelve years equaled their replacement cost. Through investigation Jefferson discovered a more cost-effective solution, one employed by the Venetians. Instead of wet storage in an open area, with its incumbent problems of preservation, the Venetians stored their war vessels in dry docks and boasted they could keep them there for eighty years without appreciable deterioration. While the Venetian claim might be questioned, Jefferson believed it and thought the scheme ought to be tried in America. He contacted a man with an inventive genius almost comparable to his own, the architect Benjamin Latrobe. Jefferson wrote to Latrobe on 2 November 1802 proposing a dry dock 800 feet long, 175 feet wide, and completely roofed over. It would be built in Washington and could accommodate a dozen frigates, all for a cost of half a million dollars. A plan was sent to a House committee, where it died a quiet death.[2]

Jefferson's proposal was not what Congress had in mind. Laying up ships was supposed to save money, not cost a half million more. As the ships did come home to Washington they were laid up, not in a Jeffersonian dry dock but at the Washington Navy Yard, where they were left with minimal crews and even less maintenance. By December 1805 Smith could report that eight frigates and the brig *Hornet* were lying in ordinary at Washington. Some members of the House thought that maintaining the vessels was a needless waste of money and asked Smith if some could not be sold. He resisted and replied that he knew "of no vessels belonging to the navy" that ought to be sold. Congress made no move to force a sale, but neither did it appropriate money sufficient to maintain or repair them properly. For the time being, at least, neither Jefferson nor the Congress was in a naval mood.[3]

It was far easier to get rid of men than ships. On 21 April 1806 legislation was approved that allowed the president "to keep in actual service, in time of peace, so many of the frigates and other public armed vessels of the United States, as, in his judgement the nature of the service may require, and to cause the residue thereof to be laid up in ordinary in convenient ports." If the Congress had stopped here, the president might well have decided to keep the fleet in operation, although it is hard to imagine Jefferson doing that; however, in the section immediately following they limited the number of officers and men who could be kept in service, thereby limiting the number of ships to be manned. The quotas were: 13 captains, 9 masters commandant, 72 lieutenants, 150 midshipmen, and 925 enlisted men, none of whom were eligible for full pay unless in actual service and under orders. The act was a victory for the antinaval element in Congress and most especially for the acerbic John Randolph of Virginia, who in debate over the measure proclaimed that "this mammoth of the American forest" ought not "to leave his native element and plunge into the water in a mad contest with a shark."[4] Randolph's sentiments reflected the majority view. On the same day Congress limited the number of men in service it also directed the president to sell any vessel that "is so much out of repair that it will not be for the interest of the United States to repair the same."[5]

While major warships in the American navy were fast becoming an endangered species, another type of vessel was proliferating at an astonishing rate. These were the gunboats.

No part of Jefferson's naval policy has received as much attention or been the subject of as much controversy as his decision to build small gunboats. No precise origin for the idea can be unearthed. Gunboats were common to the navies of all powers at the time; indeed, Americans themselves had made frequent use of them in the Revolution. Jefferson's uniqueness lay not with the concept but with the application. Where others saw them as an adjunct to the fleet he saw them as *the* fleet.

The first official mention of building the boats came as a result of trouble with Spain over navigation on the Mississippi. On 28 February 1803 Congress approved the construction of fifteen gunboats at a total cost of not more than fifty thousand dollars.[6] Secretary Smith intended that the boats would be built on the Ohio and asked Captain Samuel Barron if he would trek inland to superintend the building. Barron's response is not recorded, but at a time when war was brewing in the Mediterranean with its promise of battle and fame, it is hard to imagine that a post on the Ohio building small boats would have appeared very attractive. At any rate, nothing was accomplished, and for the time being no boats were built on the Ohio or elsewhere.[7]

One problem was precisely *what* should be built. After months of discussion on the proper model, in December Jefferson finally instructed Smith to build two experimental boats, one at Hampton Roads and the other in Washington. James

Barron would superintend the former, while John Rodgers was charged with the latter.[8] Both boats went into service in the summer of 1804, but in neither case do we know the precise dimensions. Rodgers' boat was the larger, mounting a long thirty-two and two swivels. It required a crew of thirty-two. Barron's was smaller, armed with a single thirty-two and manned by twenty-three men. Ironically, while the intention was for service on the Mississippi, neither boat would see that river. Both were ordered to the Mediterranean, although in a further twist, when surveyed, Rodgers' boat was found unfit for an ocean crossing and remained at home on coastal patrol.[9]

Jefferson and Smith were pleased and ordered construction of eight more boats. These eight were probably designed by Josiah Fox; they were rigged as ketches, armed with a single long thirty-two, and manned by approximately thirty men. In the years to come before the War of 1812, "gunboat mania" took hold; altogether, the administration sought and Congress authorized the construction of 278 gunboats. Nowhere near that number were actually built, and many of those that were launched were in the water only long enough to be taken to a nearby facility where they might be put up in ordinary. Furthermore, their design is uncertain. Since they were built all along the coast as well as at several locations on the Ohio, Connecticut, and Hudson rivers, design control was impossible. Perhaps as many as five different models were used. What they did have in common was shallow draft, fore and aft rig (schooner, sloop, or ketch), sweeps for movement in calms or adverse currents and tides, and an armament usually consisting of a single heavy-caliber gun (thirty-two-pounder) sometimes found in the bow, but often mounted amidships on a traversing mechanism.[10]

Gunboats were a very fitting expression of Jeffersonian philosophy. They were intended only for defensive purposes. Excursions to the Mediterranean notwithstanding, the intent was for most never to leave home. Since there were so many of them, every port could have its own, thus reducing the perennial problem of strident calls from local merchants about being naked to the enemy. Their numbers would also mean multiple building contracts, which might be parceled out as favors. In their defensive mode they fitted in nicely with the ongoing program of enhancing fixed coastal fortifications. They provided a sort of mobile artillery, able to move quickly to support the permanent emplacement. Not to be overlooked was their cost, for they were, judged individually, cheap. In this matter one might argue that their total cost was considerable and that Jefferson might have been wiser to invest the nation's resources in fewer but larger ships. That argument can only be made in retrospect. The commitment to gunboats was incremental. They were authorized in four separate acts of Congress stretching over a period of four years, and those voting for the first act could never know that two years later they would be asked to vote for more. Furthermore, with the exception of the last act, which was passed in the emotional aftermath of the *Chesapeake* affair, all of the gunboat appropriations taken together could not have paid for the construction of a single frigate. Even if Jefferson had wanted to, it is highly unlikely that he could ever have persuaded Congress to build anything more than "cheap" gunboats.

For his part, Secretary of the Navy Smith publicly supported Jefferson's policy, although he, like the officers who served under him, viewed the boats as an adjunct to the regular fleet. He thought the navy ought to have both defensive and offensive capabilities. Obviously, Jefferson and a majority of Congress thought otherwise; to them gunboats *were* the American fleet.

From a naval point of view, the best argument in favor of the program was made by army general James Wilkinson, in a paper entitled "Reflections of the Fortifications and Defence of Sea Ports of the United States." He shared his thoughts with Edward Preble, who agreed, albeit under the impression that gunboats were a part of the navy, not the whole navy.

It may be asked whether we are to rest the safety of our commercial towns and shipping on the pacific disposition or good faith of foreign powers? To which we may reply in the negative and add that it is certainly our duty to seek for those places of defence within the compass of our abilities which may be found most economical, most durable, and most effectual.

After as close a view of this question as can be expected from a man unskilled in naval affairs, I have formed a conclusion that, next to a superior navy, floating batteries will be found more effectual to the protection of our seaports and should, therefore, be preferred. But I speak with exception to long tidewater rivers and narrow channels, because they may be commanded by fixed batteries and chevaux-de-frise, yet cannot be secured by them against blockade.

In determining on the size, form and construction of such floating batteries regard must be had to the services to be performed and, after due experiment, the best models may be adopted for tidewater and uniform currents, for bays and harbors, narrow, wide, open, or sheltered from particular winds.

The extent of our bays and inlets, the capacities of our harbors, and the water approaches to our great cities have determined my judgment in favor of these vessels calculated to be impelled with velocity by the more powerful combination of oars and sail to enable them to make rapid transitions and to take any requisite station with promptitude.

In equipping armies and manning these vessels provision should be made to prevent their being boarded by light barges, and with submission I would recommend that they should carry battering pieces of the largest caliber and the lightest construction on their bows and sterns. I have strong prejudices in favor of a proposition of eight-inch howitzers, because one shell which takes effect will prove more destructive (generally speaking) than ten shot. I feel confident that, without extensive fortifications and proportionable military force to garrison them, that barges, galleys, or gunboats on the preceding or improved plan, with the cooperation of heavy movable batteries which may be expeditiously transferred from one part of a town or city to another by men and horses, will form our most economical, durable, and effectual means of defence and afford the best security to the objects to be protected. And in support of this opinion I beg leave to offer the following considerations:

1st. Such vessels can either attack or defend, may prove as offensive in the retreat as pursuit, and can approach or avoid an enemy at discretion.

2nd. In calm their oars will enable them to take any station with safety which may be found most advantageous.

3rd. Their mobility will enable them in smooth water to hang on the bow or stern of a vessel and avoid its batteries.

4th. Their lowness in the water will enable them to deliver their shot on a horizontal range or at a small elevation, which will give them more certainty and effect.

5th. In calm weather they may without hazard approach a vessel at anchor in a stream to the point-blank (range) of 24-pounders, 650 yards, or of 32-pounders, 850 yards, and, preserving a steady station, may give effect to every shot without fail.

6th. In light breezes, with sails and oars, they may preserve the same distance on the bow of a vessel and, if pursued, may deliver as destructive a fire as if they were stationary.

7th. Should they be hard pressed, they may escape in shoal water and renew the action at discretion.

8th. In rough weather they may take station beyond the (range) of the guns of a ship, from whence the superior elevation of their own pieces may enable them to deliver their fire with effect.

9th. Taking advantage of circumstances, they may drive intruders from our bays, roads or rivers; and, by forcing them to sea, may relieve a blockade or render it less close, constant, or pernicious.

10th. They may be employed during the calm season to transport stores or men from one port to another with safety, even should an enemy be waiting; and, lastly, in time of peace, eight out of ten may be laid up under cover, and, with due attention, instead of injury, may be improved by aid for a number of years.[12]

If, as many critics have asserted, it was foolish for America to build gunboats, it is hard to see how it would have been any less foolish to proceed ahead on a building program that would have left the nation with a number of very large and expensive warships. It was utterly impossible for the United States to build enough major ships to challenge Great Britain. If Congress had tried, it simply would have meant spending more money to provide no more security than geography already provided. Indeed, it is even possible that the very attempt to exert naval muscle would have brought the Royal Navy down on the United States in a preemptive strike. Under the circumstances, Jefferson was far more realistic than his opponents; Dumas Malone, the president's most eminent biographer, is quite correct when he says that "Jefferson's opinion, especially after Trafalgar, that a strong seagoing navy would have been an utter waste was not as silly as certain later enthusiasts for seapower were to claim."[13]

Whatever the policy of the United States might be in regard to naval matters, there could be no question as to the British position. It was arrogance based on undisputed power. Such power was most cogently brought home to Americans by the Royal Navy's practice of impressment.

Impressment was a rough and ready version of selective service. In wartime the Royal Navy had a nearly insatiable appetite for men. Volunteers might be expected to furnish some portion of this need, but they could never supply it completely. Wartime or peacetime, service in His Majesty's Fleet did not offer many attractions. Harsh discipline, low pay, long periods away from home, and the ever present specter of death or injury from combat, disease, or accident helped keep seamen away from the navy in droves. The same conditions of service enticed those already on board to desert, a practice which in the Napoleonic Wars had reached near epidemic proportions. The only way for the service to maintain itself was by the age-old but detested custom of impressment.

There was no quicker way to empty a waterfront tavern or brothel than the cry "Press gang!" Nor was there anything to make a sailor more nervous at sea than to have his vessel ordered to heave to and prepare to receive a press gang from one of His Majesty's vessels. Had the British confined this onerous practice to their own shores and ships it would have been bad enough, but the need for men and the well-known fact that many British deserters were serving aboard American merchantmen caused officers of the Royal Navy to feel justified in stopping, searching, and removing any men they considered to be British subjects, even though they might be aboard an American flag vessel.

The most nettlesome problem was how to distinguish bona fide American sailors from deserters. There was no easy way to make such a distinction, nor was there a method to determine American from British citizens with any degree of certainty. While it is true that the American government recognized "naturalization," the British government did not. Once an Englishman, always an Englishman, was the rule. Therefore, even in those rare cases where a former English subject might carry his naturalization papers to prove his new citizenship, it was all for nought.

The problems were considerable, but so too was the need for manpower in the Royal Navy. It would have taken a cadre of saints to deal fairly with the issue; no one ever thought of the officers in His Majesty's Navy as saints. Manpower took precedence over all, and as a result many legitimate American sailors found themselves unwilling denizens of a British forecastle.

Estimates on the actual number of Americans impressed vary. In the roughly ten years between 1792 and 1802, probably 2,400 men were conscripted off American ships. In the following ten years, because of the rising intensity of the Napoleonic conflict, that number nearly tripled. How many of these men were in fact British citizens or deserters is again impossible to estimate; however, by their own actions the Admiralty in the period 1802–12 did release one third of those taken, thereby admitting to having wrongfully taken them in the first place. Nevertheless, it seems certain that a large number of men taken were indeed British subjects or deserters. Bonaventure Beaussier estimated that 170 members of *Philadelphia*'s ill-fated crew were British deserters. An exaggeration perhaps, but illustrative of the problem.[14]

Those who objected most to impressment were not necessarily merchants and ship owners. After all, those men had a vested interest in maintaining trade and business as usual. The impressment of sailors was an inconvenience that many of those who remained ashore were quite willing to tolerate. Cries of outrage more often came from the hinterland and the frontier, where nationalism ran high and suspicion of all things British was endemic. The latter for good reason, since the British in Canada were in the habit of supplying guns and inciting the Indians in the northwest to attack American frontier settlements.[15]

As long as the British confined their impressment activities to merchant vessels, the issue remained a dull, chronic pain that never went away but on the other hand never got worse. On two occasions, however, the Royal Navy overstepped itself and precipitated a crisis that brought howls of anger from Americans.

The first occurred on 12 June 1805. Gunboat No. 6, commanded by Lieutenant James Lawrence, was on her way to the Mediterranean to join the squadron of Commodore Rodgers. Off Cádiz she encountered a British squadron assigned to blockade the Spanish port. As he drew near, Lawrence noticed that two of the British vessels, *Tenon* and *Dreadnought*, were leaving their normal stations and making for him. Knowing full well the British habit of taking whomever they pleased, Lawrence was immediately suspicious. They ordered him to heave to and prepare to receive a boarding party. Having no choice, Lawrence complied, and a party of British officers was soon on board. Before taking them below to his cabin, Lawrence told his second in command, Midshipman James Roach, to remain on deck and under no circumstances to allow any of the men on No. 6 to be taken off.

While Lawrence was below, three of his crew, "who had been very unruly during the passage," recognized some old shipmates in *Dreadnought*'s boat and called down that they were Englishmen and wanted off No. 6 and back into the Royal Navy. A strange request, to be sure, perhaps born of a long Atlantic crossing in their small craft. Of the three, one was an acknowledged deserter from His Majesty's Navy, while the other two had served and earned legitimate discharges.

The commotion brought Lawrence and the British officers back on deck. The officers, upon hearing the story, demanded that all three be surrendered. Lawrence refused and decided to go aboard the British flagship and take up the case with the admiral. Before leaving the boat, he reiterated his command to Roach that no one was to leave.

On board the flagship the discussion was not pleasant. The British demanded Lawrence turn over the three men. Lawrence again refused, upon which he was told that it did not matter, since a boat had already been dispatched to take the seamen. Lawrence replied that such was impossible, since he had left explicit orders that no one was to leave. No sooner had he gotten those words out when through the cabin windows he could see a small boat coming alongside with his three crewmen aboard. Midshipman Roach was a man of little spine and no resolve. Lawrence felt humiliated and offered to surrender his

command to the British. They refused and sent him away to
suffer his indignity.[16]

As soon as he arrived at Syracuse, Lawrence made his report
to John Rodgers. Rodgers, incensed at such an insult, thereupon issued a general order phrased in a fashion to allow no
misunderstanding.

### GENERAL ORDERS

An insult offered to the Flag of the United States of America on the
12th of June last, near Cadiz by a British Squadron under Command of
Admiral Collingsworth [*sic*], induces me as Commander in chief of the
United States Naval forces in this Seas to direct that you do not under
any pretence whatever suffer your Vessel to be detained or your men
taken out of your Vessel without you are compelled so to do by superior
force; in which case After having resisted to the Utmost of your power,
you are directed to surrender your Vessel as you would to any other
common Enemy, but on no account to leave her until after you have
struck your Colours; after which if you are not compelled by the Author or Authors of such Insult and Violence to quit your Vessel, you are
directed by me to do, and on going on board the Enemy to deliver your
Sword to the Commanding Officer of the Enemy's Vessel, and not to
return to your Own again, unless you are absolutely put on board of her
by force. On saying that you are not to suffer your Vessel to be detained
You are not to consider that it extends to the prevention of your giving
every satisfaction to the Vessels of War you may meet on the high Seas,
whose Nation we are at peace with, so far as a friendly intercourse will
justify, or in language more *plain* you are not to be detained by force.[17]

Rodgers' captains understood and obeyed the order. For
their part, the British acquiesced; never again in the remaining
years of the American squadron's stay in the Mediterranean
would one of their vessels be treated so roughly.

American commanders, sensitive to their rights and honor,
were angered by what had happened to Lawrence. Almost exactly two years later, they would have even more reason for
resentment.

U.S.S. *Chesapeake* was one of the original six frigates.
Launched on 2 December 1799 at Gosport Navy Yard in Virginia, she was commissioned early in 1800 and given to Captain
Samuel Barron. She went into service too late to see much
action in the Quasi War, and following the peace she was placed
in ordinary at Norfolk. *Chesapeake* came back into service in

1802, and for that year as well as part of the following she was on station with the Mediterranean squadron. Back in America by June 1803, *Chesapeake* was once again put into ordinary, this time at Washington. She was at rest until the spring of 1806, when Captain Charles Stewart was ordered to her in anticipation of sending her back to the Mediterranean as flagship of the squadron.

It turned out to be a false start. Congress would not allow the navy sufficient men to man her, so for the moment *Chesapeake* remained a lifeless hull at Washington. By January 1807, the need for her services had become more urgent. Her sister frigate, *Constitution*, had been in the Mediterranean since the fall of 1803; it was time to bring her home. *Chesapeake* was the obvious replacement. The president agreed, and on 17 January Captain Barron was ordered to wrap up his work with the gunboats and proceed to make *Chesapeake* ready for sea. Shortly thereafter Barron left Hampton Roads and rode to Washington, where his first sight of his new command saddened him. Jeffersonian austerity had provided ill for the frigate in ordinary; it would take a considerable amount of time and money to fit her for sea. After two months in Washington, Barron decided the work had progressed far enough along that he could return to Hampton Roads, where he planned to do the final fitting out. He left his frigate in charge of Master Commandant Charles Gordon, who in early June was finally able to bring the ship down the Bay. On Saturday 6 June Commodore Barron came aboard *Chesapeake* and hoisted his broad pendant. That ceremony finished, Barron went back ashore. With the apparent exception of one visit, he remained ashore for the next two weeks, content to leave the final preparations to Gordon.[18]

While Gordon was preparing *Chesapeake* for sea, another officer was engaged in recruiting men. He was Arthur Sinclair, a newly minted lieutenant who had commanded a gunboat in the Mediterranean and whose most recent duty was to oversee the ships in ordinary at Norfolk and assist Barron with the gunboats. Also present at Norfolk was Captain Stephen Decatur, commander of the Gosport yard. The command relationship is not clear; however, Sinclair, perhaps because he had worked with Barron, was charged with recruiting for *Chesa-*

*peake.* Among the men he recruited were three British deserters from H.M.S. *Melampus.* When the British learned the whereabouts of the sailors, they protested through diplomatic channels to Decatur. He avoided the issue by declaring that the matter was not within his jurisdiction. For his part, Sinclair refused to release any men unless ordered to do so by his superiors. The British lodged a protest through the American State Department that eventually found its way to the secretary of the navy, who asked Barron to investigate. Barron determined that the sailors were indeed off *Melampus,* but that they were Americans who had gotten there in the first place by being impressed; therefore he would not release them and they would continue on board *Chesapeake.* Vice Admiral G. C. Berkeley, British commander on the North American station, was less than pleased at the American response; he issued orders to his captains that should they meet *Chesapeake* at sea, they were to search her for deserters.[19]

On Sunday afternoon 21 June Barron came aboard, and at six the next morning *Chesapeake* got under way, bound for the Mediterranean station. Her voyage was short but eventful. As she came down past Lynn Haven Bay, Barron noticed two British vessels at anchor, *Melampus* and *Bellona,* "their Colours flying and their appearance friendly." Further on, at Cape Henry, *Chesapeake*'s lookout reported that one of the two ships of the line on station was making sail and standing out to sea, following after Barron. The Britisher was H.M.S. *Leopard,* fifty guns.

By four in the afternoon *Leopard* had run down to *Chesapeake* and was rounding up on her starboard quarter, all the time keeping the weather gauge. For hours Barron watched *Leopard* approach, thinking it all quite innocent and doing nothing to prepare his ship. Barron's nonchalant attitude is difficult to understand. For what purpose would she leave her station and pursue *Chesapeake*? A friendly visit? Highly unlikely. Nor could it be a matter of wishing to identify a stranger. *Leopard* knew the frigate was *Chesapeake,* and Barron knew they were aware of that; after all, the American's departure had been advertised for days. Clearly *Leopard* had a purpose for her pursuit, and Barron must have known it: they wanted their deserters back.

Given that the British navy had already taken thousands of American seamen off ships at sea, continued routinely to seize merchant vessels of other nations for alleged violation of British rules, and in the case of Lawrence had gone so far as actually to take men from an American warship, Barron should have been on the alert. All the more so when it was observed that as *Leopard* took up her position near *Chesapeake* she had taken the tompions out of her guns. Barron knew all this and still did nothing. The subsequent court of inquiry summed it up nicely when it noted that the circumstances "were in themselves so suspicious as to have furnished sufficient warning to a prudent, discreet, and attentive Officer of the probable designs of a ship of war conducted in that way and ought to have induced Commodore Barron to have prepared his ship for action."[20]

At a signal from *Leopard, Chesapeake* hove to and received an officer on board, Lieutenant John Meade, who delivered to Barron a copy of Admiral Berkeley's order and requested that he muster his crew for inspection. For more than half an hour a discussion went on in the commodore's cabin among Gordon, Barron, and Meade; still, Barron made no move to ready his ship. Finally Meade left, and it was only at this point that Barron thought the situation might be serious. He told Gordon quietly to pass the word for the men to go to general quarters. He wanted this done without drawing the attention of the British. The problem of getting nearly four hundred men to go to quarters quietly need not be explained, but even beyond that, the ship itself was in such a state of disarray that it would have taken hours to prepare for battle. Guns were not secure on their carriages, none had been fitted with their firing mechanisms, the marines lacked sufficient cartridges, and those they did have were the wrong size. The decks were littered with equipment and stores were not yet stowed. Everything was in a mess.

As soon as Meade was back aboard *Leopard* and had made his report, the Britisher fired several shots across *Chesapeake*'s bow, then ranged alongside at pointblank distance and fired a broadside. Within fifteen minutes *Leopard* poured three broadsides of solid shot and canister into the American. According to witnesses on the quarterdeck, Barron was confused and indecisive. He ordered men away from the guns to lower a boat so a message might be taken to *Leopard.* He was heard to tell some of the crew to seek cover or be cut to pieces — hardly an order in the tradition of Preble's Boys. Finally, before even a single American gun had been fired, Barron ordered the colors struck. For the sake of honor one gun was set off by Lieutenant William Henry Allen, ignited by a live coal brought up from the galley.

The British refused *Chesapeake*'s surrender, but they did come aboard and remove four men, the three in question and a fourth. For her part *Chesapeake* had three men killed, eight wounded seriously, and ten wounded slightly, including the commodore himself. At approximately eight in the evening *Leopard* departed, and *Chesapeake* limped for home. Sixteen hours later she dropped anchor at Hampton Roads.

Americans were outraged. At Hampton Roads the mob took over and destroyed more than two hundred water casks that had been sent ashore to be filled for British warships. At both Norfolk and Hampton, the militia had to be called out to control the violence. Meetings and newspapers throughout the country demanded a reckoning. Unfortunately, little could be done. On 2 July Jefferson issued a proclamation prohibiting British warships from entering American waters and demanding those present to depart. As noted earlier, he also used the occasion to summon home what was left of the Mediterranean squadron.[21]

The *Chesapeake* affair affected Thomas Jefferson profoundly. One historian has even suggested that with true British intentions now revealed, Jefferson decided, in his own mind at least, that war was both inevitable and desirable, and so moved to rearm the nation both on land and sea. A flurry of legislation designed to strengthen America came in the wake of the incident. At the same time Jefferson moved on another front to strike at the British.

On 22 December 1807 the president signed the Embargo Act, which virtually prohibited American foreign trade. By this measure Jefferson hoped to strike at British pocketbooks. Harking back to the days before the Revolution, when similar strategies had induced British merchants to bring pressure on Parliament to satisfy American demands, Jefferson believed that the same method would work now to remedy grievances. The outlook was not promising, for as Congress was debating the Embargo Act, both Great Britain and France were instituting policies quite inimical to American maritime interests.[22]

As the president and Congress saw to the national interests, the navy was attempting to put its own house in order. Charges were levied against four men on board *Chesapeake*: Commodore Barron, Captain Gordon, Captain John Hall, commander of the marine detachment, and William Hook, gunner.[23] The court, John Rodgers presiding, convened on 4 January. Barron's case was heard first. He was found guilty of "neglecting on the probability of an engagement to clear his Ship for action" and suspended from the navy for a period of five years. Gordon and Hall were found guilty of varying degrees of negligence and were reprimanded privately by the secretary of the navy. Hook was found guilty of not seeing to the proper care and mounting of the guns; he was dismissed from the service.

For the remainder of Jefferson's administration, the navy focused its attention on enforcing the embargo — a hopeless and thankless task — and on building more gunboats. On his own Smith lobbied for bigger ships, but his efforts came to nothing.

Neither gunboats nor embargo had the desired effect. Both the British and French continued blithely to ignore American neutral rights, seizing vessels and condemning them according to their own rules. The situation was precarious; a report to the House summed it up well late in November 1808, shortly before the nation was to choose a new president.

> After a period of twenty-five years of peace, hardly interrupted by transient hostilities, and of prosperity unparalleled in the history of nations, the United States are for the first time since the treaty which terminated the revolutionary war, placed in a situation equally difficult, critical, and dangerous. Those principles recognized by the civilized world under the name of law of nations which heretofore controlled

belligerent Powers, regulated the duties of neutrals, and protected their rights, are now avowedly disregarded or forgotten by Great Britain and France. Each of these two nations captures and condemns all American vessels trading with her enemy or her enemy's allies; and every European Power having become a party in the contest the whole of our commerce with Europe and European colonies becomes liable to capture by either one or the other. If there be any nominal exception it is made on a condition of tributes, which only adds insult to the injury.[24]

The election of 1808 was hardly a contest. James Madison, secretary of state, close friend and neighbor of Jefferson's, and staunch Jeffersonian, easily beat aside the other Democratic–Republican candidate, George Clinton, as well as the Federalist Charles C. Pinckney. The change was in personnel only, for in matters of public policy Madison and Jefferson were close kinsmen. Unfortunately, Madison was not Jefferson's intellectual or political equal. At a time when foreign relations were the overwhelming problem, Madison blundered badly. He continued the policy of peaceable coercion by replacing the embargo with a Non-Intercourse Act, which reestablished trade with all nations except Great Britain and France so long as both continued to violate American rights. The following year, 1810, Non-Intercourse gave way to an unusual piece of law called Macon's Bill No. 2. By its provisions trade was reestablished with both Great Britain and France; however, if either one should agree to respect American neutral rights, then trade would be cut off with the other.

Madison's policies led him into a French trap. In a bit of adroit diplomacy, Napoleon announced on 1 November 1810 that France would henceforth respect American rights. Madison accepted the French statement at face value — always a mistake when dealing with the emperor. Across the Channel, the British refused to budge. Determined to make his point in the face of British intransigence, Madison ordered the American minister in London to return home. The drift toward war was unmistakable.

As relations with Great Britain worsened, Madison and Congress gave greater attention to rearming America. Early in 1810 the new secretary of the navy, Paul Hamilton, sought to reactivate the frigates laid up in ordinary and appointed a board — Commodore Rodgers, Captain Thomas Tingey, commandant of the Washington Navy Yard, and the newly promoted Captain Isaac Chauncey — to examine the best methods of repairing and fitting for sea the frigates *Congress, Constellation, Adams,* and *New York.* In June of the same year, Hamilton sent out a general order to his captains. It was a bellicose message that helped set the stage for another bloody encounter.

> You, like every other patriotic American have observed and deeply feel the injuries and insults heaped on our Country by the two great belligerents of Europe; and you must also believe that (calculating by the past) from neither are we to expect liberality or justice but on the contrary that no opportunity will be lost of adding to the outrage to which for years we have been subjected — Amongst these stands most conspicuous the inhuman and dastardly attack on our Frigate *Chesapeake* — an outrage which prostrated the flag of our Country and has imposed on the American people cause of ceaseless mourning. That same spirit which has originated and has refused atonement for this act of brutal injustice, exists still with Great Britain; and from France like wise we have no reason to expect any regard to our rights — What has been perpetrated may again be attempted. It is therefore our duty to be prepared and determined at every hazard, to vindicate the injured honor of our Navy, and revive the drooping Spirit of the Nation.[25]

Among those who received Hamilton's message was Commodore John Rodgers. On 16 May 1811, in command of the frigate *President,* Rodgers was sailing north along the coast, bound from Annapolis to the waters off New York, where his orders instructed him to remain for the protection of American commerce. Shortly after noon, approximately forty-five miles northeast of Cape Henry, *President's* lookout called out to the deck below that a strange sail was approaching from the southeast. Rodgers knew that the British frigate *Guerrière* was in the area and had recently stopped an American merchantman and impressed one John Diggio, a native of Maine, into her crew. Rodgers assumed that the stranger now in sight and bearing down on him was the guilty Englishman.

The stranger was not *Guerrière* but a considerably smaller vessel, His Britannic Majesty's sloop of war *Lille Belt,* twenty guns.[26] Her captain, Arthur Bingham, bore down on *President* and signaled for recognition. When the American did not answer, and after Bingham had seen the commodore's broad pendant flying from the masthead, he concluded that she must be an American frigate and resumed his southerly course. Rodgers, still believing *Lille Belt* might be *Guerrière*, decided to give chase and hail her, hoping to effect the release of Diggio. How he hoped to manage that without a fight is quite unclear. It defies credulity to believe that he entertained any thought that by a simple request one of His Majesty's ships would surrender a crew member. He would have to take him, and that is exactly what he intended to do.

With a full press of sail, Rodgers gained on the English ship. Realizing he could not outrun the American and thinking there was no particular reason why he should, Bingham brought *Lille Belt* to, hoisted his colors, and in preparation for whatever might follow, double shotted his guns.

After some maneuvering to gain advantage, *President* finally rounded to on the weather side. By now it was 8:30 P.M. and dark. In later testimony Rodgers maintained he could not make out *Lille Belt*'s flag, although he admitted he could see it. Unwilling to identify themselves, as soon as they were within hail both captains called across, "What ship is that?" No answer. Both repeated the question. According to Rodgers, there then came a shot from the stranger, which was quickly answered. A general engagement followed. Who fired first? Rodgers claimed Bingham did. Bingham claimed Rodgers did. We can never know.

For three quarters of an hour the battle raged. *Lille Belt* was badly outgunned. With her sails and rigging in shreds, she finally fell off. Again Rodgers asked, "What ship is that?" This time Bingham replied. In the morning Rodgers sent Lieutenant J. O. Creighton aboard to offer aid. Bingham politely refused the offer, went to repairing his damage, and headed for Halifax. Bingham lost thirteen men, with another nineteen wounded. *President*'s only casualty was a boy slightly wounded.

Although Federalist New England was noticeably cool toward the commodore, elsewhere he was hailed, toasted, feted, and editorialized as the man who had avenged *Chesapeake*. The British took a dim view of all this. Through their minister, Augustus Foster, they protested and noted that in the case of *Chesapeake* they had provided suitable apologies; could the Americans do less? No apology was forthcoming. A court of inquiry held in August and early September on board *President* in New York harbor found, to hardly anyone's surprise, "that Captain Bingham made the attack and without a justifiable cause."

In the months after, the drift toward war accelerated. Madison informed Congress that a secret British agent, John Henry, had been fomenting trouble in the New England states. Secretary Hamilton, sensing the urgency of the moment and the spirit of Congress, presented a report calling for twelve seventy-fours and ten thirty-eights. The proposal was defeated, but only by a narrow margin.

The trouble at sea was mirrored by continuing problems with the Indians in the northwest. William Henry Harrison, governor of the Indiana Territory, was busy tracking down the Shawnee chief, Tecumseh. Bloodshed on the frontier was laid at the doorstep of the British, who were known to be inciting and supplying the Indians from Canada.

In the southeast, however, along the Florida-Georgia border, the roles were reversed. Here Madison actively encouraged settlers living under Spanish rule to revolt and place themselves under American jurisdiction. At the urging of Georgians, Captain Hugh Campbell sent *Vixen* and two gunboats to the vicinity of St. Augustine to "observe." Both Americans and British were playing a dangerous game.

Everywhere they turned, Americans saw British machinations. In the midst of these tensions, they went to the polls to elect a new House and one third of the Senate. The results indicated clearly that prowar sentiment was surging forward. A new type of Republican who espoused nationalism and expansion came to the fore, typified by the War Hawks, men such as Henry Clay, John C. Calhoun, and Peter Porter. In their campaigns they urged the nation to strong and belligerent moves, even to war.

Having in his own mind at least already declared war on the British, on 1 April 1812 Madison sent a confidential message to Congress recommending the immediate passage of an embargo. Unlike Jefferson's act, this was not a move to intimidate the British; rather it was a step to husband ships and call home those abroad in preparation for hostilities.

Madison's embargo had no difficulty getting through the House; it passed the more moderate Senate with a smaller but still significant majority. Less than a week after passage, Congress authorized the president to call up one hundred thousand militiamen for six months' service. In the days to come, futile attempts were made to seek a diplomatic solution. On 1 June Madison sent a war message to Congress. The House quickly approved. The Senate took longer, but it too agreed. Madison proclaimed a state of war with Great Britain.

# 9
## 1812 — A Year of
## Great Victories

The Americans were far less surprised at the outbreak of war than the British. From that day in early April when Madison had first proposed an embargo, a sure sign to everyone that serious measures were on the way, until the actual declaration of 18 June, American naval officers were readying their vessels for the inevitable. It was not a promising picture.[1]

No new vessels had been built since 1806, leaving the navy with a force of only ten frigates, two sloops, six brigs, and a ragged assortment of schooners and gunboats. However, even this exaggerates the actual force available, since many of the vessels were either laid up in ordinary or in such a poor state as to be only one step removed from condemnation.[2]

Since no vessels were assigned on foreign station, the active fleet spent its time for the most part in home waters. It was split into two squadrons — a northern one under John Rodgers based at New York, and a southern squadron commanded by Stephen Decatur operating from Norfolk. Both squadrons sailed under standing orders by which they were charged to protect American ships; seize any privateers being illegally fitted out in American ports; report any American providing aid to a belligerent; and, finally, assist customs officers in expelling foreign armed vessels from American waters. Despite the small size of these two forces, their high state of readiness, combined with the eagerness of their commanders to do battle, gave the Americans an early but temporary advantage.

While Rodgers and Decatur patrolled offshore, the ports themselves were protected by a combination of land batteries and gunboats. Neither was in much of a state of readiness, and indeed, their announced mission of defending the ports was a source of never-ending aggravation and anxiety. Command was a major issue. Given the relatively low degree of esteem in which the gunboats were held, their command was left to junior officers. Rank was no determinant of pride, and the captains of these cockle shells felt themselves as much the master of their wooden world as the most illustrious commander of one of His Majesty's ships of the line. Therefore, it was most irritating for them to find themselves often under the control of the local military officer, who, being their senior, thought himself quite justified in issuing commands. Adding to the painful uneasiness of the gunboat officers was the problem of men — they could not get enough — and supplies, of which they were chronically short.

All in all, despite the bellicose noises emanating from Washington, the force that was expected to take the brunt of the enemy's fury was woefully unprepared. Even more surprising, those sounding the tocsin of war made no attempt to put the fleet in readiness. Unable to focus the attention of either the president or Congress on the needs of his anemic navy, Secretary Paul Hamilton decided on a bold venture. In the midst of the jingoism and bravado, he made a recommendation that he knew would be unpalatable, especially to the nationalists who so dearly wanted war. He suggested to President Madison that since the navy was so small, it might be foolish to allow them to sortie against the British, risking the loss of all. Instead, keep them at anchor in port, where they might be safe from harm. Hamilton's idea received a very unsympathetic response, just the one he wanted. As a simple matter of national pride, the navy must engage the enemy. Ships could be replaced, honor could not.

Madison's sentiments were echoed by the captains. Hamilton heard in person from captains William Bainbridge and Charles

Stewart, both of whom happened to be in Washington during the late winter of 1811–12. Each told him of his unyielding commitment to aggressive action. After hearing from these officers, Hamilton decided to seek advice from his two senior officers, Decatur and Rodgers. Since they were at their posts, it was necessary to solicit their opinions in writing. On 21 May he wrote informing them that "As war appears now inevitable" he needed their counsel.[3] Neither Rodgers nor Decatur took long to respond.

Rodgers wrote first.[4] He told Hamilton that the supreme objective ought to be "to annoy the trade of Great Britain." To achieve that he proposed the creation of several task forces: one to harass the West India trade, another to target movements around the British home islands, and a third to focus on the East India trade. Vessels not assigned to a task force would sail separately or in company in American waters, hoping to find and destroy any enemy shipping found in the vicinity. Rodgers' plan is notable in both its ambition and its self-interest. For a navy the size and experience of the American to launch thrusts in so many directions meant taxing men, ships, and administration to the breaking point. On the other hand, it is clear to see why Rodgers favored such operations, especially the one in English home waters. As he told Hamilton, he wanted dearly to command a force to sail the waters around England.

> They have always, I perceive, honored me with a place in their lying naval chronicle with the title of *Buccaneer,* and nothing on this side of the grave would afford me more real satisfaction than to have such an opportunity as I have mentioned of affording them more bitter subject for their still more bitter and illiberal animadversions.

Hamilton also asked in his letter for opinions regarding which American ports would be most useful in war. Rodgers gave a thoughtful response and indicated that Charleston and Savannah were well placed for southern operations, although both could handle only small vessels. He recommended against ports in the Chesapeake or Delaware bays because of their vulnerability to blockade. New York had the advantage of nearness to the major sea lanes; however, the bar at Sandy Hook was an obstacle that large ships could pass over for only one hour at each high tide. Boston was a good port, but it was farther away than Rodgers would like. In the last analysis, from his perspective the best of the lot was Newport, Rhode Island. It was deep, well protected, and close enough to be of service.

Like Rodgers, Decatur urged the necessity of getting to sea as quickly as possible.[5] He had not the slightest doubt that the Royal Navy would move as fast as possible to blockade the ports. The time to get out was before their ships could take station. However, once the ships were at sea, Decatur and Rodgers parted company. Decatur viewed Rodgers' plan of squadrons sailing in British home waters as too dangerous. He preferred a *guerre de course* carried out by single vessels or at most two frigates in company. He would provision them with as much as they could carry, send them to sea, and keep them there as long as possible to harass British commerce. Decatur rightfully saw that the most dangerous time for an American warship would be the moments when she was entering or leaving port, for it was there that the enemy could be counted on to concentrate his force.

Curiously enough, in their report to Hamilton neither Rodgers nor Decatur made mention of what for most Americans was the most critical naval issue of all — who would defend the coasts? The great concentration of population and commerce along the eastern seaboard, particularly in the Chesapeake and Delaware regions as well as Long Island Sound, made those sheltered waters vital to the well-being of the nation. In plain truth, Rodgers and Decatur both knew that defense of the area was hopeless. In the face of the enemy's overwhelming force, to stand and defend the homeland was tantamount to suicide. That mission, inasmuch as it could be accomplished at all, would have to be done with the land forces and more particularly with the state militias.

To the Americans the British were formidable giants, but from the giant's point of view there were serious problems. Tremulous voices in America were quick to assert that the Royal Navy had a force of one thousand ships and had thus far

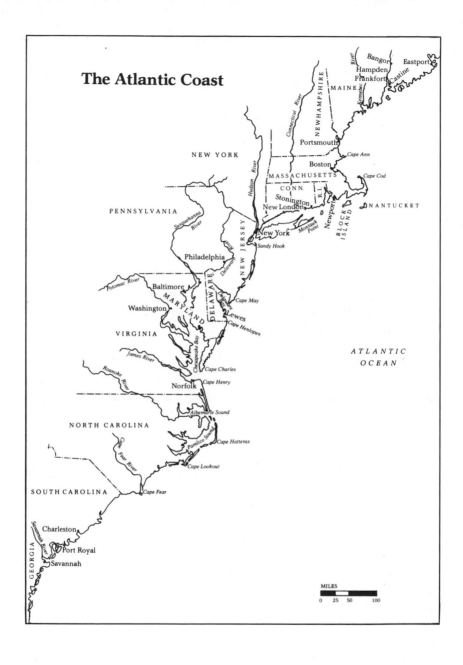

# The Atlantic Coast

MAINE

River

Bangor

Eastport

Hampden

Frankfort

Castine

Kennebec River

NEW HAMPSHIRE

Connecticut River

Portsmouth

Cape Ann

NEW YORK

Boston

MASSACHUSETTS

Cape Cod

Hudson River

CONN.

NANTUCKET

Stonington

R.I.

New London

Newport

PENNSYLVANIA

Susquehanna River

Montauk Point

BLOCK ISLAND

New York

NEW JERSEY

Sandy Hook

Philadelphia

Delaware River

Potomac River

Baltimore

MARYLAND

DELAWARE

Cape May

Washington

Lewes

Cape Henlopen

VIRGINIA

James River

Chesapeake Bay

Cape Charles

ATLANTIC OCEAN

Roanoke River

Norfolk

Cape Henry

Albemarle Sound

NORTH CAROLINA

Pamlico Sound

Cape Hatteras

Cape Fear River

Cape Lookout

SOUTH CAROLINA

Cape Fear

Charleston

GEORGIA

Savannah River

Port Royal

Savannah

MILES

0   25   50        100

managed to cow and defeat all the European navies. That was an exaggeration; nearly a third of that number were either in ordinary or still on the stocks. Even the remaining two thirds were not all fit for service, since many were in port for refitting or repairing. Nor did such alarmist reports account for the huge demands being made on the navy. The Admiralty had simultaneously to maintain a large home fleet, another in the Mediterranean, a sufficient force to blockade the Continent, plus additional squadrons and individual vessels to patrol the vital sea lanes to North America, the West Indies, Africa, and the East. Even before the American war, the Royal Navy was straining to meet its commitments.

In anticipation of hostilities, the Western Atlantic had been placed under a single commander, Admiral Sir John Borlase Warren. Each of the subordinate commands, at Halifax, Jamaica, and the Leeward Islands, still retained a fair degree of autonomy; however, they did report to Warren and were subject to his orders. The prime responsibility for control of coastal American waters, at least in the very early stages of the war, rested with the squadron based at Halifax under the command of Admiral Herbert Sawyer.[6]

Sawyer was in a difficult position. Despite the threat of war, the Admiralty had reduced the number of ships under his command. In a move designed to prevent any untoward incidents with the Americans, Sawyer had been instructed not to allow his vessels to sail any closer than fifteen leagues (approximately fifty miles) from the coast. Those instructions were effective in preventing incidents, but at the same time they effectively limited intelligence. Thus the admiral was both weak and ignorant.

Following standard operating procedures, late in the fall of 1811 most of the Halifax squadron left Nova Scotia and sailed to Bermuda where they planned to remain for the winter. Passing a winter in Bermuda was certainly preferable to enduring the blustery northeasters of Halifax; however, naval facilities on the island were few and primitive. By the time the season drew to a close in the spring of 1812, Sawyer's ships were in much need of refitting.

As Sawyer made preparations to return to Halifax, he also had to give thought to what he would do if war broke out with the United States. He had little doubt that the Admiralty's command would be for him to blockade the coast; that was obvious. The question was how. The coast was enormous. To cover it he would have to divide his force down to single ships, and even then gaps would appear by the dozens, while at the same time exposing his command to piecemeal destruction.

Lord Nelson himself would have had trouble in the Halifax command, and Sawyer was certainly no Nelson. Indeed, added to the problems of distance, weather, and lack of ships and men, the Halifax squadron suffered throughout the early years of the war with mediocre commanders and ill-trained seamen whose inabilities are testified to by an unusual record of accidents, wrecks, and losses in battle.

John Rodgers was quick to take advantage of British unreadiness. Only three days after the declaration of war, he put to sea from New York with a squadron consisting of three frigates, *President, United States,* and *Congress,* accompanied by the sloop of war *Hornet* and the brig *Argus.*

Two days to sea Rodgers spoke a vessel and learned that the Jamaica fleet, bound home to England, was in the vicinity. He signaled his captains to set every stitch of canvas available and headed eastward in pursuit. Barely three hours later a large ship was sighted, bearing straight down on the Americans. She turned out to be the British frigate *Belvidera,* whose captain upon recognizing the enemy immediately went about and fled. Rodgers pursued. After more than ten hours of dogging his prey, Rodgers was close enough to engage with his bow chasers. The commodore went forward to lay the guns and supervise the firing personally. After several rounds had gone off, some to very good effect, one of *President*'s guns blew up, killing one man and injuring thirteen others including Rodgers. The chase continued, but the Englishman proved to be a clever foe. He lightened his ship by heaving over the side spare anchors, boats, and anything else not absolutely needed. That action, combined with expert sail handling, gave him the advantage. He was soon beyond American range, and by eleven in the evening Rodgers was forced to give up the chase.[7]

Disappointed at *Belvidera*'s escape, Rodgers once again took up the search for the Jamaica fleet. It was hopeless. He remained at sea with his squadron for seventy days and in that time took eight British ships, a piddling record. By the time he returned to Boston on 31 August, more than three hundred of his men had symptoms of scurvy. All in all, it was a poor showing. The only consolation was that the mere existence of Rodgers' squadron had forced the British to deal with his threat and therefore did not allow them to move in on the American coast and intercept homeward-bound shipping.

While Rodgers was busy scouring the North Atlantic, other events of importance for the navy were taking place closer to home. The first was an unhappy affair on 17 July. The brig *Nautilus,* which had seen considerable service, especially in the Mediterranean, was sailing off the coast of New Jersey when she was seen by the British frigate *Shannon,* part of a squadron sent by Admiral Sawyer to look for Rodgers: *Shannon,* thirty-eight guns; *Guerrière,* thirty-eight guns; *Africa,* sixty-four guns; and *Aeolus,* thirty-two guns. *Nautilus* led the frigate on a seven-hour chase, but it was no use. *Shannon* drew up, and *Nautilus'* commander, William Crane, recognizing the futility of resistance, surrendered. By this action *Nautilus* earned the unenviable distinction of being the first warship lost on either side.[8]

Captain Philip Broke, *Shannon*'s very able commander, was especially pleased at the capture, for it helped in some measure to compensate for a recent unhappy adventure *Shannon* and the rest of the squadron had had with U.S.S. *Constitution.* On 18 June *Constitution* left Alexandria, Virginia, bound for Annapolis. Her captain, Isaac Hull, elected to remain behind in Washington for a few more days. As the frigate coasted downstream, she was overtaken by a dispatch boat bringing the news of war; the third lieutenant, George Read, mustered the crew and read to them the declaration of war, to which they responded with three cheers. *Constitution* then continued her passage to Annapolis. There she took on more stores and crew and was joined by Hull, who finally got her under way at noon on 5 July.

Bound for New York, *Constitution* made her way northward off the New Jersey shore.[9] As is not uncommon in those waters, the July winds were light and Hull was having trouble keeping a northerly course. Early in the afternoon of the 16th, *Constitution*'s lookout saw four sail to the north, between them and the shore. It was the British squadron, out looking for Rodgers. Hull, however, thinking it might be Rodgers, sailed for them to make an identification. For the rest of the daylight hours, *Constitution* and the strangers slowly closed on one another. As sunset approached, Hull was still uncertain; ever prudent, he ordered the ship prepared for action. In the dark he hoisted recognition signals; they went unanswered. He now knew the strangers were enemies. Hull ordered the frigate brought about and headed on a southeasterly course away from the British.

Not a few of the crew thought the situation hopeless. Hull had virtually no wind; indeed, he had lost steerage way. A light breeze brought the enemy, in overwhelming numbers, down to *Constitution*. A large section of the taffrail was cut away, and two guns moved aft to fire on the enemy. Above decks men went to work hauling up buckets of sea water, wetting down the sails so that they might trap more wind. On the gun deck, gangs labored to break open casks and dump thousands of gallons of fresh water over the side in an attempt to lighten the ship. At about eight in the morning Hull noticed that one of the frigates — *Shannon* — had been taken in tow by the small boats of the squadron and seemed to be closing. Charles Morris, Hull's first lieutenant, approached the captain and reminded him that kedging might be possible. This method, usually reserved for moving small ships in a harbor, consisted of taking an anchor forward in a small boat, dropping it, and then hauling in, bringing the vessel up to a new position. With the prospect of surrender and capture imminent, Hull was willing to try anything. A quick heave of the lead line showed twenty-five fathoms, shallow enough for kedging. The launch and cutter were lowered and the work began. It was sheer misery. As the day wore on the men strained on the oars, hauling out the 4,700-pound anchor ahead of the frigate. Not only did they have the enormous weight of the anchor to carry but several hundred yards of twenty-two-inch cable as well. As soon as the anchor was let go, the boat would pull for the ship, on the way back passing another small boat bringing out another anchor to repeat the process. For four hours they put their backs into it, driven on by the sure knowledge that, bad as they now felt, it would be even worse to rot in a British prison. Toward midday a breeze picked up and *Constitution* surged ahead, picking up her boats on the run, a tricky job. Such good fortune lasted only a few hours; by early afternoon the breeze had left, and the men were back to kedging.

Unpredictable as ever, the breeze came up again toward midnight and stayed with them. In the early light of the dawn Hull made a bold move. He tacked eastward, passing within range of *Aeolus*. The British squadron followed, but Hull's seamanship and *Constitution*'s sailing qualities told the difference. The gap was widening. Toward evening a squall line approached. Hull ordered the crew aloft, ready to take in sail, but only at the last possible minute so as to squeeze every zephyr possible. The wind and rain hit, the sails were taken in, then just as quickly the squall passed and Hull set sail again. The speed and precision were remarkable and speak well for the high state of readiness of the crew. As the squall passed astern of *Constitution* it hid her from the enemy. The British did not react as fast or as well. They were quick to take in sail but slow to reset; their slackness left them farther off. By the end of the second day Hull and his men, while not completely out of harm's way, had at least a comfortable and growing margin of safety. On the third day of this fox-and-hounds escapade, dawn found the enemy no closer than twelve miles. Finally, the British gave up the chase and tacked around to the northeast to resume their position close to New York in order to intercept Rodgers. Hull wisely decided to avoid New York and instead set a course for Boston, where he arrived safely on 27 July.

Hull's display of seamanship in escaping the clutches of the Royal Navy, while certainly praiseworthy, has been overrated. It was an escape, not a victory. Of perhaps more significance was the remarkable achievement of Captain David Porter aboard the frigate *Essex*. *Essex* left New York on 3 July with orders to sail south and intercept a homeward-bound enemy convoy reportedly carrying a large amount of specie. With a pendant proclaiming "Free Trade and Sailor's Rights" flying from the masthead, *Essex* headed to sea. Unfortunately, Porter missed the convoy, but he did stay at sea and over the course of the next two months established an enviable record. Sailing between Bermuda and Newfoundland, he took nine prizes, including H.M.S. *Alert,* the first British warship to surrender to an American. Altogether Porter netted prizes worth more than $300,000. In two months at sea with one ship, Porter accomplished more than Rodgers had in the same time with five.[10]

Having acquitted itself well in the first weeks of the war, the American navy was about to enjoy a streak of victories unknown to it in the past and rarely equaled since. From August through December 1812, the Americans managed to humiliate the British in a series of battles that sent the Royal Navy and the British public reeling. Since the beginning of the Napoleonic Wars in 1793, the Royal Navy had fought two hundred single-ship engagements, losing only five and each to a superior enemy.[11] In only a few months the minuscule American navy would equal that twenty-year record. Britannia's trident was rusty.

Isaac Hull and *Constitution* forged an early link in this chain of victories. In the days immediately following his return to Boston, Hull spent his time preparing for sea. It was clear that as soon as they could the British would seek to bottle him up, so it was essential that he move quickly.[12] The need for quick departure overrode any other consideration. Without waiting for new orders from the secretary, on Sunday 2 August, with clear weather and a kindly tide, *Constitution* slipped down the harbor and out past the Boston light, bound north to cruise the waters off Newfoundland and the Gulf of St. Lawrence and then south toward Bermuda.[13]

*Constitution* spoke several vessels in the following days. On 10 August she took her first prize — *Lady Warren,* bound from St. John's, Newfoundland, to St. John, New Brunswick. Hull ordered her burned. The next day he took a second prize and dispatched her in the same manner. The three days following were passed in routine fashion punctuated with gun drills, for which Hull seemed to have particular relish. On the 15th *Con-stitution* discovered an enemy warship, *Avenger*, in the act of destroying American vessels. On seeing the frigate, the Britisher took to her heels but did manage to burn one of the Americans. Three more routine days of operation followed. By now, however, from prisoners and others, Hull knew that an enemy frigate was sailing in the same waters.

The enemy in question was H.M.S. *Guerrière*, thirty-eight guns, commanded by Captain James Dacres. *Guerrière* was a captured French frigate that had been brought into the Royal Navy in 1806. Halifax was her station, but she had spent the winter at Bermuda and was now on her way home for much-needed refitting. At about two in the afternoon of 19 August, *Constitution* and *Guerrière* spotted one another. Captain Dacres later described for his superiors what followed.

On the 19th of August, in Lat 40° 20′ No. and Long 55° West. At 2 P.M. being by the Wind and on the starboard Tack, We saw a sail on our Weather Beam, bearing down on us, At 3 made her out to be a Man of War, beat to quarters and prepared for action. At 4, she closing fast, wore to prevent her raking us. At 4:10 hoisted our Colours and returned our Fire — Wore several times to avoid being raked, exchanging broadsides. At 5 she closed on our Starboard Beam, both keeping up a heavy fire and steering free, his intention being evidently to cross our bow. At 5:20 our Mizen Mast went over the Starboard Quarter and brought the ship up in the Wind. The enemy then placed himself on our larboard Bow, raking us, a few only of our guns bearing and his grape and riflemen sweeping our Deck. At 5:40 the Ship not answering her helm, he attempted to lay us on board. At this time Mr. Grant who commanded on the forecastle, was carried below, badly wounded. I immediately ordered the Marines and Boarders from the Main Deck. The Master was at this time shot through the Knee and Lieutenant Ready fell leading on the Men from the Main Deck and I received a severe Wound in the back. Lieutenant Kent was leading on the Boarders when the Ship coming to, We brought some of our Bow guns to bear on her and had got clear of our opponent when at 6:20 our Fore and Main Mast went over the side, leaving the Ship a perfect, unmanageable Wreck. The Frigate shooting ahead I was in hopes to clear the Wreck and get the Ship under Command to renew the action, but just as We had cleared the Wreck, our Spritsail Yard went, and the Enemy having rove new braces He wore round within pistol shot, to rake us. The Ship laying in the trough of the sea rolling her main deck guns under water and all attempts to get her before the Wind being fruitless, when calling my few remaining officers together, they were all of opinion that any further resistance would be a needless waste of Lives, I ordered, though reluctantly, the Colours to be struck.[14]

Dacres' narrative tells only part of the story; the casualty figures tell the rest. *Guerrière* lost fifteen killed and sixty-three wounded to *Constitution*'s seven and seven. The British captain laid some of his casualty figures to the fact that the American had so many marines in the fighting tops laying down a devastating fire. In terms of guns and men, the Britisher was clearly inferior. To Hull's 450 men Dacres had only 275 to 300; and to the American's 692-pound broadside Dacres could answer with only 581.

In the midst of the furor, one American seaman is reported to have seen a British ball strike *Constitution*'s side, cause a small dent, and then fall into the water. Upon which he yelled "Huzzah, her sides are made of iron!" From that came "Old Ironsides."

When the wounded Dacres came aboard *Constitution*, Hull treated him with all the respect due a gallant warrior. The two men were acquainted, and from their previous meeting an apocryphal story has arisen, indicative of their character. Before the war and in front of Hull, Dacres boasted that his ship *Guerrière* could beat any American frigate. So sure was the captain that he offered to bet his hat on the outcome of any such meeting. Now, wounded and defeated, this same captain proffered his sword to Hull. Hull refused the sword and asked for the hat instead.

American gunners had done their work well. *Guerrière* was not only dismasted but holed in several places and taking water. Through the night the prize crew attempted to save her, but it was hopeless. By daylight Hull ordered his men off and set a powder train for scuttling. At about three in the afternoon *Constitution* hove to, three miles from the wallowing hulk, so that everyone aboard might witness the sad and awesome sight. With a tremendous flash reaching up from the magazine, followed by a dull roar, *Guerrière* disappeared, her splintered remains bobbing on the North Atlantic.

Early in the morning of 30 August, Hull was back in Boston. Even in that Federalist town the news set people to celebrating — an American frigate, for the first time in the history of the republic, had beaten a major British warship. Such good news from the east helped to modify bad news from the west. On land the war was not going so well, and Bostonians had just been treated to melancholy dispatches from Detroit describing the shameful surrender of that post to the enemy. The incompetent American commander was General William Hull, Captain Isaac's uncle.

Hull's victory set the example for other officers and helped charge them with an aggressive spirit. Master Commandant Jacob Jones was such a man. On 13 October he passed the Delaware capes in command of the sloop of war *Wasp*, eighteen guns, bound toward the heavily traveled sea lanes connecting England and the West Indies. Two days later a fierce fall blow carried away his jib boom and washed two men overboard. The next night *Wasp* fell in with an enemy convoy headed for England. Although two of the convoy appeared to be large escorts, Jones elected to attack anyway. He was met by H.M.S. *Frolic*, twenty-two guns. The battle was savage and quick. At less than one hundred yards the slugfest began. So close were the two vessels that at some moments *Wasp*'s rammers banged against *Frolic*'s sides. With both vessels severely crippled aloft, the battle finally turned on boarding and bloody hand-to-hand combat. *Frolic*'s bowsprit was overhanging *Wasp*. Jack Lang — folklore claims he was once an impressed seaman aboard a British man-of-war, a remembrance that possessed him with revenge — jumped onto the spar and urged his mates to follow. By the time they hacked their way through to *Frolic*'s main deck, there were few defenders left. Jones had only a few minutes to relish his hard-won victory when a lookout spotted the other escort approaching. It was no small vessel but H.M.S. *Poictiers,* a seventy-four-gun ship of the line. With his rigging still in a jumble, Jones had no choice but to surrender. He and his crew were carried into Bermuda.[15]

*Wasp*'s misfortune was in part due to her having sailed alone. Had she been in company with a friend, the results might have

been different. The irony is that her solo voyage was an accident. In the fall Secretary Hamilton had issued orders dividing
the American fleet into three divisions of three vessels each:
Rodgers had *President, Congress,* and *Wasp*; Decatur had command of *United States, Chesapeake,* and *Argus*; and William Bainbridge, *Constitution, Essex,* and *Hornet.* Jones was ready for sea
before the others, so Rodgers had ordered him out and told
him to rendezvous with the rest.[16]

*President* and *Congress* did finally get to sea on 8 October.
They sailed from Boston in company with Decatur's two vessels
*United States* and *Argus*: *Chesapeake* remained behind, not yet
ready for sea. Rodgers and Decatur left together in order to
mislead the enemy; as soon as they got off soundings they
divided, Rodgers going eastward and Decatur turning to the
south. Four days out *Argus* parted company, leaving Decatur
alone. Bainbridge was not ready to sail until the 27th, when he
headed south with *Constitution* and *Hornet,* hoping to rendezvous with *Essex,* which sailed from the Delaware on the 28th.
Rodgers' squadron proved to be a great disappointment (again).
The action went with Decatur and Bainbridge.

On Sunday morning 25 October, *United States* was five hundred miles south of the Azores. After seventeen days at sea,
Decatur had little to show and was anxiously scanning the horizon. From the foremast lookout came the announcement of a
sail off the starboard bow. As the ship came closer, Decatur
recognized her to be H.M.S. *Macedonian,* Captain John S. Carden. Decatur knew her and her captain well from the days
before the war. *Macedonian* was only two years old, fresh out of
dry dock, and mounted forty-nine guns. Carden too recognized his adversary, and by nine in the morning both captains
had cleared for action and were maneuvering their ships for
the best advantage. Carden had the windward advantage and
used it to keep out of range of Decatur's carronades; both ships
exchanged fire with their long twenty-fours and kept beyond
range of musketry and grape.[17]

Decatur fired the first broadside, but it proved inaccurate.
Carden answered and took down a small spar. Decatur's next
broadside took effect. It brought down the mizzentopmast, and
that falling timber carried with it the driver gaff. The loss of the

driver in light winds hampered *Macedonian's* maneuverability and allowed *United States* to take up a position on the quarter and riddle her. Within a short time the ship became first a brig, then a sloop, and by eleven just a rolling hulk. Carden surrendered, having suffered 104 casualties compared to Decatur's twelve.

Since Hull had had to sink his frigate, Decatur had the chance to be the first American captain to bring one of His Majesty's frigates into port. For two weeks *Macedonian* and *United States* lay rafted to one another while the crews worked to repair the damage. The repairs held, and on 4 December *United States* proudly entered Newport escorting her vanquished enemy.[18] Jubilation was everywhere. To take the news to Washington, Decatur selected one of his junior officers, Lieutenant Hamilton, who happened also to be the son of the secretary. Decatur was as good a politician as captain. The lieutenant arrived at the capital to find his father and several senior officers attending a ball. He interrupted the festivities to announce the news, causing a general uproar and a flood of congratulations, music, and toasts, capped by a presentation of the captured colors to Mrs. James Madison.[19]

Family problems prevented Isaac Hull from going to sea again as commander of *Constitution,* so on 27 October, when she once more passed Boston light outward bound, the frigate had a new commander — William Bainbridge.

Thus far in his naval career, success had eluded William Bainbridge. That did not mean he was not well known; quite the contrary. He was the first American naval commander to surrender his vessel to the enemy, the schooner *Retaliation* in the Quasi War. He was the commander of *George Washington* when she was pressed for the voyage to Constantinople, and of course it was Bainbridge who commanded *Philadelphia* when she ran aground at Tripoli. In each of these instances, Bainbridge had been absolved of any blame. He was just considered very unlucky, leaving many to believe he must have a Jonah in his sea bag. Undoubtedly, as they put to sea, many of the men aboard *Constitution* and her consort *Hornet* must have been contemplating their own fate under this captain.

*Constitution* and *Hornet* plowed south toward their rendezvous with *Essex*. Once the squadron was united, the plan was to move into the vicinity of the Cape Verde Islands, sail west to the Portuguese island of Fernando de Noronha, and thence prowl along the coast of Brazil. It was a promising cruise track that would put them across some very busy sea lanes. If all went well, it was even contemplated to send the squadron off St. Helena to intercept homeward-bound East Indiamen, or perhaps round the Horn and attack British whalers in the Pacific.

*Essex* was under the command of David Porter, the officer who had rallied the crew of *Experiment* during the Quasi War. He and Bainbridge knew one another well, for Porter had served on *Philadelphia* and had been imprisoned with her captain. On 14 December *Essex* dropped anchor at Fernando de Noronha. Porter fooled the local governor into believing his ship was the English merchantman *Fancy,* upon which the governor informed Porter that he had been recently visited by two English warships, *Acasta* and *Morgiana,* the captain of the former having left a letter for Sir James Yeo. From the description of the vessels and the mention of Yeo, an old adversary, Porter knew that the two vessels were *Constitution* and *Hornet,* who had apparently also been able to delude the witless governor. Porter sent a message ashore that he would be glad to deliver the letter to Sir James. Porter must have been chuckling as he read it.

> My dear Mediterranean Friend,
>     Probably you may stop here; don't attempt to water; it is attended with too much difficulty. I learnt before I left England, that you were bound to the Brazil coast; if so, perhaps we may meet at St. Salvadore or Rio Janeiro: I should be happy to meet and converse on our old affairs of captivity; recollect our secret in those times.[20]

Appended to this note was another message written in invisible ink.

> I am bound off St. Salvadore, thence off Cape Frio, where I intend to cruise until the 1st January. Go off Cape Frio, to the northward of Rio Janeiro, and keep a look out for me.

Because of the reported presence of a large British man-of-war in the vicinity of Rio, Porter elected to bypass the Brazilian capital and instead head for another rendezvous, St. Catherine, about five hundred miles south of Rio. He arrived there on 19 January. On the 26th a Portuguese vessel came into port with news of *Constitution* and *Hornet*. According to his intelligence, *Hornet* had been taken by H.M.S. *Montagu,* and a British squadron was on its way to hunt down the other Yankee ships. *Constitution,* on the other hand, had fared well. According to the Portuguese, she had beaten an English frigate. The implications for Porter were clear: *Hornet* was gone. *Constitution* would undoubtedly return home with her prize. All this left *Essex* the lone American in a sea swarming with the enemy. Porter's decision was clear, and probably one that he had been thinking about for some time. He decided that he would take his frigate round the Horn and go hunting in the Pacific.

Porter made a good decision on information that was only half correct. In fact, both *Constitution* and *Hornet* were safe.

Having left Fernando de Noronha on 4 December, *Constitution* and *Hornet* made the coast of Brazil on the 6th. By the 13th they had reached São Salvador. To gain the latest news, Bainbridge ordered Master Commandant James Lawrence, commander of *Hornet,* into port to make contact with the American consul. Lawrence returned with a most fascinating piece of information. At anchor in the harbor was *Bonne Citoyenne,* an old French prize now in British service, commanded by Captain Pitt Barnaby Greene. She was somewhat larger than *Hornet,* but even so, close enough to an even match with the American to be worth a challenge. What was most interesting about her, though, was her cargo — specie, and a lot of it, with some estimates going over a million dollars.[21] As long as *Bonne Citoyenne* was snug at São Salvador, she was safe under the blanket of Portuguese neutrality. Bainbridge took note and decided to sail the coast looking for other prey. Ten days later, while chasing a vessel, *Hornet* again entered São Salvador. Having had no luck at sea and seeing *Bonne Citoyenne* still at anchor, Lawrence could not restrain himself. With Bainbridge's consent he sent a message to Greene, offering to meet him at sea in a single combat. To further entice the Britisher, Bainbridge pledged that no matter how the battle turned he would not intervene. Greene would have none of it. The risk was too great. His mission was to transport specie, not play knight errant. Besides, was it reasonable to assume that if *Bonne Citoyenne* was winning, Bainbridge would stand idly by and watch *Hornet* go down to defeat? How would he explain that to the secretary? Given his past record, such an outcome would probably have ended his career. Greene was too wise to fall for the trap. He declined the invitation. At the same time the Portuguese governor, who was in an awkward position since his nation was an English ally against the French, made known his displeasure at the arrivals and departures of American warships. Frustrated, Bainbridge ordered Lawrence to remain behind and stake out Greene. If he should leave, Lawrence was to attack as soon as he passed into international waters. In the meantime Bainbridge took his own ship back to sea to look for the enemy.[22]

Four days after Christmas, about thirty miles off Brazil, Bainbridge spotted two vessels inshore sailing in a southerly direction. One of the vessels, the larger one, apparently saw him as well, for she changed course and made for the American; the other held her course. Bainbridge immediately suspected she was British and soon became convinced of it. His main worry was the size of the enemy — she might well be a ship of the line. Rather than sail toward her, Bainbridge headed offshore, enticing the stranger to follow. If she turned out to be of equal or inferior rate, this tactic would draw the enemy far enough to sea that she would be unable to run for refuge in a Brazilian port. By 1:20 P.M. Bainbridge had made his identification — it was a British frigate. At that point he came about, and the two ships closed.

H.M.S. *Java* was the enemy, like her erstwhile sister, *Guerrière*, a captured French frigate rated at thirty-eight guns.[23] She was on her way to India and had aboard numerous extra seamen who were to be distributed among the fleet on the Indian station. In addition, *Java* carried a very distinguished passenger, Lieutenant General Sir Thomas Hislop, as well as his staff, who were en route to Bombay. The frigate was under command of Captain Henry Lambert.

Within approximately one mile of *Java*, Bainbridge tacked again. Now the two frigates were sailing southeast on a parallel course. Shortly after two in the afternoon, when the two frigates were within half a mile of one another, the battle started. In the opening salvo *Constitution* took the brunt of the damage. *Java*, the faster of the pair, tried to use her speed to maneuver into a raking position; however, Bainbridge displayed fine ship handling and managed to elude the trap. On one of his attempts to rake Lambert lost his jib boom, causing a momentary pause that enabled Bainbridge to pass off his stern, raking as he went.

Bainbridge, though, had his own problems. One of *Java*'s broadsides had blown away *Constitution*'s wheel, with a fragment striking Bainbridge. Unable to control her from the deck, steering passed below to a jury-rigged tiller in the wardroom pantry.

*Java*'s speed advantage was all but eliminated by the loss of the jib boom. Sensing that *Constitution*'s superior gunnery might win the day, Lambert decided to close and board. As he bore down on the American, he miscalculated and the stub of his bowsprit became entangled in *Constitution*'s mizzen. The position was most awkward, since it left *Java* at an exposed angle to the enemy's main battery but gave her no such advantage. Bainbridge took good aim, his heavy guns wreaking havoc while the marines in the fighting tops sent down a hail of lead onto the deck. In the melee *Java* lost her foremast and the main topmast. The spider's web of wreckage and debris on the deck made it even more difficult to handle the guns.

After their brief encounter, the two frigates staggered apart. The rest reads like an exercise in target practice. "At forty-five minutes past three shot away his mizzenmast nearly by the board."[24] Along with the spars, the captain went down too. Lambert was wounded mortally by a marine sharpshooter, Adrian Peterson.

By four, *Java* was a floating wreck. Bainbridge fell off to repair his own damage in the expectation of coming back to force the final surrender. *Java*, whose command had passed to her first lieutenant, Henry Ducie Chads, was incapable of action. Chads watched the remains of the mainmast go over the side and then ordered the colors affixed to the mizzen stump.

When *Constitution* moved in again, Chads gave some consideration to defending but quickly thought the better of it when he
saw the American coast to a position off his bow from which he
could deliver raking shot. He ordered the colors lowered.

Salvage was impossible. After transferring the crew, Bainbridge ordered *Java* blown up. At three in the afternoon on the
last day of 1812 *Java*, or what was left of her, exploded and
went to the bottom. The casualty figures reflect the tenor of the
engagement. Out of a crew of 480 men, Bainbridge had nine
killed and twenty-five wounded, including the commodore.
The accuracy of *Java*'s figures is in question, although it seems
clear that she suffered five to six times the casualties of her
adversary.

In all of this, however, *Constitution* did not escape unscathed.
Her injuries were not severe, but they were serious enough to
make it impossible for her to continue her cruise. With *Hornet*
in attendance, *Constitution* returned to São Salvador, offloaded
her prisoners, effected repairs, and then set sail for home.
Bainbridge's parting orders to Lawrence were to remain off the
port in the hope that the still tempting morsel *Bonne Citoyenne*
might yet venture out.

The year 1812 was a wonderful year for the American navy
and a disaster for the British. The London *Times*, hardly an
impartial observer, summed it up well.

> Had any one last year predicted such a result (the loss of three frigates
> and 500 merchant vessels to the enemy) he would have been treated as a
> madman or a traitor. He would have been told that long ere seven
> months had elapsed, the American flag would have been swept from
> the seas, and the contemptible navy of the United States annihilated,
> and their marine arsenals rendered a heap of ruin.[25]

Admiral John Borlase Warren was well aware of his failure to
turn in a creditable year. He certainly had good reasons to
explain what seemed to many inexplicable. On 29 December,
even before he knew of the *Java*'s fate, Warren wrote to the
Admiralty from his headquarters in Bermuda. He told them
that the American frigates were larger than their British
counterparts, heavier in construction, manned with more siz-

able crews, and carrying a greater number of heavier guns. To combat these "superfrigates" he suggested taking some older ships of the line and using them as razees.* Bigger ships were only part of the solution. He also needed more. There was simply no way he could cover the coast with the few ships allotted. He had troubles enough with the American navy; he found it impossible to cope with the swarm of Yankee privateers.[26]

Admiral Warren at least understood his problems. The Americans did not, for the euphoria of victory made reality difficult to perceive. The great frigate victories were spasmodic and only momentary, albeit glorious, episodes. The loss of *Guerrière, Macedonian,* and *Java,* while psychologically important, was in fact a mere pinprick to the Royal Navy. Furthermore, in each case the American frigate was larger, had more weight of metal, and was manned by a more numerous crew. If these battles had taken place between two major powers, the results would have been far less noteworthy. What stunned the British and elated the Americans was that a minor power like the United States had in fact smited the much-vaunted Royal Navy.[27]

As the Americans pondered their success, one fact was clear: relying on gunboats would not help them against the British. In a letter of 12 November, Captain Charles Stewart, Isaac Hull, and Charles Morris urged Secretary Hamilton to push for a mixed force of both large and small vessels. Ships of the line were best suited to defend the coast, they argued, not small gunboats.

> It cannot be supposed that in a war with a foreign maritime Power that Power will only send to our coast frigates and smaller cruisers, because we possess no other description of vessels. Their first object will be to restrain, by ships of the line our frigates and other cruisers from departing and preying upon their commerce; Their next object will be to send their smaller cruisers in pursuit of our commerce; and by having their ships of the line parading on our coast, threatening our more exposed seacoast towns, and preventing the departure of our small cruisers, they will be capturing what commerce may have escaped

*Razees were ships of the line that were reduced by one deck.

theirs, and recapturing what prizes may have fallen into our hands. Thirdly, they can at any time withdraw their ships of the line, should a more important job require it, without hazarding much on their part; and return in sufficient time to shut out our cruisers that may have departed during their absence. Fourthly, they can at all times consult their convenience in port time and number; and will incur no expense and risk of transports for provisions and water, but can go and procure their supplies at pleasure and return to their station ere their absence is known to us.[28]

Two weeks later, these views found their way into Congress, and a House committee was urging the full body to foster and care for the naval establishment. Big ships were the answer, gunboats were forgotten. Still, the issue of how to use them was not fully resolved. Would it be Rodgers' squadrons or Decatur's solitary raiders? Little formal discussion seems to have taken place on this question, perhaps because time and events at sea had already in great measure settled the issue. Rodgers' squadron cruise had been a disappointment.[29] The three solitary frigate victories told all.

## 10

# 1813 — A More Sober Time

Despite the spectacular victories of 1812, not everyone was enthusiastic. In the waning days of December, as Congress debated naval policy, it was clear that some members had strong misgivings about building seventy-fours. The old antinaval lobby had pretty much resigned themselves to the building of the frigates and smaller vessels, but with the line of battleships they saw a chance to stem the tide. What they feared most was what might come after the war — a large permanent naval force that would be both expensive and mischievous, inasmuch as it would encourage the government toward foreign adventures. Left unsaid, at least on the floor of Congress, was another concern — the secretary himself.

Paul Hamilton was a mediocre administrator whose grasp of naval issues depended almost entirely upon advice from his captains. He was solicitous and at times almost fawning in his relations with the senior officers. Furthermore, it was rumored that he was a heavy drinker whose personal habits interfered with his professional capacity. All in all, Hamilton was a political liability for Madison and certainly not the man to run a growing naval establishment.[1]

Indeed, Hamilton's days were numbered. On 28 December the president commented to the secretary offhandedly that he had received complaints about mismanagement in the Navy Department. The next evening Hamilton was summoned to a more formal interview, where Madison told him bluntly that he was an obstacle to congressional approval for naval appropriations. Hamilton defended his record, but it was no use; the president told him "this was a government of opinion and when the popular current set against an officer he could not be useful." Hamilton offered the commander in chief his resignation. It was accepted.[2]

Hamilton's departure helped pave the way for considerable naval expansion. On 2 January an act was approved providing for the construction of four seventy-fours and six forty-fours at a cost of two and one half million dollars. In his retirement from public life, Hamilton could take some solace from having laid the groundwork for this ambitious building program. His successor would inherit the task of trying to carry the project to completion, a business that was to prove most difficult. Not one of the ten vessels authorized would ever see service against the British.

On 19 January 1813 William Jones took the oath as the republic's fourth secretary of the navy. Jones was a Philadelphia sea captain and merchant who had sailed as a privateer under Thomas Truxtun. He was now in his fifties, and this was not the first time he had been offered the post of secretary. In his first administration Jefferson had approached Jones, but he declined, not wishing to preside over what he viewed as Jefferson's dissolution of the navy. Matters were quite different now — war had brought expansion, a policy Jones was much disposed to support. In him Madison found a strong advocate for continued naval expansion.[3]

Jones was quick to take the helm. A perusal of the account books brought him his first bad tidings — the department's budget was in the red to the tune of more than one million dollars. That news was delivered to the House on 7 February. While assessing the financial situation, Jones also looked carefully at the administrative structure and moved to make several alterations in the way in which the department did business. With the geometric expansion of the fleet and the men manning it, there was a clear, yet unfilled, need to augment support activities. Jones called for more pursers to handle the details of contracts and procurement; more clerks to manage correspondence and bookkeeping; and more captains since there were at the time no spares. He also alluded to the need for additional small vessels to provide convoy escort in American waters. He wanted to continue work on the seventy-fours, but in the meantime smaller vessels could be built and launched to harass the British and perhaps draw some of their blockading ships away from the coast. Congress agreed, and with hardly a whimper enacted a bill on 3 March providing for the construction of six sloops and the sale of several gunboats. The latter was done not out of any admission that the "Jeffs" (a popular nickname for the boats) had failed, but rather as a simple method for saving money that might be allocated to larger ships.[4]

It was fortuitous that Jones moved so rapidly, for Congress was still heady with the victories of 1812. Had Jones been a more cautious man and bided his time, the results would have been quite different. Eighteen thirteen was not a good year.

Still hoping to encourage separatist feeling in New England, the British refrained from imposing a tight blockade north of Cape Cod. To the south, however, it was a different matter. In the Chesapeake and Delaware Bay areas British warships patrolled close in, making it difficult for American ships to put to sea. Some vessels did manage to get out, but for the most part they consisted of privateers whose success at eluding the enemy could hardly be celebrated by naval officers, since their crews were made up of men who otherwise would be aboard public warships. As for the gunboats, they proved next to useless and sat idle at the dock wanting crews. When they did sail, they often had to hurry back home to escape being taken by the enemy.[5]

While captains in port fretted about getting to sea, those at sea worried about getting home. One such commander was James Lawrence aboard *Hornet*. He had been left behind by Bainbridge with instructions to lay off Bahia, Brazil (the modern city of Salvador), on the lookout for the enemy. He was to be especially cautious of running afoul of a seventy-four rumored to be in the area. At his discretion Lawrence was to take *Hornet* north following the coast to points near Pernambuco, Cayenne, and Surinam, timing his itinerary so as to arrive back in Boston early in April.

On 6 January, while patrolling off Bahia, *Hornet* took the

merchant schooner *Ellen* with a cargo of specie. At nearly the same time, however, Lawrence learned that the phantom seventy-four had materialized in the form of H.M.S. *Montagu,* whose arrival sent him scurrying for cover in Bahia. Under no illusions that the Portuguese would permit him to stay, Lawrence slipped out to sea the same night, evaded *Montagu,* and laid a course for the north.

On 24 February, off the Demerara River in British Guiana, *Hornet* met H.M.S. *Peacock.* The two moved on one another from opposite tacks. They passed close and exchanged broadsides. *Peacock,* though about the same size as *Hornet,* suffered from a fatal flaw; her broadside weight was only two thirds of *Hornet*'s (198 versus 297 lbs.). Following the opening gambit, *Peacock* came about and sailed parallel to *Hornet.* Lawrence saw his chance and put his vessel on the enemy's starboard quarter. The battle was brief, only eleven minutes by some accounts. *Peacock* surrendered with six feet of water in her hold and more rushing in. She was doomed. The water being shallow, not more than six fathoms, both vessels anchored. What then followed is a matter of dispute. Lawrence reported that he immediately sent his small boats to rescue *Peacock*'s crew. *Peacock*'s purser, Joshua Keene, disagreed. According to him, Lawrence waited more than a half hour before sending help, and then when they arrived the Americans were more interested in looting *Peacock* than saving her crew. The English ship went down carrying nine of her crew and three of *Hornet*'s. According to Keene, one American sailor went to the bottom clutching *Peacock*'s silver service.

Whatever the truth about the behavior of the men, it was still a magnificent victory for Lawrence. In contrast to the sloppy gunnery on board the *Peacock, Hornet*'s gun crews had exercised their weapons with considerable skill. That, coupled with the greater weight of the metal, made for a short battle.[6]

While Lawrence was battling *Peacock,* Captain David Porter faced a challenge of a different sort. He was preparing to take *Essex* into the Pacific via Cape Horn. Since the days of discovery, rounding the Horn had been viewed as the next best thing to a voyage in hell. Storms, ice, wind currents, and an inhospitable shore made the region feared by all intelligent mariners. Porter completed the necessary preparations for the passage, which at first encounter promised to be relatively routine:

> . . . some of my guns were put below, the spars taken from the upper and put on the gun-deck, and the weight considerably reduced aloft. Added to these measures, the best sails were bent, preventer shrouds got up to secure the masts, and every other means adopted that prudence could suggest, or our ingenuity invent, to render our passage as free from disaster as possible. We were entering the bourn of all our dread with a pleasant breeze from the northward and a smooth sea, felicitating ourselves on our fortunate and pleasant passage through the streights, and our prospect of a safe and speedy one around the Cape.[7]

Having lulled Porter into believing he was on a yachtsman's passage, the Horn then turned on *Essex* with the fickleness and violence for which she was infamous:

> . . . the black clouds, hanging over Cape Horn, burst upon us with a fury we little expected, and reduced us in a few minutes to a reefed foresail, and close-reefed main top-sail, and in a few hours afterwards to our storm-staysails. Now was the violence of the winds the only danger we had to encounter; for it produced an irregular and dangerous sea, that threatened to jerk away our masts at every roll of the ship . . . the gales blew hard from the northwest, accompanied with heavy rains, cold disagreeable weather, and dangerous sea. We were never enabled to carry more sail than a close reefed main-topsail and reefed foresail, and were frequently under our storm-staysails.[8]

On 24 February *Essex* was far enough west that Porter could declare his ship "fairly in the Pacific," the first American warship ever to claim that honor. They cruised north along the coast of Chile on the lookout for British whalers. On 6 March they anchored close to the shore of the island of Mocha, where they hoped to find British whalers taking on water and meat. They found none, but being low on provisions themselves, men from the *Essex* went ashore for water and to hunt the feral pigs and horses that roamed the island. In the hunting melee a nearsighted lieutenant, Stephen Decatur McKnight, fired at a horse and hit the beast, only to have the ball pass through it and strike gunner's mate James Spafford, who fell to the ground crying, "Sir, you have shot me! I am a dying man; take me to the boat." Spafford's self-diagnosis proved all too correct.

*Essex* left Mocha and resumed her northerly course along the bleak and barren Chilean coast. On the 15th Porter put into Valparaíso. He expected a cool if not hostile reception, since Chile was Spanish and Spain a British ally against Napoleon. What the captain did not know was that the spasmodic revolution that had been tearing the country apart for some time had, for the moment at least, put Valparaíso in the hands of rebels who gave a warm welcome to the Americans.

Porter spent nine days in Valparaíso provisioning and partying. He was anxious to get out to sea. His greatest ally, surprise, would vanish quickly as the British learned of his presence. Like Francis Drake more than two centuries before, he planned to ravage the enemy before they even knew of his whereabouts. Before he left port Porter conferred with Benjamin Worth, master of the American whaler *George* out of Nantucket. The captain told him the best places to hunt British whalers were off the port of Payta in Peru and in the Galápagos Islands. Porter decided to follow the captain's advice.

On the morning of the 25th, as they were running down the coast, Porter encountered the American whaler *Charles* from Nantucket. Her captain told Porter that two other American whalers had just been taken by a ship flying Spanish colors. Porter set off in chase, with British colors hoisted so that he might not scare off the culprit. The ruse worked. *Essex* found the ship, *Nereyda,* whose lieutenant, believing that he was addressing an English officer, blithely told Porter how they were cruising for American ships. Porter listened politely, then hoisted his true colors and proceeded to pull *Nereyda*'s fangs by dumping all her guns into the Pacific. He then sent her into port with a stinging letter to the local viceroy.

From *Nereyda* Porter liberated a number of American seamen, most of whom he had put on board *Charles*. Not wishing to keep those men against their will, he decided to send *Charles* into Coquimbo, Chile, with any men who wished to be put ashore. Those who did not could come over to *Essex* and sign her articles. Before bidding farewell to the whalemen, he asked

them to list for him all the American and British whalers they
knew to be in the area. The list was impressive. According to
their best recollections the whalemen could count twenty-three
American ships whaling in the region and ten British, including the infamous *Nimrod,* a British privateer cruising the coast.

With this information Porter was more convinced than ever
of what his mission ought to be. It was twofold: protect the
Americans and smite the British. The former might best be
done by eliminating the British threat in the area. In the short
term this was possible, since the British naval force in the region was small and widely scattered. With surprise as an ally,
Porter might well best the enemy; time was the real foe. As
soon as the British realized Porter was loose in the Pacific, they
would undoubtedly take heroic measures to track him down;
he needed to strike quickly and then make good his escape.

On 28 March off Callao *Essex* came within sight of three
ships. Two got away, but the third was overtaken. She turned
out to be the American whaler *Barclay,* a British prize that Porter could now reclaim. With *Barclay* in company, Porter continued his search for *Nimrod.* It was a wistful venture that
made little sense when by all reckoning the Galápagos were full
of fat British whalers ready for plucking. After wasting nearly
two weeks, on 11 April *Essex* and *Barclay* headed west for a
descent on the islands.

En route Porter laid plans for his attack and even began
rehearsals. Since the islands were known for their calms, he
thought there might be a need to attack with the small boats.
He assigned Lieutenant John Downes with seventy men and
seven boats to make preparations for such as assault.

On 17 April they made their first landfall at Chatham Island,
the easternmost member of the archipelago.[9] Downes was sent
in with a small boat to reconnoiter. He found nothing except
the marvels of nature; indeed, for the next several days David
Porter's journal reads more like a chapter from Darwin than
the record of a naval expedition.

> Here wood is to be obtained, and land tortoises in great numbers . . .
> These islands are all evidently of volcanic production; every mountain
> and hill is the crater of an extinguished volcano . . . we went on shore,

and to our great surprise and no little alarm, on entering the bushes, found myriads of guanas, of an enormous size and the most hideous appearance imaginable . . . In some spots a half acre of ground would be so completely covered with them as to appear as though it was impossible for another to get in the space; they would all keep their eyes fixed constantly on us, discovered them to be the most timid of all animals and in a few moments knocked down hundreds of them with our clubs, some of which we brought on board, and found to be excellent eating . . .[10]

Porter went on to describe the limitless number of docile seals and lizards with red heads and "plenty of birds called shags." The abundance of it all seemed to amaze him most.

The rocks were every where covered with seal, penguins, guanas, and pelicans, and the sea filled with green turtle . . . Multitudes of enormous sharks were swimming about us . . .

There were "multitudes" of everything except what he wanted most — British whalers.

Finally, on 29 April, *Essex*'s visit began to pay off. On that day Porter was roused from his cabin by the cry "sail ho." At first only one sail was in sight, but soon after they took up the chase two more appeared. Porter had no doubt that they were British. The first, soon under the American guns, was *Montezuma*, with 1,400 barrels of oil. Having subdued her easily, Porter set after the other two. When he was still eight miles away, a calm set in; no matter, he had trained his men well. Two divisions of small boats were lowered, one under Downes, the other in command of Lieutenant James Wilmer. Within a mile of the enemy, who themselves were close aboard one another, the divisions drew together and set down on the larger ship. The first surrendered without a fight, and the second quickly followed suit. They were *Georgiana*, six eighteen-pounders, and *Policy*, ten six-pounders.

These captures launched a roll of good luck for the Americans. From the captured vessels Porter was able to resupply and refit his own ships. *Georgiana* was given additional armament and put under Downes's command, with instructions to cruise independently. In the meantime *Essex*, in consort with her two prizes and *Barclay*, continued to hunt through the islands.

For the next month Porter's chief enemy turned out to be boredom. No British whalers could be found, so the time was spent in leisurely cruising (light winds made uneventful sailing) and in working up the ship. Finally on 28 May a sail was sighted. *Essex,* which had been towing the sluggish *Montezuma,* cast her off and gave chase. As sunset approached, Porter could see his quarry plainly from the deck; at the same time, however, he realized that in the darkness he might well lose her. He hove to and waited for the other vessels, *Barclay, Montezuma,* and *Policy,* to join him. He then organized his flotilla into a seagoing skirmish line, thereby covering miles of ocean and making it impossible for the Englishman to escape detection. It worked. The vessel turned out to be the English whaler *Atlantic.* When Porter came alongside, he hoisted English colors and ordered the captain to come aboard. The commander, Obadiah Wyer, formerly of Nantucket, obliged and when invited to Porter's cabin even went so far as to tell gleefully this ersatz Englishman where he might go to take American whalers. It gave Porter no end of pleasure to tell Wyer that there was no need to go in search of Americans, for they were already here.

Barely had Porter come down on *Atlantic* when another vessel was sighted. It was the letter of marque *Greenwich.* Porter made no pretense with her and fired a warning shot. That was quite enough; she struck, giving the Americans their second prize of the day.

Porter now had under his command:

| | |
|---|---|
| *Essex* 46 guns | 245 men |
| *Georgiana* 16 guns | 42 men |
| | (cruising under Downes) |
| *Atlantic* 6 guns | 12 men |
| *Greenwich* 10 guns | 14 men |
| *Montezuma* 2 guns | 10 men |
| *Policy* 10 guns | 10 men |

After shifting men and supplies, Porter decided to head his squadron east toward the mainland. On 14 June they arrived and spent a few days looking for water and Lieutenant Downes.

After more cruising *Essex* dropped anchor at Tumbez, a small port on the south side of the Bay of Guayaquil. The local governor was friendly enough; still, Porter was sensitive to the fact that the British and Spanish were allies, and no friend of Britain could be a friend of America.

On the 24th Downes made his long-awaited appearance. His report sustained Porter's judgment — that in this lieutenant he had a fine officer. Downes had taken three enemy vessels:

| | | |
|---|---|---|
| *Hector* 11 guns | 25 men | |
| *Catherine* 8 guns | 29 men | |
| *Rose* 8 guns | 21 men | |

*Hector* and *Catherine* proved worth keeping, but *Rose* was not worth the trouble, so Downes had her made into a cartel vessel* and dispatched her with the prisoners off to St. Helena. With the new arrivals Porter's squadron now numbered eight vessels. The requirements for officers aboard them so reduced the American cadre that Porter was forced to appoint a twelve-year-old midshipman to command *Barclay*. The midshipman more than proved his worth and promise. His name was David Glasgow Farragut.

At Tumbez Porter decided to reorganize his squadron. Since *Atlantic* was better suited for a warship than *Georgiana*, he put his men to work piercing her for guns and strengthening her bulwarks. He renamed her *Essex Junior* and placed the trusty Downes in command. After more cruising, Porter decided to head west toward the Galápagos again. *Essex, Georgiana,* and *Greenwich* laid a course for the islands, while Downes took *Junior* and accompanied the remainder of the prizes — *Catherine, Hector, Montezuma,* and *Policy* — to Valparaíso in the hope of selling them. It was a vain hope, and Downes ended up sending *Policy* with her oil off to America and leaving the rest at anchor in the harbor, while he hurried off to join Porter.

*Cartel vessels were used in the age of sail to send messages or prisoners to the enemy. They generally flew a white flag to identify themselves. Ideally, prisoners would be exchanged, but in this case Porter was anxious just to get rid of his nuisance cargo and did not expect American sailors in return for his British prisoners.

Porter's return to the islands was unwelcome news for the British. Within a few days he had netted three prizes, *Charlton, Seringapatam,* and *New Zealander.* More reorganization followed, resulting in the dispatch of *Charlton* and *Georgiana* back to the United States and the converting of *Seringapatam* to a twenty-two-gun auxiliary. On 15 September he took a fourth prize on this leg of the cruise, *Sir Andrew Hammond.* In her hold she had a cargo beyond value — "two puncheons of choise Jamaica spirits."

By now *Essex* had been at sea for almost a full year. Her rigging was worn, rot had set in, and her bottom was foul. But perhaps most annoying of all, at least to the crew, was the plague of rats that infested her.

> These had increased so fast as to become a most dreadful annoyance to us, by destroying our provisions, eating through our water-casks, thereby occasioning a great waste of our water, getting into the magazine and destroying our cartridges, eating their way through every part of our ship, and occasioning considerable destruction of our provisions, clothing, flags, sails, etc. etc. It had become dangerous to have them any longer on board; and as it would be necessary to remove everything from the ship before smoking her, and probably heave her out to repair her copper, which in many places was coming off, I believed that a convenient harbour could be found among one of the groups of islands that would answer our purpose, as well as furnish the crew with such fresh provisions and vegetables as might be necessary during our stay here, by which means we should be enabled to save our salt provisions.[11]

Porter had in mind the Marquesas Islands as a refuge. All that delayed his embarking was *Essex Junior.* On 30 September she arrived with the news that convinced Porter more than ever of the need to find a safe harbor where his men could rest and his ships refit. Not surprisingly, the Admiralty had finally reacted to Porter's Pacific terror. Downes reported that en route to the area was a British squadron consisting of the frigate *Phoebe,* thirty-six guns, two sloops of war of twenty-four guns each, *Raccoon* and *Cherub,* in the company of a store ship of twenty guns.

All that held him now was adverse wind. On 2 October the

wind shifted, and Porter's squadron made sail westward toward the Marquesas.

Washington Islands is the name by which Porter referred to the Marquesas, since that was the name given them by Joseph Ingraham, the American captain who claimed the islands in 1791 for the United States. Over the next twenty years several explorers visited the archipelago, including British and Russian. Sovereignty, therefore, was anyone's guess.[12] The only thing about the islands that could be said with any certainty was that they were remote — 2,500 miles southeast of Hawaii and 850 miles northeast of Tahiti.

On 25 October Porter's squadron entered Taiohae Bay on the southern coast of the island of Nukahiva. It was here that Porter decided to establish his base. After dropping anchor in the bay, Porter was startled to see a canoe approach with three white men in it. One was John Minor Maury, a former naval midshipman, the second was an American sailor, and the third an English beachcomber named Wilson. Maury and the seaman had been put ashore to gather sandalwood, with the expectation that they would be picked up again. The war, however, had intervened and their ship had not returned. Wilson, who had been on the island for years, spoke the local language fluently and proved invaluable, once Porter got over his revulsion at Wilson's completely tattooed body. Wilson had gone native.

For seven weeks Porter remained at Nukahiva. With the assistance of natives, the Americans refitted and repaired their ships, while at the same time enjoying a chance to regain their health. Of course, not every minute was spent in work, and there was ample time for liberty ashore. Lush tropical paradise, beautiful native women, men who had been at sea for more than a year — it does not require much imagination to conjure up an image of what the private side of life in Nukahiva was like after the American invasion. Even Porter, circumspect as he was, makes several incriminating references in his journal.

> With the common sailors and their girls, all was helter skelter, and promiscuous intercourse, every girl the wife of every man in the mess, and frequently of every man in the ship; each one from time to time

took such as suited his fancy and convenience, and no one among them formed a connection which was likely to produce tears at the moment of separation . . .

. . . the girls, from twelve to eighteen years of age, rove at will, this period of their lives is a period of unfounded pleasure, unrestrained in all their action, unconfirmed by domestic occupations, their time is spent dancing, singing, and ornamenting their persons to render themselves more attractive in the eyes of man, on whom they indiscriminately bestow their favors, unrestrained by shame or fear of the consequences. That terrible disease which has proved so destructive to mankind, is unknown to them, and they give free scope to the indulgence of their passions, living in the most pleasurable licentiousness.[13]

Not even the captain himself could remain chaste among so many occasions of sin.

Porter may be forgiven his carnal transgressions and those of his men; indeed, it is difficult to imagine how matters could have gone otherwise. But in another area he should be brought to accountability. Porter allowed himself to become involved in the tribal warfare endemic to the island. He felt he had no choice but to go to war to protect his position — an arguable point. The result was pitiful. The natives could offer little resistance to the superior weapons and organization of the invaders, and were slaughtered easily. Porter soon had matters under control, a situation that encouraged him on 19 November to stage a dramatic scene by which he annexed the island for the United States. Nukahiva would henceforth be known as Madison's Island, the settlement Madisonville, and the American base Fort Madison. Porter proudly forwarded copies of these proceedings to Washington, where the president promptly ignored them.

For the Americans, the stay at Nukahiva was a smashing success. As a haven for rest, relaxation, and repair, Porter could not have chosen more wisely. For the Nukahivans it was something else. Whatever Porter's intentions for them, the sojourn of the squadron can only be called — as one historian has done — "baleful."

By early December Porter came to a decision. Originally, he had intended to refit in the islands in order to prepare for the long voyage home. He now altered that scheme and instead determined to take *Essex* and *Essex Junior* back toward the coast of Chile, in the hope of encountering the British who had been sent out to find him. At the same time, he ordered the remaining ships to stay at Nukahiva with twenty-two men under the command of Marine Lieutenant John Gamble. Porter intended to keep the base at the island in anticipation of the need for a refuge after his engagement with the British.

By 9 December the vessels were ready to sail, and they got under way on the 13th. It was like a scene from a Hollywood movie. The band played "The Girl I Left Behind Me," while tearful maidens waved and wept from the shore. There must have been a wet eye or two aboard the ships as well. Indeed, three men who had swum ashore at night "determined to have a parting kiss" had to be returned to *Essex* by force.[14]

The passage back to Chile was, in Porter's own word, "uninteresting." They picked up the coast and sailed into Valparaíso harbor on 3 February 1814. David Porter was quite foolish. He knew that he was already outgunned by the British, and he must have suspected that enemy reinforcements were on the way. The most rational course was simply to run and do what damage he could on the retreat home; seeking out the enemy deliberately made no sense except that it offered a path to glory. Porter was no different from most of his peers, British and American: hubris was as common as scurvy in these navies; honor and glory was everything, even at the expense of sound strategy.

To cultivate the local dignitaries, Porter threw a ball aboard *Essex* on the evening of 7 February. In the hazy dawn of the next morning the party was literally over. Downes reported that two warships were on their way into the port. Porter quickly went aboard *Essex Junior* and with his lieutenant identified the intruders. To no one's surprise, least of all Porter's, they were British, the frigate *Phoebe* and her consort, the sloop of war *Cherub*. Their blithesome names belied their bellicose purpose and the determination of their commander, Captain James Hillyar, to have a go at the Americans.

It was one of the fortunes of war that Hillyar should be sent to deal with Porter, for the two officers were close acquaintances. They had served at the same time in the Mediterranean, Hillyar in command of the ship *Niger,* based at Gibraltar, and Porter commanding *Enterprize.* Hillyar was highly regarded by all who knew him, Tobias Lear referring to him as "an excellent man." When in Gibraltar, Porter made it a practice to visit Hillyar and his family, with whom he "spent many pleasant hours."[15]

Hillyar knew the situation full well: his enemy had taken refuge in a neutral port, and legally he was bound to respect that neutrality. That did not prevent him from taunting Porter, however, by coming within a few feet of *Essex.* Porter ordered his men to stand at their posts with cutlass and pistol at the ready. He warned his old friend that if the two frigates touched there would be much "bloodshed." *Phoebe*'s jib boom did come across *Essex*'s forecastle, but no damage was done and no shots were fired. Hillyar then moved over to the eastern side of the bay and dropped anchor at a spot from which *Phoebe*'s eighteen-pounders could reach *Essex* but where the American's carronades could not touch her. *Cherub* dropped her hook at closer range but was well covered by *Essex Junior.*

For the next week the British and Americans had ample opportunity to size one another up. A comparison of the relative strength of the two sides indicates clearly that with warships things are not always what they seem. *Essex* carried forty-six guns manned by 255 men. *Phoebe* carried the same number of major-caliber cannon, along with a half dozen or so lighter pieces. Thus, at first glance the two frigates would seem to be relatively equal, with the Britisher having an edge in crew size with approximately three hundred men. Equality, however, is an elusive matter, and in one respect *Essex* was fatally flawed. Forty of her guns were heavy carronades, thirty-two-pounders, which could heave a mighty shot but only for a small distance. *Phoebe,* on the other hand, had in her battery thirty long guns capable of sending eighteen- and nine-pound balls a considerable distance. The two consorts, *Cherub* and *Essex Junior,* were more disparate. As a converted warship *Junior* carried only twenty guns, half eighteen-pound carronades and half six-pound long guns. *Cherub* had a total of twenty-seven or twenty-eight guns (records disagree), of which only two were long and the rest carronades. The combined weight of metal for each side was not much different; the two British could heave approximately 1,700 pounds, and the Americans could toss about 1,600 pounds. Statistics would not decide the outcome; skill and fate would.

After a week of testing the Americans and trading verbal barbs, the British left port to establish an offshore blockade, hoping that Porter would either sortie to engage or attempt an escape. For the time being he did neither.

Holding station off the rugged Chilean coast was no easy task. Gale winds and a hostile shore put Hillyar's seamanship to the test. He was not found wanting. Porter wanted dearly to bring *Phoebe* into single combat with *Essex,* so that he might close and batter her to pieces. Hillyar was too clever for that and adamantly refused to move his command into any position where his superiority might be jeopardized. Time was clearly on the side of the British, for, as Hillyar knew for certain, and Porter only suspected, help was on the way.

On 27 March Porter ordered his ship prepared for sea. His plan was to sail the following day. He hoped that both *Phoebe* and *Cherub* would take the bait, follow him, and thereby let *Junior* escape. The plan might have worked had it not been for an ill wind that came up the next day, parting the port cable and then dragging *Essex* seaward, with her starboard anchor still down. Porter quickly got on sail and made an attempt to pass the enemy to windward, but as he tried a heavy squall hit, carrying away the main topmast. With no chance of outrunning Hillyar, Porter decided to head back into neutral waters and repair the damage. Unable to get back to his original anchorage, Porter took refuge in another nearby bay, where he dropped anchor close to shore. Hillyar, feeling perhaps that this might be his one and only chance to get Porter before the other British units arrived to share the glory, moved in on his wounded prey. At 3:54 P.M. *Phoebe* and *Cherub,* carefully keeping beyond range of *Essex'* carronades, opened a brisk fire. Unable to swing on a cable, *Essex* found herself with her stern to the enemy, ideal for them but death to her. With great effort Porter and his men moved three long guns to the stern ports, from which they were able to deliver accurate fire on the British, forcing them to withdraw and repair. Within a short time, though, they were back to deliver more devastating fire. Porter moved *Essex* for the lee shore, in the hope of running her aground and letting the crew escape ashore. Not even the wind would cooperate. As they came within musket shot of the beach, the wind veered to seaward and drove *Essex* back into the clutches of the enemy. Downes, who had been unable to maneuver *Junior* close enough to offer support, came aboard to relieve Porter of some of his wounded. *Essex* was in her death throes. Porter described his parlous state:

> . . . as I was informed the fire was near the magazine, and the explosion of a large quantity of powder below served to increase the horrors of our situation — our boats were destroyed by the enemy's shot; I, therefore, directed those who could swim to jump overboard, and endeavor to gain the shore . . . I was informed that the cockpit, the steerage, the wardroom and the birthdeck, could contain no more wounded; that the wounded were killed while the surgeons were dressing them, and that, unless something was speedily done to prevent it, the ship would soon sink from the number of shot holes in her bottom.[16]

Unable to strike at the enemy, both because of his awkward position and the limited range of his carronades, Porter submitted to the inevitable. At 6:20 P.M., after almost three hours of near-constant bombardment, *Essex* struck. *Essex Junior* had no choice but to follow suit.

The aftermath of the battle was nearly as rancorous as the combat, both sides continuing the battle in print long after the war. Hillyar allowed Porter and his crew to return home in *Essex Junior*; the senior *Essex* was taken into the Royal Navy and remained on duty with the fleet for nearly two decades.

As an ocean warrior, David Porter had turned in a remarkable accomplishment. He had virtually destroyed the British whaling fleet in the Pacific. He had shown the American flag in distant waters, annexed a bit of property, and all in all made a very favorable impression on the emerging leaders of the Latin American republics. What he had not done, however, was to divert a significant part of the Royal Navy from the Atlantic to the Pacific.

Time and distance prevented Americans at home from

knowing much about Porter's exploits until long after they were over. In the meantime, there was much going on along the Atlantic coast to rivet attention, particularly at Norfolk and Boston, where the bulk of the American force was concentrated.

Norfolk was in an especially unpleasant situation. The British had concentrated a considerable number of vessels there, whose presence not only made it difficult for ships to pass in and out of the Bay but provided a constant threat to the folks onshore who feared attack. All the prewar promises of how gunboats would defend the coast had evaporated. Altogether there were only fifteen boats in service along the entire coast, and even those were having great difficulty staying on duty because of lack of men. It was clear the navy had no hope of defending the coast; for that the citizens would have to turn to local authorities and hope that the militia might man the fortifications and artillery batteries. Pressed by local authorities to send a naval force to defend the neighborhood, Secretary Jones took the stance that his resources were stretched to the limit and that to "increase . . . the force at any one point must . . . necessarily reduce that of another . . ."[17] Furthermore, although he was not inclined to announce it publicly, the secretary had little interest in using the navy as a coastal defense force. He saw American ships playing their most important role as offensive weapons carrying the war to the enemy, rather than as floating forts waiting for the enemy to come and sink them at their moorings.

With virtual impunity the British were able to harass shipping and make sporadic raids in the Chesapeake and Delaware bay region. By mid-spring 1813, all water traffic had been halted as far up as Reedy Island in the Delaware and on a good part of the Chesapeake as well. In June 1813 British soldiers from Bermuda arrived off Norfolk under the command of Brigadier General Sir Sidney Beckwith. Their target was Norfolk, but the town was spared by the timely action of bringing the frigate *Constellation* to anchor at Craney Island, where in cooperation with the gunboats and Virginia militia it was able to repel the assault. Still, Norfolk's preservation did nothing to break the blockade and open a seaward passage. American ships continued to be bottled up.[18]

For the British, Chesapeake Bay offered special attractions, since it allowed them to use their superior naval power to penetrate deep into America. Admiral Sir George Cockburn, commander of the enemy forces, found particular relish in tormenting the people along the Maryland and Virginia shores. After the repulse at Craney Island, Cockburn moved farther up the Bay and in a series of unopposed amphibious raids panicked the local populace.

At Boston there was more hope. By March 1813 four frigates were in the harbor: *Congress, President, Constitution,* and *Chesapeake.* Still in command of *President* was the indefatigable John Rodgers, who had brought her and *Congress* back after their cruise of October-December 1812. *Chesapeake* had come in on 9 April and was in the process of refitting, as was *Constitution,* still recovering from her engagement with *Java.*

It was no small miracle, and a testimony to American seamanship, that all the frigates that had gone cruising in 1812 came home safely. The question now was, what next? By early 1813 the only major ship at sea was *Essex.* On 22 January Jones addressed a circular letter to his captains, inviting their suggestions for cruises. Not surprisingly, among the first to respond was John Rodgers, with one of his spacious plans, outlining five different locations that he thought promising.

> Namely on the eastern edge of the banks of Newfoundland in the direction of their trade between England, Nova Scotia, and Newfoundland — between the Manilla reef and the south western most part of the banks of Newfoundland — between Cape Clear and Ushant — between the Noose of Norway and Jutland, and on the equator, between the longitude of 24° and 31° west.[19]

By mid-April Rodgers had decided on a plan for *President.* He was bound for Halifax, the Grand Banks, and then to the Azores and the coast of Portugal. From thence he would head north around Iceland, down through St. George's Channel along the east coast of Scotland, and thence toward the Baltic to look for the Baltic fleet.[20]

It was a plan reminiscent of John Paul Jones's foray in 1779, a voyage that had climaxed with Jones's famous victory over *Serapis* off Flamborough Head. Perhaps Rodgers hoped fate would be as kind to him. On 30 April, a strong gale having temporarily rid the coast of British cruisers, *President* headed to sea, accompanied by *Congress.* They parted company about six hundred miles out, *President* off on her cruise northward, while *Congress* pressed on toward the Cape Verde Islands.

Despite his grand plans and strong effort, after a five-month cruise Rodgers dropped anchor in Narragansett Bay on 27 September and could report taking only twelve prizes, none of great significance. *Congress* had similar mediocre luck. She was at sea nearly seven and a half months, but her report upon coming into Portsmouth was only four small prizes. The best explanation for the poor showing is that the British were relying more on convoys, thus reducing the chance of a lone merchantman being picked off by an American ship.

The next frigate to get out of Boston was *Chesapeake.* Her commander, Samuel Evans, asked to be relieved on account of a malady affecting his eyesight. In his letter asking for relief, Evans recommended James Lawrence, captain of *Hornet,* to replace him. Having proven himself, Lawrence was certainly entitled to the larger command; however, *Chesapeake* was not his first choice. His wife was ill, and in order to remain with her Lawrence asked that he be given *Constitution,* whose sailing date was some time in the future, rather than *Chesapeake,* which he understood was almost ready to leave. He suggested that he and *Constitution*'s commander, Charles Stewart, simply swap commands. The change was not made; Lawrence remained in command of *Chesapeake* and prepared her for sea.[21]

While Lawrence busied himself preparing his command offshore, two British frigates were patrolling the approaches — *Shannon* and *Tenedos,* under the command of the former's captain, Philip Vere Broke. By all accounts Broke was one of the best frigate captains in the Royal Navy. Quick advancement, a product of political connections as well as competency, brought him command of *Shannon* before he was thirty years old. At the time of his station off Boston he had been in command of the frigate for seven years; in that period, unlike most of his peers, he had drilled his men incessantly. The crew of *Shannon* were without doubt among the best trained in the entire Royal Navy.[22]

Ever since the embarrassing escape of *President* and *Congress*, Broke had been feeling pangs of shame and was anxious to find recompense. As May drew to a close, he realized that he was running short on water and would have to return to Halifax within a few days for reprovisioning. From his intelligence sources he knew that *Chesapeake* was near ready for sailing and that in his absence she would undoubtedly escape. Broke rightly decided that his best course was to entice *Chesapeake* out as soon as possible for combat.

Lawrence was ready. His orders were to cruise off Nova Scotia and the Gulf of St. Lawrence to intercept incoming supply and troop ships. It was an important mission that, properly carried out, could have a significant effect on the land campaigns along the Canadian border. Because of the tightening blockade, Lawrence was told to destroy his prizes rather than take the risk of sending them in.[23] There is some dispute over how ready *Chesapeake* and her crew were, some suggesting that many of her seamen were that in name only and that her fitting out had not been complete. Lawrence's most sympathetic biographer disagrees and suggests that the tragedy that followed had nothing to do with the readiness of the ship or the men.[24] What there is no dispute about is that Lawrence's mission was to destroy enemy shipping, not seek the honors of war in gladiatorial combat with *Shannon*.

On Sunday morning 30 May *Chesapeake* cast off and stood down Boston harbor on her way to meet *Shannon*. At the same time Broke was tacking to and fro off Boston light. He had sent *Tenedos* away as a gesture to further entice Lawrence. The challenge was unmistakable, but to eliminate any doubt on 1 June Broke sent a written challenge inviting Lawrence to battle. Ironically, Lawrence never saw the note, since it arrived at the navy yard after his departure.[25]

Dressed in full uniform, Lawrence addressed his crew, urging them to heroic endeavors. From his masthead flew a banner calling for "Free Trade and Sailor's Rights." Having finished his charge to the crew, he then went below to his cabin and wrote two final letters, one to the secretary and a personal note to his brother.

On the anniversary of "the Glorious First of June," the day in 1794 on which Admiral Lord Richard Howe beat the French, *Shannon* and *Chesapeake* met off Boston. The ships were fairly evenly matched, but the duel was quick. A miscalculation on Lawrence's part brought his ship up on the weather side of *Shannon* at too great a speed. The American came alongside and both exchanged furious broadsides not more than fifty yards apart; however, because of her greater speed, instead of remaining parallel *Chesapeake* drew ahead until she was off *Shannon*'s weather bow, thereby preventing her full battery from coming to bear. At this point Lawrence attempted to slow her down by coming up into the wind and luffing. While he tried this, the sailing master (the officer responsible for sail handling) was killed and Lawrence wounded. The lapse of command was fatal. *Chesapeake* luffed, lost headway, and was stern to *Shannon,* giving Broke a fine angle for raking fire. The results were devastating. Broke moved his ship closer in and gave the command for boarding. It was over in a few minutes. Lawrence, mortally wounded in his cabin, urged his men, "Don't give up the ship." It was hopeless. *Chesapeake* struck. With Lawrence lying below, the life ebbing out of him, Broke proudly took his prize to Halifax. A few days later Lawrence died and was buried with full naval honors.[26]

The loss of *Chesapeake* was a severe blow to American morale. Since she had been beaten in a fair fight, her surrender put an end to any myths about the superiority of American ships and commanders. Lawrence's death, too, had a heavy personal impact, especially among the young American officers who looked upon him as one of their own. The nation might have been better served if Captain Lawrence had avoided *Shannon* and gone on his business rampaging through northern waters. But that would not have served the cause of honor and glory, the polestar by which these men guided their lives. In death Lawrence achieved the immortality that he might never have earned in life.

Two more American naval heroes fell in 1813.

On 18 June the brig *Argus,* under command of Lieutenant William H. Allen, sailed from New York on her third cruise of the war. She had been with Rodgers on the abortive cruise of July-August 1812 and had then gone to sea on her own from October to December, netting five prizes. Her mission was to deliver William H. Crawford to France to take up his duties as American minister. After depositing Crawford, *Argus* bore north to patrol the waters between England and Ireland. Allen had spectacular success. In thirty-one days he captured nineteen prizes, the best record of any American vessel during the entire war and proof of Rodgers' early scheme for sailing through the British Isles. Allen overstayed his welcome, however. Thirty-one days was ample time for the Royal Navy to react to his presence, and had he been a more prudent captain, he might have given thought to escape. He did not, however, and on 14 August, while setting fire to his latest prize, Allen was caught in the act by a British brig, *Pelican.* At about 6 A.M., off St. David's Head on the coast of Wales, *Pelican* and *Argus* joined combat. The advantages of size and armament were with *Pelican,* and in less than an hour *Argus* was subdued. Among the casualties was Allen, who was mortally wounded and taken below. Like his brother officer Lawrence, Allen was buried by the enemy with full naval honors, at Plymouth, England.[27]

The third officer to enter the American naval pantheon in 1813 was Lieutenant William Burrows, commander of brig (formerly schooner) *Enterprize.* Burrows had been dispatched to Portland, Maine, in order to protect the coast from British privateers operating out of Nova Scotia. It was also a well-known fact that, contrary to the law and patriotism, New Englanders were carrying on a brisk trade with the maritimes. *Enterprize*'s presence was intended to protect legal commerce and restrain the illegal variety.

Also in the neighborhood was the British brig *Boxer,* under command of Captain Samuel Blyth. *Boxer* had been prowling off Sequin Island at the mouth of the Kennebec. It is quite possible she was in the neighborhood to play a role in a little charade, pretending to chase American vessels as they entered the river in an attempt to give credence to the claim that they were on a legal passage, when in fact they were just returning from the Canadian maritimes. At any rate, it was the sound of cannon fire that drew *Enterprize* toward Sequin. Early on the morning of 5 September, she spotted *Boxer* just off Pemaquid Point, only a few miles north of Sequin.

In light airs the two brigs maneuvered for position. At about three in the afternoon they let loose at one another. In some ways the battle was similar to the one between *Chesapeake* and *Shannon,* in that the decision came as a result of gunnery. In this case, however, the roles were reversed, and victory went to the Americans.

Although hard fought, the battle between *Enterprize* and *Boxer* was hardly of earth-shaking importance; nevertheless, it has achieved a bit of fame because of the human drama connected to it. Both captains died, each falling victim to the other. Both men were brought into Portland, where with great ceremony and pageantry they were laid to rest beside one another. If the victory off Pemaquid dulled the edge of sadness still felt over *Chesapeake*'s fate, there was yet another thought to reflect on — only a few weeks before, Captain Samuel Blyth had served as pallbearer for Captain James Lawrence.[28]

For the Americans, 1813 was a year of unpleasant reality. The euphoria of the 1812 frigate victories was faded as the Royal Navy recovered from its initial shock and took the offensive.

Just getting to sea was difficult. *Constellation* at Norfolk had been reduced to a floating fort. The captured *Macedonian,* along with her captor *United States* and the sloop *Hornet,* had sortied from New York in May, only to be chased up Long Island Sound by a British squadron. They were lucky to find refuge at New London, but with the British patrolling outside, that haven had become a prison. The three vessels spent their time swinging at anchor.

The tightening noose of the British blockade was felt all along the coast. In February, Chesapeake and Delaware bays had been declared officially blockaded, effectively closing the ports of Philadelphia and Baltimore. In March, Admiral War-

ren extended the closure up to Sandy Hook, and in November
he extended it to New London. New England, because of its
British sympathies, was for commercial purposes still not blockaded, but by May 1814 that coast too would be "stopped." All in
all, the prospects were dismal. By the end of 1813, only four
major American vessels were at sea: *Essex,* whose days were numbered, *President, Constitution,* and *Congress.* All others were in
port and under blockade.

Privateers also felt the British pressure. While the Royal
Navy was slow to establish a commercial blockade along the
coast, it was quick to sense the danger of letting those rascals get
to sea. One third of all prizes taken by American privateers
were captured in the first ten months of war; after that, the
number diminished quickly as privateers found themselves
confronted with a well-organized convoy system and aggressive
patrolling.

Everywhere along the coast, from Georgia to New Brunswick, the British navy was present and operated at will. American warships were holed up, and American trade was fast di-
minishing.

While the saltwater navy faced an uncertain future — if any
— to the west among the green hills and on the freshwater
lakes, the story was quite different. Here the American navy
would dominate.

## 11
# Perry and Macdonough

In the spring of 1812 John Randolph of Virginia rose in the House and in a mocking tone attacked those who seemed determined to shed blood. He told them that the reason for war was lust: a craving, gnawing, unrelenting desire for land — Florida for the south and Canada for the north. He was right, for Canada was much on the minds of Americans. It was a plum that could be plucked easily. Even Thomas Jefferson agreed to that, remarking that "the acquisition of Canada . . . as far as the neighborhood of Quebec, will be a mere matter of marching."[1] However, any movement north or south, in or out of Canada, would be forced to hurdle watery barriers: the Great Lakes in the west, Lake Champlain and the St. Lawrence River in the east.

Useful as barriers, the lakes were also most important as highways. North-south shipment of goods and people from New York to the St. Lawrence was impossible except via the Hudson River–Lake Champlain corridor. Those going west might follow the Hudson to Albany and then head west along the Mohawk River en route to Oswego on Lake Ontario. A short portage around Niagara Falls would bring them to the eastern edge of Lake Erie and an easy passage to Detroit. For the movement of heavy goods and large numbers of people in the northern regions, the waterways were absolutely indispensable.

In neither the United States nor Great Britain did strategists

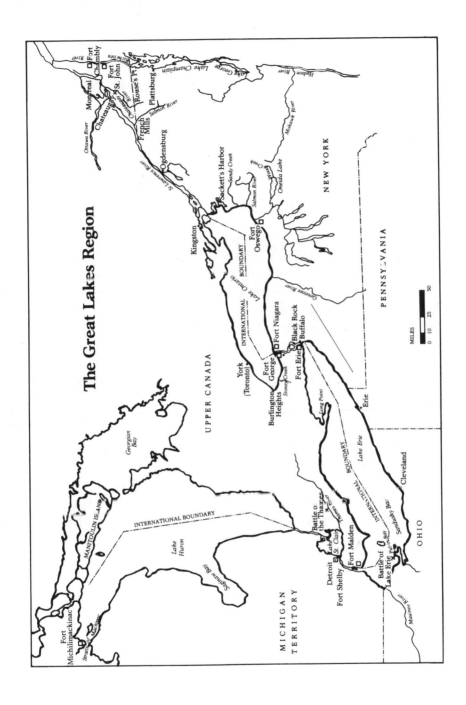

The Great Lakes Region

need to be reminded of geography. The American plan was to invade Canada in a two-pronged movement, one army to cross the border at Niagara and the other at Detroit. Near the end of December 1811, anticipating war, the secretary of war submitted a detailed proposal for the invasion.[2] It called for a holding force organized in six military districts along the entire border, to remain in position while twenty thousand regulars with ten thousand in reserve attacked at Niagara and Detroit. In order to coordinate and control the armies, both operations would be under the same commander. If all went well, once into Canada they would link up and effectively surround Lake Erie. The plan for the land operation was a good one; however, in one particular it was noticeably lacking: little, if any, thought had been given to the need for naval support. At the time, the United States had no naval force on Lake Erie and only one vessel, the sixteen-gun brig *Oneida,* on Lake Ontario, under the command of Melancthon T. Woolsey.[3] The absence of naval support concerned the American commander at Detroit, Brigadier General William Hull, who as early as 1809 had asked for vessels on Lake Erie to protect his lines of communication. The request had gone unheeded.

Failure to provide naval support contributed to the British capture of Fort Michilimackinac in July 1812 and in August to Hull's surrender of Detroit. Hull's ineptness or worse at Detroit threw plans for a Canadian invasion askew and forced the Americans to switch quickly to a defensive mode and to consider the requirements of a long campaign. One such requirement was control of the lakes.[4]

Early in September after the Detroit debacle, Captain Daniel Dobbins arrived in Washington. He bore dispatches from the lakes describing the situation in detail. More important than the documents was the bearer, for Daniel Dobbins was an experienced lake man who had for some years commanded vessels in the lake trade. Almost as soon as he arrived, Dobbins was summoned to a meeting with President Madison, Secretary of War William Eustis, Lewis Cass, a prominent Ohio politician, and several members of the cabinet. It was clear from what they already knew, now buttressed by Dobbins' report, that the situation was critical. With little discussion they decided to exert every effort to seize control of the lakes. At the captain's suggestion, the town of Presque Isle (Erie), Pennsylvania, was designated as the main base on Lake Erie. Some at the meeting thought the harbor might be too shallow, but Dobbins insisted and was sent back to Erie with $2,000, a commission as a sailing master, and orders to build four gunboats.[5]

Overall command was given to Captain Isaac Chauncey, then in charge of the New York Navy Yard. From his New York City command post, Chauncey immediately began to forward men and supplies to Lake Ontario via Albany and the Mohawk River. He also sent ahead Lieutenant Jesse Elliott, whose task was to establish a base on Lake Erie. Elliott arrived at Buffalo and immediately reported to the headquarters of General Stephen Van Rensselaer, the local army commander, who, much to the lieutenant's chagrin, told Elliott he had never heard of him or his mission. He referred the young officer to General Peter Porter, who, as it turned out, was of considerable aid since he was "perfectly acquainted with every part of the lake." Elliott's conversations with Porter convinced him that Black Rock, near the mouth of the Niagara River, was the only place on all of Lake Erie suitable for an American base. That, of course, ran counter to the opinion of Dobbins, who was busily building his gunboats at Erie. Nevertheless, Elliott persisted and convinced Chauncey of his correctness, with the unfortunate result that American forces on the lake were divided between the two locations, with more than two hundred miles of potentially hostile water between them.

Despite the scarcity of supplies, Elliott went to work building two three-hundred-ton vessels and converting several merchantmen. The work went slowly. He was hampered particularly by the abysmal condition of the roads, which made it impossible to bring in heavy ordnance that had been ordered up from New York. Until cold weather froze the ground, there was no hope of bringing supplies into Black Rock. Under the circumstances, both Elliott and Chauncey agreed that since moving material to Lake Ontario presented fewer handicaps, at least for the time being, they ought to concentrate resources there. Guns previously destined for Erie were now diverted to Ontario. Realizing that the decision to concentrate on Ontario might not be well received in Washington, Chauncey wrote to assure the secretary that his decision was only a temporary expedient, and that as soon as possible Lake Erie would get equal attention.[6]

On 6 October Chauncey arrived in Sackett's Harbor on Lake Ontario. Like Elliott, he first surveyed the situation carefully to decide where he would establish his base. From the south side Sackett's Harbor was a virtual island. Located many miles to the north, almost at the entrance to the St. Lawrence River, it had no good land access and was approachable only via the lake. Roads leading to the south, the direction from which supplies would have to come, were rough trails passable only when frozen in winter or when hardened by drought in midsummer. Chauncey appreciated the problem of accessibility, but from another point of view Sackett's Harbor had an indisputable virtue — it was easily defensible. With a few earthen bulwarks and cannon, any enemy attacking would have to pay dearly. The only other potential location was Oswego, a convenient spot fronting the lake, with its back to the river connecting it to Lake Oneida and thence to the Mohawk River. In times of high water, supplies could be brought into Oswego from the rear by water. Such advantage, however, was countered by the town's extreme exposure along the lakefront, making it most difficult to put up a credible defense. Chauncey decided wisely to concentrate at Sackett's, even though it meant moving men and supplies the forty miles along the lakefront from Oswego. Under the circumstances it was the best plan possible.

Having decided where to concentrate, Chauncey wasted no time. *Oneida,* Woolsey's command, was already present and in good shape. In addition the commodore purchased five schooners and set to building two more ships. It was a promising beginning. Between Elliott and Chauncey, the Americans already had a respectable force on the lakes, and if the building program went ahead as planned, there was every hope that by spring they would attain naval superiority.[7]

British reaction to the American push on the lakes was slow

and feeble. At Black Rock they did manage to make a show of force. The post itself was in range of enemy land batteries entrenched across the river at Fort Erie, which prevented American vessels from getting to the lake. That uncomfortable situation was made intolerable on 8 October, when two British brigs arrived from Fort Malden, near Detroit. The two visitors were *Detroit,* formerly *Adams,* taken by the British at the fall of Detroit, and *Caledonia,* a vessel of the Canadian Provincial Marine. Elliott decided that their presence was too serious a threat to ignore and too great an opportunity to miss. Early on the morning of the 9th, he pushed off from Black Rock in two large open boats with one hundred men. Pulling with difficulty against the current, finally, to the complete surprise of the enemy crews, they came alongside the two brigs and boarded. Within a few minutes the vessels were subdued and on their way to the American base. *Caledonia* made it back safely, but *Detroit* did not; caught by the current and under heavy fire from her former owners, she had to be burned.[8]

The loss of *Detroit* and *Caledonia* put the British at a distinct disadvantage on Lake Erie, and for the time being they had to be satisfied simply to hold their positions and build vessels for the spring campaign. The Americans too were content, and Elliott's triumph ushered in a winter of relative calm on the lake.

On Lake Ontario the sparring was more frequent. Chauncey assumed that control of Ontario was more important than the struggle over Erie; therefore, he took personal command and directed resources to Oswego and Sackett's Harbor.[9]

British headquarters for Ontario were at Kingston, only a short sail of thirty miles from Sackett's. Such proximity caused Chauncey to fret that the enemy might take advantage of his exposed lines to Oswego. In the evening of 2 November the commodore received an intelligence report that a strange vessel was prowling the coast. He immediately suspected her to be British and set out with *Oneida* to intercept. By morning he was within a few miles of Kingston. In the distance he could see at anchor an enemy ship of twenty-one guns, *Royal George,* and two schooners. Since they were to windward, Chauncey decided to head back to Sackett's. The view of Kingston tempted him, though, and a few days later, when he received more information confirming that his fleet was superior to the British, he made up his mind to attack. On 8 November, accompanied by six schooners, *Oneida* left Sackett's. Chauncey intended to sweep the enemy from the lake and then descend on Kingston. On the 9th he found *Royal George* under sail and making for Kingston. He pursued her into the harbor and for nearly two hours put her and several other vessels under heavy fire. He could not, however, move in close, because of a heavy cannonading from the shore batteries. He withdrew, planning to return the next day. Unfortunately, heavy weather set in and his pilots warned against navigating in a confined area where he might be driven ashore; accordingly, Chauncey took to the open lake and headed for Sackett's. Although he had not accomplished all he wanted, as a result of his sortie he now knew that he had command of Lake Ontario and so informed the secretary.[10]

In the days following, as the weather held fair, the men in the Sackett's yard were busy constructing the fleet. Under the careful eye of master builder Henry Eckford, they worked to finish a large ship, *Madison*, twenty-four guns, whose launch on 26 November gave Chauncey indisputable command of Lake Ontario. Even as she slid into the lake, ice was already forming. Within a few days Chauncey informed the secretary that the season was over and his ships would be laid up shortly. He went on to paint an optimistic picture for the spring campaign. He intended, he told the secretary, to move in the spring, as soon as the ice broke up, with a large contingent of troops and take Kingston. The plan was a good one and pleased Jones, who even before he had received the commodore's report was instructing him to build another vessel on the scale of *Madison*. In no uncertain terms he told Chauncey, "you are to consider the absolute superiority on all the Lakes the only limit to your authority."[11]

On the other side of the lake, reports were not so sanguine. Chauncey's success had pushed the British force into making a classic strategic blunder. In the face of a superior enemy, they divided their force; one part was sent to York and the other to Kingston. Compounding the problem was the dismal performance of the Provincial Marine, a lake-going version of the Canadian militia. Morale was virtually nonexistent, causing Captain Alexander Gray, the assistant quartermaster general, to report that "the officers of the marine seem to be destitute of all energy and spirit and are sunk into contempt in the eyes of all who know them."[12] Through the winter, Gray worked diligently to add to the British force on the lake. At both Kingston and York, keels were laid for two large vessels whose completion would bring the British force to a level equal to that of the Americans. Finding men to command and man the ships was difficult. It was pointless to build good ships if they were to be manned by inferior men. Admiral Warren was sympathetic and responsive. Four vessels in his command, two at Halifax and another two at St. John's, were laid up and their crews dispatched to the lakes. Warren also ordered some "active, zealous, young officers" to the lakes, namely, captains Barclay, Finnis, and Pring, along with six lieutenants. Overall command went to Sir James Lucas Yeo. In a subsequent division of authority, Barclay took command of the forces on Lake Erie.[13]

British reaction to the American challenge, while energetic, was not timely. They had waited too long to commit their resources. Logistics for them were even more difficult than for the Americans; movement of men and supplies through the Canadian wilderness in midwinter was a nightmare under the best of circumstances, and in the worst simply impossible. It took weeks to cover the distance between Kingston and Montreal. The trip to York was even worse. The Americans had started sooner, were better organized, and in the beginning at least were under more able command. Thus, as the ice began to break on the lake in April, despite their best efforts the British were still undermanned and ill equipped.

On 25 April 1813 the Americans made the first move. Sailing from Sackett's were *Madison*, the flagship, joined by *Oneida*, sixteen guns, in command of Lieutenant Jesse Elliott; schooner *Hamilton*, ten guns, Melancthon Woolsey; a schooner *Scourge*, nine guns, Mr. Osgood; and a ragtag fleet of nine smaller vessels. On board were 1,800 troops under the charge of General Henry Dearborn, with his second in command, Brigadier General Zebulon Pike. Contrary to the previous plan, their target was not Kingston. They had learned recently that the governor general of Canada, Sir George Prevost, was at Kingston with a large reinforcement. As it turned out, the information was greatly exaggerated: Prevost was at Kingston but with not nearly as many troops as the Americans believed. Nevertheless, the focus now turned to York (the present-day Toronto), where targets were tempting and lightly defended.

On 27 April Chauncey and company arrived at York. It was an easy victory, but with one tragic result. General Pike was killed in a magazine explosion, depriving the American forces of a talented and brave officer. In the euphoria of victory Dearborn found it difficult to control his men, and they turned to arson and plunder, a favor the British would be pleased to return at Washington in 1814.

Chauncey took considerable satisfaction from his role in the attack. His crews had performed well and had accomplished much, including the burning of a large ship on the stocks laid down by Gray and the capture of the *Gloucester*. What neither he nor Dearborn could know was that their victory had considerably more impact than the mere capture and destruction of an enemy post and vessels. The most valuable accomplishment of the descent on York was the burning of a large quantity of naval supplies intended for the building of a fleet on Lake Erie. It was a serious setback for the British.

Once the lake warriors finished their work at York, they moved southeasterly to Fort Niagara, on the American side of the Niagara River. Here Chauncey landed the troops and then took his squadron back to Sackett's, arriving home on 11 May. From Sackett's he sent four schooners down to Oswego to bring up some much-needed stores recently arrived from New York. Having resupplied and taken on board troop reinforcements, Chauncey took his fleet once again to the Niagara River. Under a withering fire delivered from the American vessels, General Dearborn was able to land his augmented force on the British side of the river. Faced with a vastly superior enemy, the British retreated all along the Niagara.

Since both banks of the river were now in American possession, Chauncey had an opportunity to free the vessels trapped
at Black Rock. He ordered Oliver Hazard Perry to proceed
immediately and move them down the shore to Erie, where
they could join up with the remainder of the Lake Erie squadron. Even without the enemy, just getting out of Black Rock
proved to be an arduous chore. With the help of oxen and
soldiers sent by Dearborn, Perry had to drag his vessels against
a four-knot current setting toward the falls. Not until 12 June
were they free on the lake. Six days later Perry and his squadron made Erie and there joined Dobbins, who was busy readying vessels for service.

With the British in retreat, Dearborn had an opportunity to
pursue and wreak more havoc; however, any movement along
the shore would have had to be aided and covered by Chauncey. That proved not possible, for on 30 May the commodore
received distressing news that caused him to plan an immediate
pullback to Sackett's.

Chauncey's decision to attack York and leave Kingston un-
molested might well have been an error. Although Kingston
was better defended, with his superior weight on both land and
lake Chauncey could have taken the town. That he chose not to
attack left the British with their principal base secure and in a
position to threaten Sackett's. Chauncey's sail to the other end
of the lake left his rear unguarded; it was too good an opportunity for the enemy to miss.

At Kingston the British made good use of their time. On the
20th of April they launched a new ship, *Sir George Prevost,* a
name that the governor general, with uncharacteristic humility,
promptly insisted be changed to *Wolfe.* On the same day *Wolfe*
got her bottom wet, Captain Barclay arrived. At the same time
the indefatigable Gray was already gathering timber to build a
vessel as a replacement for the one burned at York. In a buoyant mood, Gray reported that he had "every reason to believe
we shall be able to cope with the enemy."[14]

Preparations went along very nicely at Kingston. On 16 May
Sir James Yeo and his retinue of officers arrived. His commission from the Admiralty placed him in command of operations
on all lakes. Since he planned to take personal command on

Ontario, Barclay was displaced to Lake Erie and Pring to Champlain.

When Yeo learned that Chauncey had sailed from Sackett's with his entire fleet, he proposed an attack. With a hastily put together force, he sailed to Sackett's and landed. The American garrison offered a fierce resistance. They were eventually forced to retire, but not before they had put their ships and buildings to the torch. Altogether, the Americans lost about a half million dollars in supplies; nevertheless, they did save a good deal and at the same time forced the British to pay a high price for a small victory. More than a third of their men were casualties, including several officers, among them Captain Gray, who was wounded mortally.

For the moment the British had managed to turn the tables, and they now enjoyed a slight superiority on Lake Ontario. On 2 June Chauncey wrote to the secretary to tell him of his concern.

> I beg to call your attention to the situation of the naval forces on the lakes. I have under my command on this lake 14 vessels of every description, mounting 62 guns, well manned and well appointed. The enemy have seven vessels and six gunboats mounting 106 guns, well officered and manned. If he leaves Kingston I shall meet him. The result may be doubtful but worth the trial.[15]

A few days after announcing "I shall meet him," Chauncey had the chance and turned it down. Yeo sailed out of Kingston and paused for a while off Sackett's, hoping to draw the Americans out; failing at that, he sailed toward the Niagara. Chauncey's initial timidity is inexplicable, but within a few days he had ample reason to take a cautious course. On 6 June the American army on the Niagara peninsula suffered a severe setback at the battle of Stoney Creek. That began a vast unraveling of their whole position on the peninsula. On 9 June they abandoned and burned Fort Erie and withdrew from all their posts along the Niagara. The only one they continued to hold was Fort Niagara, but that was small comfort, since they had neither the force nor the will to move beyond the palisades.[16]

Given the precarious land position, Chauncey was not about

to risk his fleet, and career, against Yeo. Instead, he decided to wait while *General Pike,* a large ship on the stocks at Sackett's, was finished. Then, or so he thought, he could attack; unhappily, that never came to pass. Both Chauncey and Yeo were cautious men who saw more to be gained by keeping their fleets intact than by risking all in an Armageddon on the lake. With such men in command, there would be no decisive action on Lake Ontario, only occasional engagements broken off quickly as the commanders returned to port.[17]

Isaac Chauncey was the kind of commander who attacked only when there was a moral certainty of victory. Against an active and clever enemy, he could never have that assurance.

For his part, Yeo was more venturesome than Chauncey; however, his commander, Governor General Prevost, was the most timid man on the lake. He saw nothing but problems, provided limited and at times grudging support to Yeo, all the while urging him to act. Under these circumstances, it is not surprising that both officers saw more to be gained in preserving than in risking their fleet.

Although both sides had initially viewed Lake Ontario as the arena for decisive combat, the relative balance of naval power in that region combined with the reluctance of the two commanders meant stalemate. Such was not the case on Lake Erie, where an aggressive and able American commander faced a British force with no choice but to fight or die.

Lieutenant Oliver Hazard Perry had an impressive naval pedigree. Born in Rhode Island, he was the eldest son of Christopher Perry, commander of the frigate *General Greene* in the Quasi War. Young Perry took his commission as a midshipman and served under his father until the elder Perry retired in 1801. After serving in the Mediterranean, he was promoted to lieutenant in 1807 and posted to Newport, Rhode Island, as commander of the gunboats stationed there. The duty was hardly exciting, but it did have the advantage of allowing him to be at home with his family. It also provided him with considerable experience in the problems of building and operating a flotilla of small boats.[18]

The outbreak of war raised Perry's hopes for a greater command, and Hamilton promised him command of the brig *Argus*. Unfortunately for Perry, Hamilton left office in December 1812. In the meantime, *Argus* had been stationed at New York as part of Decatur's squadron. Decatur appointed Lieutenant William Allen to command her and the new secretary, William Jones, unaware of his predecessor's promise, confirmed the appointment. Perry explained his position; Jones, trapped and embarrassed, found a quick escape when he learned that Chauncey wanted Perry for the lakes. He happily issued orders dispatching Perry to Chauncey's command.[19]

With a large contingent of Rhode Islanders, Perry arrived at Erie on 27 March, where he found two remarkable gentlemen at work: Daniel Dobbins, the lake sailor and builder; and Noah Brown. Brown was an experienced New York shipbuilder who had recently completed five gunboats for the navy. He had arrived only a short time before Perry. Despite shortages of nearly everything, except snow and cold, he and his small gang of men had laid into their work.

Perry's arrival helped speed progress, but things really began to spurt forward in April, when Brown's brother Adam arrived with more men, followed a few weeks later by a large contingent of skilled workmen from Philadelphia. Altogether, at Erie the Browns had under construction six vessels: two brigs, *Lawrence* and *Niagara*, plus four schooners, *Porcupine, Scorpion, Tigress,* and *Ariel.* They also were responsible for the construction of a blockhouse to guard the yard and several other buildings including a cook house, barracks, and office, along with all the gun carriages and fourteen small boats.[20]

Construction proceeded briskly. By the time Perry returned from Black Rock with additional vessels, his fleet was nearly ready for service. The one thing lacking was men. Perry complained bitterly that he must have experienced seamen. On one occasion when Chauncey did send men to him, Perry responded by telling his commander, "The men that came are a motley set, blacks, soldiers, and boys. I cannot think you saw them after they were selected." Chauncey rightly shot back, "I regret you are not pleased with them; for to my knowledge, a part of them are not surpassed by any seaman we have in the fleet; and I have yet to learn that the color of the skin, or the cut and trimmings of the coat, can affect a man's qualifications or usefulness.[21]

Suitably chastised, Perry turned to the next issue — how to get out onto the lake. One of the reasons Dobbins had favored the selection of Erie was that it fronted on a large bay with only one entrance to the lake. It was a narrow passage that was constricted even further by the presence of a sandbar that allowed not more than six feet of water. The only way to get across was to strip the vessels of all their equipment, including guns, and ease them out. But in the case of the two brigs, even that was not enough. Noah Brown provided the solution — camels. These were large buoyant floats filled with water, which could be lashed to the hull of the vessels and then pumped dry, thereby lifting the hull higher in the water. That remedy left still another problem — the enemy. The American fleet would be coming out unarmed, and interception at this point would be a turkey shoot.

Fate was kind to Perry. The British had been cruising in a menacing fashion off Erie since 20 July, but on Friday the 30th they disappeared. According to one account, they took their leave so that Captain Barclay might attend a dinner in his honor at Port Dover, where in the course of the evening he replied to a toast that he expected to return to Erie "to find the Yankee brigs hard and fast aground on the bar at Erie . . . in which predicament it would be but a small job to destroy them."[22]

When he learned that the British were absent, Perry ordered immediate preparations for getting the fleet over the bar. Even with camels, it was no easy task; a number of bottoms got knocked badly going over. Perry's men spent all day Monday and Tuesday tugging, hauling, pumping, and praying. They took the shallow-draft vessels over first so that they could put them out on line in case the enemy returned. *Niagara* and *Lawrence* were the most difficult, and by the time they reached deep water their bottoms had been bumped more than once. As feared, Barclay did come back before the Americans were ready. He arrived when *Niagara* was still without her guns.

Perry, however, had positioned her cleverly so that she looked as if she were ready for battle. Barclay was taken in; not wanting to risk battle with an apparently superior force, he withdrew.

On Wednesday evening 4 August, Perry wrote to the secretary:

> I have great pleasure in informing you that I have succeeded after almost incredible labor and fatigue to the men, in getting all the vessels I have been able to man over the bar, *Viz.*, *Lawrence, Niagara, Caledonia, Ariel, Scorpion, Somers, Tigress,* and *Porcupine.*[23]

For the next few days Perry continued to fit out his fleet and drill his crews. On the 10th a welcome reinforcement of 102 men arrived from Chauncey. The commander of the contingent was Jesse Elliott, who now became second in command of the squadron and captain of *Niagara.* Manned and ready, Perry's fleet headed for the open lake on 12 August.

For the British the problem of logistics, difficult enough on Lake Ontario, became even worse on Lake Erie. They had decided to make their main base at Amherstburg on the Detroit River. It was a post at the end of a very long and thin supply line. Compared to the Americans, the British were in a far worse situation with much less to overcome it.

The man fated, or cursed, to command this distant and forgotten part of the empire was Captain Robert Heriot Barclay. A veteran of Nelson's victory at Trafalgar, where he had lost an arm, Barclay was an able and well-regarded officer. He was among those officers sent by Admiral Warren to the lakes early in 1813. He had arrived at Kingston and been assigned to command *Wolfe.* He was superseded in that command a scant three weeks later, when James Yeo arrived to take his place. As senior commander Yeo approached Captain William Mulcaster to take control of the fleet on Lake Erie. Mulcaster knew only too well the difficulties of the post, and seeing no glory in being sent there, he declined. Barclay was then "offered" the post — an offer he could not refuse.[24]

Upon arriving at his new post, Barclay wrote immediately to Yeo requesting more men and supplies. Thereupon began a

Charles Stewart. Artist unknown

"Battle of Lake Borgne," by Thomas Hornbrook

David Porter by Orlando Lagman

Frigate *Essex*. Artist unknown

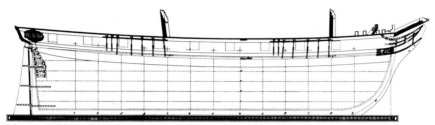

Lines of the United States Brig *Argus*

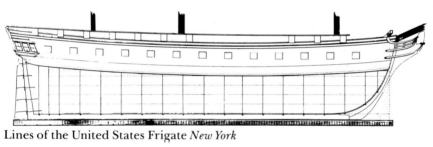

Lines of the United States Frigate *New York*

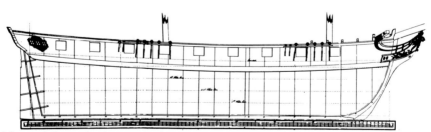

Lines of the United States Brig *Siren*

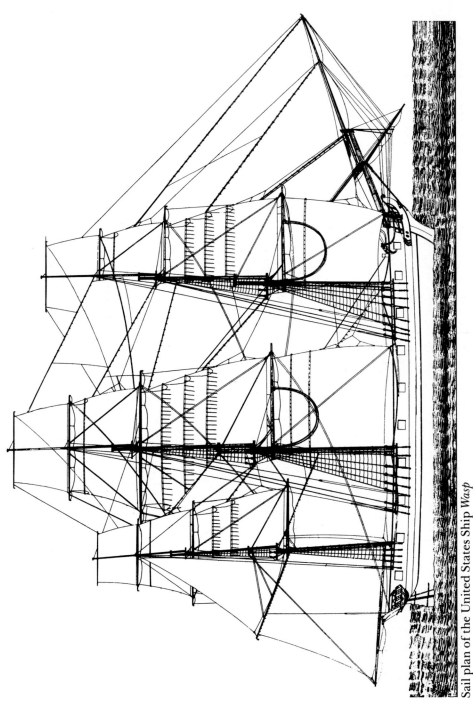

Sail plan of the United States Ship *Wasp*

*Wasp* and *Frolic*. Drawing and engraving by F. Kearny from a sketch by Lieutenant Claxton of the *Wasp*

"Macdonough's Victory." Lithograph by Nathaniel Currier.

Isaac Chauncey by Gilbert Stuart

*Constellation* and *L'Insurgente* by William Bainbridge Hoff

*United States* and *Macedonian* by Alonzo Chappel

precipitous deterioration in relations between the two. They had an uneasy bond that made the cool cooperation between Perry and Chauncey seem like a match made in heaven. Barclay's pleas for reinforcements brought him one officer, Captain Robert Finnis, and the captain's servant. Some solace might be taken from the fact that Barlcay did at least have a good association with the local British army commander, General Henry A. Proctor. Nevertheless, whatever comfort Barclay might take from that, it could in no measure mitigate the unending pain of dealing with Prevost.

Initially, Barclay had the superior force, but that edge gradually vanished. His failure to stop Perry from slipping through with the Black Rock squadron was a classic blunder, which, coupled with his break in the blockade allowing Perry to cross the bar, thrust him into the inferior position. He then had no choice but to withdraw and avoid combat, while at Amherstburg his men struggled to finish a large new brig, *Detroit,* that he hoped would give him a fighting chance.

Time was Barclay's worst enemy. With provisions running short, both he and Proctor knew full well that they could not last the winter. The army at least had the option of retreating. If Barclay opted to join Proctor, he would have to destroy his vessels or see the Americans take them — an unacceptable course. He had no choice. Short on provisions, with vessels manned in great measure by inexperienced landsmen, boys, and soldiers, Barclay sailed with a heavy heart on the afternoon of 9 September to seek the enemy. He was not disappointed.

Shortly after dawn the next day, the two fleets came in sight of one another at a place called Put-in-Bay in the southwest corner of the lake. The British were to the west of the Americans, and there was a slight southwest wind. With a fair breeze Barclay bore up toward Perry, but then the wind shifted, giving the Americans the windward advantage. As the fleets closed, Barclay was in a difficult spot. In every category save the number of long guns, which proved unimportant, Perry had the advantage; small wonder that Barclay fought only as a last resort.

### Perry's Squadron[25]

| | Tons | Crew | Weight of Metal | Armament |
|---|---|---|---|---|
| *Lawrence* (brig) | 480 | 136 | 600 | 2 long 12s<br>18 carronades 32s |
| *Niagara* (brig) | 480 | 155 | 600 | 18 carronades 32s<br>2 long 12s |
| *Caledonia* (brig) | 180 | 53 | 80 pivot | 2 long 24s<br>1 carronade 32 |
| *Ariel* (schooner) | 112 | 36 | 48 pivot | 4 long 12s |
| *Scorpion* (schooner) | 86 | 35 | 64 pivot | 1 long 32<br>1 carronade 32 |
| *Somers* (schooner) | 94 | 30 | 56 pivot | 1 long 24<br>1 carronade 32 |
| *Porcupine* (schooner) | 83 | 25 | 32 pivot | 1 long 32 |
| *Tigress* (schooner) | 96 | 27 | 32 pivot | 1 long 32 |
| *Trippe* (sloop) | 60 | 35 | 24 pivot | 1 long 24 |
| TOTAL | 1,671 | 532 | 1,536 | |

With the winds still light and baffling, Barclay was hove to facing in a southwest direction. His squadron was in a close column formation, with *Chippeway* in the van, followed by *Detroit*, on which Barclay flew his flag, *Hunter*, *Queen Charlotte*, *Lady Prevost*, and *Little Belt*. Perry's squadron came down on Barclay in an oblique column, with the wind on the port side. The American order was *Ariel*, *Scorpion*, *Lawrence*, *Caledonia*, *Niagara*, *Somers*, *Porcupine*, *Tigress*, and *Trippe*. Perry flew his flag from *Lawrence*, which also bore a banner proclaiming the heroic words of her namesake: "Don't Give Up the Ship." Perry's second in command, Jesse D. Elliott, was on board *Niagara*.

At a quarter before noon *Detroit* opened the action with her long guns. The shot was directed at *Lawrence*, but soon the others opened up and the action became general. Perry found himself in a difficult situation. *Detroit* had his range, but because of his large number of short-range carronades, he could do little to her. Rather than wait and suffer, he pressed ahead to close the distance. As he did, he became separated from his supporting vessels. *Detroit*, *Queen Charlotte*, and to a lesser de-

## Barclay's Squadron

| | Tons | Crew | Weight of Metal | Armament |
|---|---|---|---|---|
| *Detroit* (ship) | 490 | 150 | 252 | 1 long 18 |
| | | | | 2 long 24s |
| | | | | 6 long 12s |
| | | | | 8 long 9s |
| | | | | 1 carronade 24 |
| | | | | 1 carronade 18 |
| *Queen Charlotte* (ship) | 400 | 126 | 366 | 1 long 12 |
| | | | | 2 long 9s |
| | | | | 14 carronades 24s |
| *Lady Prevost* (schooner) | 230 | 86 | 141 | 1 long 9 |
| | | | | 2 long 6s |
| | | | | 10 carronades 12s |
| *Hunter* (brig) | 180 | 45 | 60 | 4 long 6s |
| | | | | 2 long 4s |
| | | | | 2 long 2s |
| | | | | 2 carronades 12s |
| *Chippeway* (schooner) | 70 | 15 | 9 | 1 long 9 |
| *Little Belt* (sloop) | 90 | 18 | 24 | 1 long 12 |
| | | | | 2 long 6s |
| TOTAL | 1,460 | 440 | 852 | |

gree *Hunter* were able to concentrate their fire on *Lawrence*. *Caledonia,* a sluggish and ill-sailing tub, could not move fast enough to provide cover; even if she had had her light armament, she would not have been of much help. The only hope was *Niagara.* Elliott chose to hold his place in line and not come forward to help his commander. For more than two hours the battle continued, in the words of Captain Barclay, "with great fury."[26] Finally, with *Lawrence* a perfect and unmanageable wreck, Perry left her and carried his flag to *Niagara.* Not long after her abandonment *Lawrence* surrendered. By that time Barclay had too many other worries to take any pleasure from this small triumph. He himself had been wounded severely; indeed by the battle's end, every British commander and second in command was either wounded or dead. *Lawrence's* wretched condition was mirrored in *Detroit* and *Queen Charlotte.*

From the deck of *Niagara,* which, thanks to Elliott's ineffectiveness, was still very much intact, Perry continued to command.[27] Elliott was dispatched in a small boat to bring the other vessels up. In stronger hands *Niagara* bent to the attack and poured a fierce fire into *Detroit* and *Queen Charlotte,* making them unmanageable and causing them to run afoul of one another. By three in the afternoon, Barclay realized the situation was hopeless. To continue resistance in the face of such overwhelming firepower was reckless suicide. He hauled his flag down, and shortly thereafter the whole British squadron followed suit. The American casualties were 123, two thirds of them on board *Lawrence.* The British counted 145 dead and wounded.

Less than one hour after accepting Barclay's surrender, Perry sent his famous message to General William Henry Harrison: "Dear General — We have met the enemy and they are ours. Two ships, two brigs, one schooner and one sloop."*

With Erie now an American lake, the British had no choice but to withdraw from their positions along the shore. On 23 September they burned what stores they could not carry and marched out of Amherstburg. On the 27th the scene was repeated at Detroit. Proctor then took his army back across the Detroit River on an eastward march. He was pursued by Harrison, until finally the two armies met at the Battle of the Thames, where the Americans were not only victorious but the great Indian chief Tecumseh, a British ally, was killed. His death demoralized the Indians and swayed them from their British friends. Perry on the lake and Harrison on the land had together delivered a crushing blow to British hopes in the west.[28]

As far as Prevost and Yeo were concerned, the reverse on Lake Erie confirmed them in their opinion that the decisive point was not in the west but in their own theater on Lake Ontario. Chauncey would have agreed.

Since the British attack on Sackett's in May, Chauncey had

---

*According to most accounts, *Hunter* was the only brig in Barclay's command.

been unwilling to leave port and engage Yeo. That could wait until the completion of his newest ship, *General Pike,* which was launched on 12 June and joined Chauncey's squadron on 21 July. With her considerable power now available, the commodore set out on the lake. What followed was a sort of aquatic ballet. For nearly three months Chauncey and Yeo toyed with one another. Three times they actually exchanged fire, but in no instance did either side seem to have enough fortitude to close, board, and destroy.

Early in August, as the two commanders maneuvered off the Niagara peninsula, Chauncey was struck a double blow, one by nature and the other by the enemy.

The first tragedy occurred in the early morning hours of 8 August, when the two schooners *Hamilton* and *Scourge* were hit by a sudden squall. Both vessels were heavily armed, too heavily as it turned out, for the weight of the cannon made them unstable. Blown over on their beam ends, the schooners were unable to right themselves. In minutes they were swamped and went to the bottom, three hundred feet down, carrying more than one hundred men to a watery grave.[29]

Only two days later Chauncey suffered a second bit of bad luck. With the wind in his favor Yeo decided to attack. Chauncey withdrew, but in the process he lost two more schooners, *Julia* and *Growler.*[30]

The loss of four schooners in two days shifted the balance of power on the lake to Yeo. Six weeks later, however, on 28 September, during a running battle near Burlington Bay, the Americans managed to inflict heavy damage on Yeo's flagship, *Wolfe.* With that the balance was restored.

For this inability or unwillingness to provide history with a grand battle on Lake Ontario, both Yeo and Chauncey have suffered heavy criticism. It has been particularly so in the case of Chauncey, probably because he has had to live in the shadow of his two junior contemporaries, Oliver Hazard Perry and Thomas Macdonough.

Since neither side was able to come to any real advantage during the campaign of 1813, both Yeo and Chauncey retired to winter quarters to wage a war of shipwrights. The reluctance of both commanders to engage in serious combat was summed up finely by Chauncey in one of his letters to Perry:

> The first objective will be to destroy or cripple the enemy's fleet; but in all attempts upon the fleet you ought to use great caution, for the loss of a single vessel may decide the fate of the campaign.[31]

In his analysis of the war, Alfred Thayer Mahan credits the somnolence on Lake Ontario to three factors:

1. The relative equality of the two fleets. In battle it was unlikely that either would emerge victorious, only bloody.
2. Unlike the situation on Lakes Erie and Champlain there were no compelling circumstances that arose to force, or make inescapable, combat.
3. The two commodores, Yeo and Chauncey, were by personal inclination not anxious to fight.[32]

Eighteen fourteen saw little change on Ontario. Both sides continued to spar and build. Chauncey did come under heavy strictures from General Jacob Brown, who asserted that the commodore failed to support him during his Niagara campaign in the summer of 1814. In addition to all his other problems, Chauncey was seriously ill at the time and unable to assist Brown, but even had he been well, it would have been highly unlikely that he would use his ships as transports for the army. For his part, Yeo showed not much more desire. The ever cautious Prevost gave him little cause to think he ought to risk. He did, however, outbuild Chauncey. At Kingston he launched *St. Lawrence,* 102 guns. The thought of that behemoth loose on the lake sent Chauncey back to Sackett's, where he continued to build until the war was over.

Unlike Ontario and Erie, where very little of crucial naval importance had taken place before the War of 1812, Lake Champlain had a colorful and violent past. It was a critical link in the Hudson River–Lake Champlain corridor between Canada and the United States. From the days of the Iroquois wars down through the Revolution, it had been a favorite route for invasion from both north and south.

In the minds of British strategists, 1814 was the year of decision. Having bested Napoleon in Europe, the ministry was anxious to finish off the American war, and by early 1814 plans were already being made to send veteran troops off to America for the final push. The overall strategy would eventually emerge as a three-pronged attack: from the north via Champlain; at the midsection via the Chesapeake; and from the south through New Orleans. In the case of the Chesapeake and New Orleans, aside from some American gunboat harassment, the British had complete command of the waters.[33] At Champlain, however, they would have to fight for it.

The battle for the lake had begun very early in the war. On 12 September 1812 Lieutenant Thomas Macdonough was ordered to proceed to Champlain and take command. The selection of Macdonough was a good one. He had served in the Mediterranean as one of Preble's Boys and had helped Decatur put *Philadelphia* to the torch. Following his tour in the Mediterranean, Macdonough took leave from the navy and commanded a merchantman. The outbreak of war brought him back into service. He was first posted to the frigate *Constellation,* then fitting out at the Washington Navy Yard. Her ill condition promised a long wait before she could get to sea, so Macdonough asked to be sent to Portland, Maine, to take charge of a gunboat flotilla, a command similar to the one Perry held in Newport before his assignment to Erie. That had lasted only a short time when the lieutenant was told to report to Champlain and take command of the naval forces on the lake. He left Portland and "proceeded . . . across the country through the Notch of the White Mountains, partly on horseback, carrying my bundle with a valise on behind, and a country lad in company to return with the horses. Arrived fatigued at Burlington on the lake, in about four days, and took command of the vessels . . ."[34]

Macdonough's vessels were an odd and unkempt lot. There were two gunboats whose condition was best described by the governor of New York, Daniel P. Tompkins, who noted that "the seams of both of them so open as almost to admit the hand."[35] Six small trading sloops were also at the dock. They had been chartered by the army to carry troops and supplies. Macdonough's task was to make fit what he had and build more. Although poorly prepared, the new commodore could take encouragement in that, as rickety as his fleet appeared, it was superior to what the British had on the lake.

Only a few weeks after his arrival at Burlington, Macdonough left Vermont to attend to personal business. He traveled to Middletown, Connecticut, to marry his love, Ann Shaler. Their marriage on 12 December 1812 was followed by a honeymoon sleigh trip to Burlington.[36]

By spring 1813 Macdonough had at his service three armed sloops, *Growler, Eagle,* and *President,* with which he took to the lake as soon as the ice was out. For the time at least the British, who were in position at the northern end of the lake, were content to leave the Americans unchallenged. Finally, on the first of June 1813, the enemy decided to break the calm. A squadron of gunboats came prowling down the lake toward Plattsburg on the New York side. Macdonough immediately sent orders for *Growler* and *Eagle* to sail to the attack. Lieutenant Sidney Smith, commander of *Growler* and the senior officer present, advanced with more bravery than judgment and landed in a good deal of trouble. As the British gunboats withdrew, Smith pursued them up the river Chambly and across the border into Canada. In his exuberance he failed to take into account that he was now in British territory, which was brought home to him when his sloops began to take fire from the shoreline. He had gone up the river as far as Isle aux Nois before deciding to come about. Getting out of the river proved to be far more difficult than getting in. Although he had a fair breeze, his sloops could not move against a strong northerly current. In the battle *Eagle* was sunk and *Growler* surrendered. The former was raised easily and repaired for service with the British. Since they were captured at about the same time as the epic battle between *Chesapeake* and *Shannon,* their new owners named them *Broke* and *Shannon.* According to the Admiralty, however, such pretension was reserved for larger vessels, and their names were changed to the more prosaic *Chub* and *Finch.* Whatever the names, as a result of this capture the British now enjoyed naval supremacy on Lake Champlain.

While Macdonough withdrew to Burlington to lick his

wounds, the enemy decided to take advantage of their gains. On 4 July Prevost sent an urgent request to the senior naval officer at Quebec, asking that men be sent to Champlain so that an attempt might be made on the lake to take some of the pressure off Ontario. Captain Thomas Everard from H.M.S. *Wasp* responded, as did Captain Daniel Pring, recently arrived from Ontario. With remarkable speed an expedition was launched down the lake. Escorted by *Chub, Finch,* and three other armed boats, several transports with nine hundred troops moved toward Plattsburg. In the presence of the regulars, the American militia evaporated. With no resistance the troops quickly destroyed the "Block house, Arsenal, Barracks and public buildings at Plattsburg . . ."[37] With that done, Everard sailed across the lake to look in at Burlington, and if lucky draw Macdonough out to decide once and for all who would command Champlain. Although he lost some small vessels to the marauders, Macdonough was too wise to be drawn out. Everard was able to destroy four of the American fleet, but the rest remained safe behind a well-positioned land battery. Captain Everard returned up the lake and was back behind British lines by 3 August. In retrospect the Everard expedition stands as a good example of what a small force well led and moving quickly can accomplish. In less than a week they had managed to strike a heavy blow at Plattsburg, disrupt and alarm Macdonough, and return to their own lines with only slight losses. Everard was back on *Wasp* in the St. Lawrence before the Americans fully appreciated the daring of his attack.

The British raid made Macdonough cautious. Fearful that his position at Burlington was too exposed, he decided to move his squadron to a safer refuge. He needed a location that might be easily protected but at the same time suitable for shipbuilding. He found that combination in the small town of Vergennes, located about eight miles up Otter Creek on the east side of the lake. The town had for some years been a shipbuilding center. It sat at the first falls of the creek, which provided a prime source of waterpower for gristmills, saw mills, and other water-powered industry. Iron from the neighboring town of Moncton was brought to Vergennes, where it was worked at the local forges, blast furnace, and rolling mill. There was no better place on the entire lake at which to build warships.

Work began at once. In the yard of the Steamboat Company of Lake Champlain, Macdonough found a large vessel on the ways, the steamboat *Vermont*. He bought her, took the engines out — thus denying himself the distinction of being the first American naval officer to take a steam warship into action — and converted her to a schooner rig under the name *Ticonderoga*.

*Ticonderoga*'s conversion, as well as the other work at the yard, was under the close eye of the Brown brothers, those indomitable builders who had been indispensable to Perry. In his wonted terse fashion, Noah Brown recorded events.

> In March, 1814, received orders from the government to proceed to Lake Champlain, and there build a ship and nine gunboats, and do what Commodore MacDonough [*sic*] thought proper, to be able to meet the British fleet on the lake. I proceeded on to Lake Champlain, to the City Verg'l, set up a ship of 180 feet keel and 36 feet beam, which was furnished, and nine gunboats and a schooner that was set up for a steamboat; and repaired all the old fleet, and the Commodore thought he had force plenty to meet the English, and we, with all our men, returned to New York.[38]

At the other end of the lake the enemy was not idle. Along the shore of Isle aux Nois they had two vessels under construction, a large ship pierced for thirty-six guns with an additional gun on a pivot and a smaller brig mounting sixteen guns. The ship was christened *Confiance,* in honor of a French prize once commanded by Yeo. The brig was named first *Niagara* and then *Linnet*. Unhappily for the British, they had no one to match the Brown brothers, nor did they enjoy the resources available at Vergennes. Progress for them was very slow.

The raid on Plattsburg, accompanied by the news that the British were busy at Isle aux Nois, caused Macdonough to reevaluate his situation. Having only a few weeks before sent Brown and his workers home, he now had second thoughts. At the end of June, Noah and Adam Brown received orders to return to Vergennes, this time to build a brig. As usual, they worked wonders. It took Adam Brown nineteen days to build and launch the brig *Eagle*.

Naval supremacy on the lakes was only a means to an end, that being either the facilitation or frustration of invasion. Perry had managed to frustrate the British in the west; Chauncey was posing problems in the center; the only route left untried was Champlain. In the summer of 1814 Sir George Prevost, governor general and commander in chief, turned his attention toward Champlain.

Prevost had good reason to be optimistic. Troop transports were arriving daily in the St. Lawrence, bringing thousands of veterans from the war against Napoleon, men who, according to their former commander, the Duke of Wellington, "could go anywhere and do anything." Ten thousand of these regulars were assigned to the Champlain campaign. The invasion might take one of two routes, either along the east shore and through Vermont or down the west side through New York. Since the Yankees in Vermont had for some time been most cooperative in supplying the British with food and animals, Prevost saw no point in marching in that direction. The better and more strategically important route was the one that aimed directly at Plattsburg.

Plattsburg, already attacked once, was a critical location along the lake. Foolishly, the Americans had drawn off most of the defending force and left as a garrison fifteen hundred regulars and a motley assortment of local militia. At the very most, Brigadier General Alexander Macomb, the commander, could raise thirty-five hundred effectives, and most of them were decidedly second rate. By any reasonable estimate Prevost was in for an easy victory.

That victory would in fact elude George Prevost is a measure of his character. In a blunt but accurate observation, one historian has noted, "Whether Prevost's natural character was warped by circumstances, weakened by strain, and perhaps by incipient illness, or simply broken down by what it had no force to master, will never be known."[39] Cautious to the point of paralysis, Prevost held it as an abiding rule that whenever joined with the navy in a combined attack, the army would wait for their brethren in blue to clear away any obstacles before troops were committed. This was a convenient philosophy, since in effect it put all the burden on the naval commander. If

### Macdonough's Fleet

| | Tons | Crew | Weight of Metal | Armament |
|---|---|---|---|---|
| *Saratoga* (ship) | 734 | 240 | 828 | 8 long 24s |
| | | | | 6 carronades 42s |
| | | | | 12 carronades 32s |
| *Eagle* (brig) | 500 | 150 | 480 | 8 long 12s |
| | | | | 12 carronades 32 |
| *Ticonderoga* (schooner) | 350 | 110 | 328 | 8 long 12s |
| | | | | 4 long 18s |
| | | | | 5 carronades 32s |
| *Preble* (sloop) | 80 | 30 | 63 | 7 long 9s |
| 6 gunboats (*Borer,* *Centipede, Nettle, Allen,* *Viper, Burrows*) | 70 | 246 | 444 | 1 long 24 |
| | | | | 1 columbiad 50 |
| Row galleys (*Wilmer,* *Ludlow, Aylwin, Ballard*) | 40 | 104 | 48 | 1 long 12 |
| TOTAL | 1,774 | 880 | 2,191 | |

he did not succeed, then Prevost could withdraw without risking his army and place the blame for failure on others. This was his method of operation on Erie and Ontario. Nothing would change on Champlain.

Through the summer Prevost prepared to invade.[40] At Vergennes Macdonough was prevented from taking to the lake by ice. Finally, on 29 May, following an ineffectual try by the British to get at his ships while they were still at anchor, the commodore got onto the lake and made sail for Plattsburg. With *Confiance* and *Linnet* still on the ways, the British were no match for the Americans. They wisely withdrew to the protection of their batteries on Isle aux Nois, leaving Macdonough in possession of the lake.

Although the carpenters worked furiously at Isle aux Nois, the British were not able to launch *Confiance* until 25 August. Eager to begin the campaign lest he be trapped by winter, Prevost, against the advice of his naval officers, ordered the army to move on 1 September, while *Confiance* was still in a state

## Downie's Fleet

| | Tons | Crew | Weight of Metal | Armament |
|---|---|---|---|---|
| *Confiance* (ship) | 1,200 | 325 | 920 | 27 long 24s |
| | | | | 4 carronades 32s |
| | | | | 6 carronades 24s |
| *Linnet* (brig) | 350 | 125 | 192 | 16 long 12s |
| *Chub* (sloop) | 112 | 50 | 162 | 3 long 6s |
| | | | | 8 carronades 18s |
| *Finch* (sloop) | 110 | 50 | 150 | 4 long 6s |
| | | | | 6 carronades 18s |
| | | | | 1 columbiad 18 |
| 7 gunboats | | | | |
| *Yeo* | 70 | 41 | 56 | 1 long 24 |
| | | | | 1 carronade 32 |
| *Prevost* | 70 | 41 | 56 | 1 long 24 |
| | | | | 1 carronade 32 |
| *Blucher* | 70 | 41 | 50 | 1 long 18 |
| | | | | 1 carronade 32 |
| *Wellington* | 70 | 41 | 36 | 1 long 18 |
| | | | | 1 carronade 18 |
| *Murray* | 70 | 41 | 18 | 1 long 18 |
| *Drummond* | 70 | 41 | 18 | 1 long 18 |
| *Beckwith* | 70 | 41 | 18 | 1 long 18 |
| Four boats | 160 | 160 | 128 | 1 carronade 32 each |
| TOTAL | 2,422 | 997 | 1,804 | |

of unreadiness. The army crossed the border on their march toward Plattsburg. On 2 September Captain George Downie arrived to take command of the lake squadron. Prevost insisted the vessels stand ready for battle. Downie objected and asked for time. Prevost said no and ordered him to hoist his flag aboard *Confiance* and sail to support the army.

Captain Daniel Pring was made second in command assigned to *Linnet*. With carpenters still hammering away on his flagship, Downie set sail accompanied by *Linnet, Chub, Finch,* and eleven gunboats to provide support for Prevost. All the time he protested his unreadiness, but the governor general paid no heed.

By 6 September the army was at Plattsburg, but Prevost refused to attack until Downie had destroyed Macdonough's fleet, which was anchored in the bay. In a series of testy letters he goaded Downie, placing the blame for the delay on him and urging him forward. Downie planned an attack on the 10th, but a headwind held him back. Prevost wrote him, "In consequence of your letters the troops have been held in readiness since six o'clock this morning to storm the enemy's works at nearly the same moment as the naval action begins in the bay. I ascribe the disappointment I have experienced to the unfortunate change of wind, and shall rejoice to learn that my reasonable expectations have been frustrated by no other cause." The letter infuriated Downie and he told Pring, "The letter does not deserve an answer. But I will convince him that the naval force will not be backward in their share of the attack."[41] Downie clearly expected that it would be a joint attack. The British commodore had his work cut out for him.[42]

Macdonough was in an exceedingly strong position. He had anchored his fleet in Plattsburg Bay behind Cumberland Head. The bay was open to the south but closed at the north; thus any breeze from the north (common at this time of year) would make it extremely difficult for an enemy force to approach the Americans. The fleet was anchored in line with springs and kedges so that they might reverse their broadsides if necessary. Macdonough also took advantage of nearby shoal water and placed himself in a position that forced the British to sail within range of his carronades or run aground. At the head of the line Macdonough put his two most powerful vessels, *Eagle* and *Saratoga*. This, too, was carefully thought out, for with a northerly breeze they could easily move southward to lend a hand down the line. Next in line after *Saratoga* were *Ticonderoga* and *Preble,* with the gunboats generally arranged so as to cover the spaces between the major vessels.

By anchoring not only did Macdonough force the enemy to come to him, but he also augmented his own force. None of his crews had to work at sail handling; every man was at a combat station.

Downie was fully apprised of Macdonough's dispositions, and he laid his plans with care. *Confiance* was to lead the attack.

Taking the van, Downie intended to bring her on a windward leg up the bay, come around, pour a broadside into *Eagle,* and then pass down to *Saratoga* and anchor in a position to deliver heavy broadsides. If all went well, *Confiance* could then grapple and board, or if that was not possible she might stand off beyond range of *Saratoga* and pummel the ship with long guns. At the same time, *Linnet* and *Chub* would work on *Eagle,* while *Finch* and the gunboats would open up on *Ticonderoga* and *Preble.*[43]

On Sunday morning 11 September the wind was light from the north, the sky was clear, and there was a bit of an early fall chill in the air. Not long after breakfast the American picket boat off Cumberland Head sent the signal everyone had been anxiously awaiting: "Enemy in sight." From the fighting tops of the squadron sailors could make out over the trees the moving mastheads of the British. Macdonough, a deeply religious man, summoned his officers to the quarterdeck and in British tradition offered a prayer:

> Thou givest not always the battle to the strong, but canst save by many or by few — hear us, thy poor servants — imploring thy help that thou wouldst be a defence unto us against the face of the enemy. Make it clear that Thou art our Saviour and Mighty Deliverer, through Jesus Christ, Our Lord.[44]

The men went to their stations.

Downie came up the bay on the port tack. *Eagle* fired first, and within minutes a general engagement was under way. Downie was unable to follow his original plan, as American fire and light winds prevented *Confiance* from taking her planned post. Instead she came abreast of *Saratoga* at about three hundred yards' distance. Her first broadside against Macdonough did savage damage, taking out forty men or nearly one fifth of the crew. *Saratoga* gave as well as she received, and among the first casualties on *Confiance* was Downie himself, who was killed by one of his own guns thrown back at him when struck by American shot. Despite the death of her commander, *Confiance* held her place in the slugfest. The same cannot be said for

*Chub,* which under a not very able captain lost her place in line and drifted through the American squadron, finally hauling down her colors. *Finch,* too, had an unhappy and early fate in the battle; she ran aground on the shoals and was unable to affect the battle much at all. Gunboats on both sides were hotly engaged, but the real battle finally resolved down to a contest between *Confiance* and *Linnet* versus *Eagle* and *Saratoga.* About one and a half hours into the battle *Eagle* cut her cable, came about, and moved to a position south of *Saratoga.* By accomplishing this she was able to show her port, and thus far unengaged, battery to the enemy. A short time later *Saratoga* managed a similar maneuver by swinging around in place. Neither *Confiance* nor *Linnet* could do the same. By showing in effect two new batteries to the enemy, Macdonough took a decisive advantage. *Confiance,* badly mauled, had no choice but to surrender. *Linnet* did the same, and soon the entire British fleet was in American hands. Shortly after the battle Macdonough wrote to Secretary Jones:

> Sir: The Almighty has been pleased to grant us a signal victory on Lake Champlain, in the capture of one frigate, one brig, and two sloops of war of the enemy.[45]

For his part, having done absolutely nothing to assist Downie, Prevost ordered his army to break camp and return to Canada. Much bitterness followed the debacle on Champlain. In the naval court-martial that followed, the court found Downie and his officers blameless and leveled their charges at Prevost.

> The court is of the opinion that the capture of His Majesty's said Confiance the brig Linnet and the remainder of the said squadron by the said American Squadron, was principally caused by the British Squadron having been urged into battle previous to its being in a proper state to meet its enemy by a promised cooperation of the Land Forces, which was not carried into Effect and by the very pressing letters and communications of their Commander in Chief . . .[46]

In retrospect the damnation of Prevost seems entirely justified. The pity is, he did not live long enough to present his own defense (if any). He died 5 January 1816.

## 12
# 1814 — The War Ends

Eighteen fourteen was not a good year. No matter how loud the cheers from Champlain, they could not drown out the cries of distress from Washington. It was the year in which the British, released from their heavy continental commitments against the French, were able to send units of the fleet and army to tend to matters American.

No one appreciated America's naval difficulties more than Secretary Jones. Indeed, he knew them all too intimately, for he had very little staff with whom to share his burdens. When he first took office, the entire staff numbered only twenty. The chief clerk, holding a position akin to that of the modern under secretary, was Charles W. Goldsborough, who had been present literally at the creation of the department in 1798 under Stoddert. His long tenure in office made him an invaluable, but not always pleasant associate. Jones found it difficult to work with him, and after several unhappy clashes he finally dismissed him. At first Goldsborough refrained from a counterattack, but on reflection, and perhaps a bit of agitation from friends, he decided to appeal his firing. Not without influence, Goldsborough applied all the techniques of bureaucratic infighting he could muster; nevertheless, although he annoyed Jones, he could not beat him and the dismissal stood.[1]

Goldsborough's departure and sniping made a difficult situation worse. Jones was swamped with a flood of detail, forcing him to attend personally to the minutiae of administration. At the same time Madison relied on him to handle the Department of the Treasury in the absence of Albert Gallatin, the regular secretary, who was away on a diplomatic assignment.[2] There can be little doubt that William Jones was the workhorse of the Madison administration.

The tortures of day-to-day operations did not dull Jones to broader questions of naval strategy and policy. More than any of his predecessors, he took a keen and direct interest in shaping wartime strategy. He was a strong advocate of attention to the lakes and on this account took a fair amount of criticism from coastal dwellers, who saw lake operations draining resources away from their own defense. Thankfully, Jones held his course and in the end was wonderfully vindicated by Perry and Macdonough.

His experience with the disposition of the coastal gunboats was equally troublesome. As always, each port, no matter how small, thought itself entitled to complete naval protection. Despite the clamor, Jones resisted the temptation to follow political expedience by scattering resources everywhere. Instead he followed a well-thought-out plan.

Huzzas over the great frigate victories notwithstanding, Jones rightly saw that such events had more psychological than strategic importance. He believed that the navy's best hope lay with commerce raiding and that single-ship engagements on the line of *Constitution* and *Guerrière* ought to be avoided even when victory might be had. Such sentiments were not well received by either the officer corps or the naval supporters in Congress. Further, Jones felt that money and material devoted to the construction of large seventy-four-gun ships was misspent. While he had no objection to ships of the line, he saw America's needs as immediate and such behemoths would take years to build; better to build small and quick. Shortly before he took office Congress had gone ahead and authorized four seventy-fours and six forty-fours. Although doubtful that they could be completed in time to help the war effort, Secretary Jones could hardly gainsay such enthusiasm. Two months later he did get what he wanted when Congress, as part of the effort to build a force on the lakes, also authorized construction of six sloops for ocean service.[3]

Events at sea in 1814 vindicated Jones's judgment. The British blockade was growing ever stronger. In 1813 four frigates managed to get to sea; in 1814 only two saw action, *President* and *Constitution*, and in neither case were their cruises particularly successful.

*President* left on her fourth cruise, still under command of John Rodgers, on 4 December 1813. He cleared Block Island and, once off soundings, shaped a southwesterly course in the direction of the West Indies. *President* took up a station to the windward side of Barbados and from there cruised along the coast near Cayenne; following the chain of the Windward Islands, she went north to Puerto Rico and thence through the Mona Passage to the east coast of Florida. Rodgers continued up the coast, carefully eluding the British, and finally crossed the bar at Sandy Hook to the safety of New York harbor on 18 February. The cruise netted very little, a few paltry merchantmen but nothing more.[4]

*Constitution* had a similar fate. After her return to Boston following the victory over *Java*, Bainbridge was transferred to command of the navy yard, and the frigate went in for a badly needed overhaul. In the spring a new captain, Charles Stewart, was appointed to command *Constitution*. On the last day of 1813 he got her to sea, bound for the West Indies. He sailed toward the mid-Atlantic, hoping to intercept East Indiamen heading home. He found none and so cruised toward Barbados, where in mid-February he overtook and captured His Majesty's schooner *Pictou*, as well as the merchant vessels *Lovely Ann*, *Phoenix*, and *Catharine*.

From there Stewart laid a course along the coast of Guiana up to and then through the Mona Passage and north to home. For a crew hungry for prize money, the voyage was depressing. On 2 April Stewart picked up the light at Portsmouth, New Hampshire, and bore down toward Boston. Now the real peril began. In December, when he had left, winter weather had worked to keep the British blockading force away; spring's arrival brought them back. Not only was their return certain, but so were the locations where they might be found. The Admiralty was after big game, namely the American frigates, and since these ships drew considerable water they knew they could be expected only at the major ports. Stewart's problem, and that of any other frigate captain lucky enough to get to sea, was how to get home early enough in the spring to avoid blockaders. Such a strategy necessitated short cruises, few prizes, and a high risk of interception.

At 8 A.M. on 3 April, with a light wind out of the northnorthwest, *Constitution*'s lookout sighted two large vessels coming up from the east-southeast. There could be no question of their nationality. Stewart hoisted every inch of canvas to escape. By now he was off Cape Ann, heading into Massachusetts Bay. Had the wind been cooperative, the best course would have been to hug the shoreline and head west, sliding between Bakers Island and Misery Island into the sanctuary of Salem harbor. The wind was perverse, however, and Stewart was forced to head more southerly toward Marblehead harbor. The race was on to see who would arrive first — the British coming up from the south or the Americans running down from the north. As *Constitution* pressed ahead Stewart ordered extra equipment, provisions, and even some prize goods cast overboard. By midday he had passed Halfway Rock and was almost within Marblehead harbor; a few more minutes and he would be safe. Meanwhile, Marbleheaders and others from the neighborhood had crowded the shoreline to watch the race. Militia manned the guns at Fort Sewall and saluted as the great frigate passed by them. As soon as it was obvious that *Constitution* was safe, the British stood offshore and then departed. A few days later Stewart moved his ship into Boston harbor, where she would be locked up by the enemy for the next eight months.[5]

Although disappointed, Jones was not greatly surprised by the poor performance of the frigates. Whatever the merits of their captains and crew, they simply were not suited to the work at hand. The secretary could take comfort and satisfaction from the reports arriving from the vessels he had long urged America to build — fast and well-armed sloops of war. Dispatches from two, *Wasp* and *Peacock*, were particularly pleasing.

*Peacock* was built at the New York Navy Yard by none other than those remarkable shipbuilders Noah and Adam Brown. She was one of the sloops authorized by the March 1813 act and was launched on 19 September 1813, only seventy-two days after her keel-laying. For a vessel her size she was heavily armed, fitted out with eighteen thirty-two-pound carronades and two long eighteens. *Peacock* made three wartime cruises, all under the command of Lewis Warrington, a Virginian and veteran naval officer.

After taking aboard guns, crew, and provisions, Warrington received his sailing orders early in March 1814. Jones had a grand design for *Peacock*. She was first to deliver stores to the naval station at St. Mary's, Georgia. From there Warrington was instructed to cruise off Florida and after an appropriate period track east to European waters and search for prizes among the British Isles, coast off Norway and south to Portugal, eventually crossing back for a visit to the West Indies and then home.

On 12 March 1814 *Peacock* left New York on her maiden cruise. After offloading supplies at St. Mary's, she continued south along the coast and on the morning of 29 April near Cape Canaveral met His Britannic Majesty's brig *Epervier*. They were near equals, the English ship having the same number and weight of carronades as Warrington. What told the difference was the training and discipline of the Americans, reflected by the high volume and accuracy of their fire. The melee lasted less than three quarters of an hour. In that time *Epervier* suffered heavy damage aloft and was taking water below. Having the choice to sink or surrender, the British captain chose the latter. Warrington sent a party aboard, and through the night they managed to control the damage and put *Epervier* in condition to sail. Warrington and crew received a hero's welcome at Savannah, where they finally put in on 4 May. The degree of joy there and in Washington was not lessened by the discovery, upon search of *Epervier*, that her strongbox contained $118,000 in specie.[6]

Port time was relatively brief for Warrington; on 4 June he took *Peacock* to sea again. As instructed, he bore east toward Europe, visiting everywhere Jones had ordered, with the exception of Norway, where the presence of both the British and Swedish fleets made cruising too risky. In the Irish Sea, gales from the southwest made sailing hazardous and forced *Peacock* on several occasions to stand far out to sea in order to keep off a lee shore. At the same time, such foul weather kept enemy merchantmen to home, depriving Warrington of his prey. He sailed the waters between Cape Clear and Waterford, taking three prizes, and then came up around the west coast of Ireland and north toward the Faeroe and Shetland islands. Taking a southerly course, Warrington sailed to the Bay of Biscay, along the coast of Portugal, across the Straits of Gibraltar, and then west via the Madeiras and the Canaries. Continuing west, he picked up the coast of Guiana and turned northwest, finally arriving at Cape Henlopen, his first American landfall, and reaching the safety of New York on 30 October. In 147 days at sea he had taken fourteen prizes, valued at more than half a million dollars. Most remarkable of all was that in his cruise to Europe and the West Indies he had lost only one man.[7]

As in Savannah, Warrington was acclaimed and toasted. He was also promoted — to the rank of captain. Had a frigate with a reasonable chance of getting to sea been available, Warrington might well have bid for her. Such was not the case, however, and he had to be content to remain with *Peacock*.

In November, while she lay at anchor in New York, *Peacock* was joined by the brig *Hornet*, Captain James Biddle, recently escaped from New London, where she had been blockaded since June.[8] Also in the harbor were the frigate *President*, under Stephen Decatur, and the store ships *Tom Bowline* and *Macedonian*. Jones had a plan for these vessels on the model of *Essex* — a far-flung cruise to the East Indies, a part of the world where the enemy least expected attack, and where fat Indiamen might be found.

As commodore of the squadron, Decatur ordered his captains to sail separately and then rendezvous at Tristan da Cunha, a remote island fifteen hundred miles west of the Cape of Good Hope. In that way, if the blockading force discovered them breaking out, only one vessel might be lost, instead of the entire squadron. *President* was the first to get under way, setting out on the evening of 14 January 1815. With a New York pilot guiding her, she made her way through the night with a stiff breeze and a fair tide. About eight, as she was passing over the bar, the most critical part of her exit, she came down hard in a trough and struck bottom. Again and again she hit. For two hours *President* was in agony, slamming against the sand bottom. Finally, she slipped off and Decatur ordered the carpenters to check for damage. Although no final call could be made until her bottom could be inspected, it was clear from the way *President* handled that some damage had been done.

While Decatur was agonizing over the damage done to his ship, the British blockading squadron was on the alert. The commander, Captain John Hayes, suspected from various pieces of intelligence that the Americans in New York might make a run for it. He put his own ship, *Majestic*, with fifty-six guns, as well as three accompanying frigates on notice to be watchful.

At about five in the morning, as the sun rose and the sky cleared, *President* spotted three of the British squadron dead ahead and only two miles distant. The chase was on, and for the next eighteen hours *President* was dogged by her pursuers. *Endymion*, the lead frigate, drew within range of *President*'s guns. For two hours they exchanged a fierce fire, but it was no use. Out of the dark and smoke Decatur could see the other enemy ships drawing near. Certain that he was doomed, he saw no point in sacrificing lives. At eleven-thirty in the evening he struck.

*President*'s misfortune did not deter the remainder of the American squadron, and together they got to sea on 20 January. Six days out they parted company when *Hornet* decided to chase down a strange sail.

*Peacock, Tom Bowline,* and *Macedonian* continued to plow southeast toward the rendezvous.[9] *Hornet* and *Tom Bowline* arrived first, about mid-March, but were driven away from the anchorage by bad weather. On the 23rd *Hornet* was back, preparing to drop anchor, when her lookout called to the deck to announce an unidentified vessel standing down toward them. She was at such a great distance that Biddle felt no need yet to beat to quarters and ordered his crew to dinner. When they finished, he ordered them to general quarters. About 1:40 the stranger, the British sloop of war *Penguin,* drew within pistol range and hauled to the wind, coming up on a starboard tack. Biddle followed suit, and the two sailed a parallel course. Aboard *Hornet* was a young midshipman, Mr. Skiddy, who many years later published his journal recounting the action.

> The moment his guns flashed, ours were in operation; and strange to say, in five minutes I perceived the blood running from his scuppers.[10]

Skiddy's prose might be a bit melodramatic, but it does present a reasonable sense of the battle. Although *Penguin* and *Hornet* were fairly matched, the struggle was decidedly one-sided. *Penguin* closed to board and thrust her bowsprit between *Hornet*'s main and mizzen masts. Biddle ordered his men to that point, where they laid down a withering fire on the British, whose boarding party, massed in the confines of the foredeck, fell like tenpins. *Penguin* pulled clear, but at the cost of her foremast and bowsprit. Crippled, she had no choice but to surrender. The entire action lasted barely twenty-two minutes. The next day Biddle scuttled *Penguin.*

*Tom Bowline* was sent to Rio as a cartel vessel, while *Peacock* and *Hornet* continued their cruise toward the Indian Ocean. On 27 April, at approximately 38°30′ south latitude and longitude 33° east, they sighted what they hoped was an East Indiaman. Unfortunately, it turned out to be a ship of the line, H.M.S. *Cornwallis.* Both Americans took to their heels, with *Cornwallis* electing to run down *Hornet.* Only by jettisoning everything they could, including guns, did *Hornet* manage to escape. With her sting gone over the side, Biddle decided to head for home. Lucky *Peacock* was able to continue into the Indian Ocean, taking several valuable prizes along the way.

On 30 June *Peacock* entered the Straits of Sunda and there encountered the British East India Company armed vessel *Nautilus.* Her captain tried to persuade Warrington that the war was over, which in fact was true. He refused to listen and suspected a ruse was being tried on him. It was an unequal battle, *Peacock* having the advantage in size and armament. *Nautilus* had seven men killed and eight wounded. In the aftermath Warrington was finally convinced that the war was indeed over, so he returned his prize.[11]

The success of *Hornet* and *Peacock* sustained Jones's faith in small vessels. It also proved the wisdom of getting ships to sea and keeping them there, rather than short cruising and day sailing. If the triumph of these two warships was not enough to convince the unbelieving, then the activities in 1814 of another of Jones's pets completed the conversion.

*Wasp* was commissioned early in 1814 at Newburyport, Massachusetts. She was a sloop of war mounting the now nearly standard armament of twenty thirty-two-pound carronades and two long twelve-pounders. Her captain, Johnston Blakely, was an Irishman by birth — County Down — who had come to America with his parents in 1783. He joined the navy as a midshipman in 1800 and served with distinction in both the Quasi and Barbary wars. During the early phase of the War of 1812, he commanded *Enterprize*, and left her to take *Wasp* only sixteen days before the former's epic battle with *Boxer*.[12]

At four in the afternoon on the first of May 1814, *Wasp* took the ebbing tide out of Portsmouth harbor and headed to sea. Blakely, following Jones's instructions, was on his way to cruise the British Isles. On the first of June he made the Channel and began to wreak havoc. In three weeks *Wasp* took seven prizes, sinking six and sending the seventh to port with prisoners. On 28 June, at position 48°36′ north latitude and longitude 11°15′ west, *Wasp* fell in with the Royal Navy brig *Reindeer*, the "pride of Plymouth." William Manners, captain of the brig, was a gallant but unlucky officer. As he closed on the American, he could see how badly outclassed he was. In weight of shot, Blakely had a 50 percent advantage and carried at least that many more men. Nevertheless, true to orders and tradition, Manners elected to fight. The event was brief, only nineteen minutes. Manners and twenty-two of his men were killed, forty-two others were wounded. *Wasp* lost five men, with another twenty-one left in the care of the surgeon. The next day *Reindeer* was sent to the bottom, and *Wasp* headed for Lorient to land prisoners and refit.[13]

Blakely remained in France until the end of August. His

protracted visit was not by choice but dictated by a long delay in securing repairs and supplies. Finally, on Saturday 27 August, *Wasp* was on the hunt again. On the third, fourth, and fifth days out she took prizes, an auspicious start for the second leg of an already successful cruise. The last of this string of three captures, His Majesty's sloop *Avon*, was a difficult catch.

The battle took place between Kinsale and Cape Clear, beginning about eight-thirty in the evening. They fought at close quarters for more than two hours, with *Avon*, slightly inferior to *Wasp*, getting the worse of the action. At the point of surrender the Englishman was granted a reprieve when another vessel of His Majesty's navy hove into view, *Castilian*. *Wasp* wisely departed, unaware that a few hours later *Avon* went to the bottom.

With the Royal Navy thoroughly aroused, Blakely thought it best to leave the crowded waters around the home islands and sail south. On 12 and 14 September off Portugal he took two prizes. Those were followed on the 21st by the capture of *Atalanta*. Because of her value, Blakely decided to send her into Savannah and for that purpose put a prize crew aboard, sending with them his latest dispatches. That is the last official word ever heard from *Wasp*. She disappeared at sea with all hands.[14]

The British reaction to the success of these small American vessels was reminiscent of their earlier shock over the victories of a few fir-built frigates: a mixture of disbelief and self-flagellation. Curiously enough, they understood the effect of American strategy better than the Americans themselves. One contemporary English observer assayed the situation well.

> The depredations committed on our commerce by American ships of war, and privateers, has attained an extent beyond all former precedent.
> It will be seen in our correspondence, that A. D. affirms they have literally swept our seas, blockaded our ports, and cut up our Irish and coasting trade. Another of our able epistolary friends, resident at Greenock, expresses his fears lest some enterprising American should enter the Clyde and destroy the shipping in that estuary. We refer our readers to the respective letters. The insurance between Bristol and Waterford or Cork, is now *three times higher* than it was when we were at

war with all Europe! The Admiralty Lords have been overwhelmed with letters of complaint or remonstrance; public meetings have been held at Liverpool and Bristol, by the merchants and shipowners, and many severe strictures passed upon the public conduct of those at the head of the naval department. The answers returned by the lords of the Admiralty to the *remonstrances* of the merchants of Liverpool and Bristol, state that three or four frigates, and fourteen sloops, were cruising at the time of the captures of which they complained, off the Irish station. But the truth is, that our navy contains scarcely a single sloop that is fairly a match for the weakest *American built* vessel of that class of ships of war . . . The system of maritime warfare adopted by the United States consists in burning, scuttling, and destroying every thing they capture. The eagerness with which they seize on the papers of the ships they take, points out the proofs they must exhibit in America to attain their remuneration. By this system America loses the amount of the premium and also the duties she would otherwise derive from the sale of the prizes, and the services of such warlike stores as they may chance to capture; but, on the other hand, *they make destruction sure;* cut off the chance of recaptures by our cruisers, whilst their own remain longer at sea, and by retaining all their force, commit more extended devastation.[15]

It had taken American naval planners two years to learn how to fight. If William Jones had only been secretary at the beginning of the war, instead of at the end, how much better the performance might have been.

While Jones was enamored of small, he did not forget big. The effort to get *President* to sea is demonstration of his interest in getting the frigates back into the war. The continuing blockade at New London, where *United States* and *Macedonian* were confined, was frustrating.[16] At Boston, however, luck prevailed. In mid-December the harbor was left uncovered, and, taking that opportunity after more than nine months in port, *Constitution* darted to sea.

Charles Stewart was still in command, having remained with his ship after the narrow escape at Marblehead harbor. From Boston Stewart took his frigate to Bermuda, and from there to waters off the coast of Portugal. Early in February he decided to run toward the southwest off Madeira. It was here that *Constitution* fought her last battle of the war.

On the 20th of February, at one in the afternoon, a sail was seen off the port bow. Stewart pursued, and at two a second sail came into view. The first sighting was H.M.S. *Cyane*, a small frigate of thirty-four guns under the command of Captain Thomas Falcon. The second was *Levant*, a corvette of approximately twenty-two guns, Captain George Douglas. Taken together, the two English ships could muster a slight advantage over *Constitution* in broadside weight, but such an edge hinged entirely on their being in complete cooperation and concert during the battle. For all practical purposes, that was an impossibility.

Stewart set out in chase, hoisting as much sail as possible. At four in the afternoon, *Constitution* lost her main royal mast, causing her to take in sail and make repairs. The chase then resumed. Stewart opened fire with his bow chasers, but the range was still too extreme, so after a few ineffectual shots the guns were secured. *Levant* and *Cyane* tried to move to a windward position; failing that, they shortened sail and went into a line formation to await *Constitution*'s arrival. At 6:05 Stewart ranged up along the starboard side of *Cyane* and let loose with a broadside, which was ably answered by both enemies. For fifteen minutes the battle raged, "then the fire of the enemy beginning to slacken and the great column of smoke clearing away we found ourselves abreast of the headmost ship, the sternmost ship luffing up for our larbored quarter." At this point Stewart was in danger of being pinned between the two. He acted quickly, pouring a broadside into the headmost ship; then, backing his sails, he moved his frigate rearward to come abreast of the sternmost ship, filling her with a broadside. The ballet continued, with Stewart displaying extraordinary ship handling, maneuvering between the two ships while hammering them with his guns. At 6:50 *Cyane* struck. With her consort lost, *Levant* was making her best to leeward. By eight Stewart had finished his business with *Cyane* and took up the chase. Realizing the difficulty of escape, *Levant* bravely turned to face *Constitution*. They came at each other on opposite tacks and traded broadsides. Stewart then came under her stern and raked. Douglas crowded all sail and tried to make good an escape. With her bow chasers thundering, *Constitution* took up the pursuit. The American gunners did their work skillfully and repeatedly sent well-directed shot tearing through the rigging. It was hopeless. At ten *Levant* lowered her colors.[17]

Stewart's victory over *Cyane* and *Levant* ranks as one of the most remarkable American naval victories ever. A nice combination of clever ship handling and expert gunnery, both the products of careful training, worked to give *Constitution* a well-deserved victory. "Old Ironsides" had begun the war in glory and ended it on the same note.

There is some irony in that while the American navy was enjoying success on distant stations, at home it was powerless to protect the American shore. The Royal Navy had little or no difficulty invading the bays and rivers of the coast. Such power was visibly demonstrated on the Chesapeake during the summer of 1814.

Aside from the occasional escape of a swift Baltimore privateer, Chesapeake Bay was effectively closed by the enemy, who roamed at will. The only force capable of causing them any difficulty, and very little of that, was the gunboat flotilla, made up of an assortment of barges and galleys under the command of the redoubtable Joshua Barney. Age and reputation gave Barney the kind of authority rank alone could never confer, and he reported directly to the secretary. For the most part, his force was confined to the region of the Patuxent River. They made occasional gnatlike forays against the enemy, but in point of fact they were no more than a nuisance to the British.[18]

Thus far in the war, the British had been content merely to blockade and maraud in the region, but in the summer of 1814 that policy turned to a more serious effort at the capture of Baltimore and Washington. Rumors of the British intent caused Madison to summon Barney and General William Winder, the local military commander, to a cabinet meeting to discuss defense of the capital. Their discussions might more profitably have centered on evacuation rather than defense, for when the British finally landed on 19 August, the American quickly retired. Barney blew up his gunboats to prevent capture and then moved with his men to join the capital's defenses. Under attack by the British veterans fresh from the Napoleonic

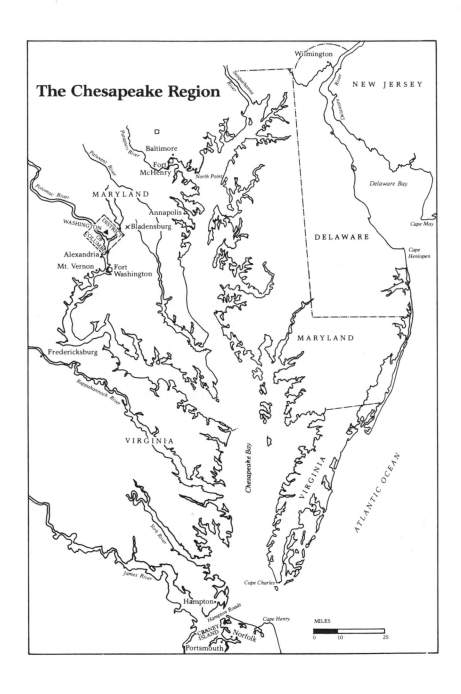

# The Chesapeake Region

Wilmington

NEW JERSEY

*Susquehanna River*

*Delaware River*

*Patapsco River*

Baltimore

Fort McHenry

*Patuxent River*

North Point

*Potomac River*

MARYLAND

Delaware Bay

Cape May

Annapolis

WASHINGTON
DISTRICT
OF
COLUMBIA

×Bladensburg

DELAWARE

Cape Henlopen

Alexandria

Mt. Vernon

Fort Washington

Fredericksburg

MARYLAND

*Rappahannock River*

VIRGINIA

*Chesapeake Bay*

VIRGINIA

ATLANTIC OCEAN

*York River*

*James River*

Cape Charles

Hampton

*Hampton Roads*

Cape Henry

MILES

0    10    25

CRANEY ISLAND

Norfolk

Portsmouth

War, the inexperienced Americans collapsed; the British took the city and made every attempt to burn what they could not carry away. The only bright spot in this fiasco was the gallant fight put up by Barney and his seamen-turned-soldiers.

While Washington still lay smoldering, units of the Royal Navy came up the Potomac to attack neighboring Alexandria. On 29 August two frigates and five smaller vessels anchored in the stream abreast of the town. Under the command of Captain James Gordon, the vessels remained at Alexandria for three days, collecting merchandise and merchantmen. When they finally sailed, the Americans, with the help of three eminent naval officers, Rodgers, Perry, and Porter, made attempts to harass their retreat. Rodgers attacked to no avail with fire ships, while Perry and Porter commanded land batteries. Despite the American efforts, Gordon proceeded down the river to safety, suffering only very light casualties.

Having finished their work at Washington, the British headed up the Bay to Baltimore, where they hoped to repeat the drama. On Sunday evening 11 September the fleet came to anchor at the mouth of the Patapsco River about five miles below the city. In command at Baltimore was the very able former interim secretary of the navy, Samuel Smith, who was about to prove himself as good a general as politician.

Landing at North Point, fourteen miles from the city, the army began its march, only to discover the American forces well prepared. Early warning and good planning had enabled the Americans to set up earthen defenses along the route of march. At the same time, the British navy moved in as close as it could to begin a bombardment of Fort McHenry, the linchpin for the harbor defense. The plan was for the army and navy to support one another; however, both elements ran into such stiff opposition that they had quite enough to do by themselves and could ill afford to lend aid.

After heavy attack "by the dawn's early light," the American flag could still be seen flying from the ramparts of Fort McHenry, encouraging to the defenders, dismaying to the attackers. On the morning of 15 September British forces began their withdrawal.

While concentrating their major forces in the Chesapeake region, in the summer of 1814 the British did not neglect to vex other parts of America, particularly New England. In April a raiding party moved up the Connecticut River and burned several vessels. In June Wareham, a small port on the south side of Cape Cod at the head of Buzzards Bay, came under attack.

British activities made New Englanders anxious, but nowhere was anxiety higher than among the Quakers on Nantucket Island. They were at the complete mercy of the Royal Navy. Their only hope was appeasement, and to that end "in August 1814 representations from Nantucket reached an agreement with British naval officers on the details of the island's neutrality and renounced all support to the United States for the duration of the war."[19] The Nantuckers provided eloquent testimony to the impotence of the American navy.

Farther to the north, in Maine the enemy elected to do more than just raid. Since the days of the American Revolution, the British had cast covetous eyes on that portion of Maine that juts northward, interposing itself on a direct line between Halifax and Quebec. In August Sir John Sherbrooke, governor of Nova Scotia, was ordered "to occupy so much of the District of Maine as shall insure an uninterrupted communication between Halifax and Quebec."[20] On this basis Sherbrooke took Machias and sent a force into Penobscot Bay. With no difficulty they captured Castine and even ventured up the Penobscot River as far as Bangor. As elsewhere, the Americans were impotent, and the British remained in the area until April 1815, when, as part of the final peace settlement, they returned the territory to the United States.

An unintended victim of the British attack was the frigate *Adams*, commanded by Captain Charles Morris. She was returning from a successful cruise on the Grand Banks when Morris decided to run into Penobscot Bay to "avoid" British cruisers. As *Adams* entered the bay, she ran ashore on Isle au Haut and damaged her keel. To make repairs Morris took her upriver to Hampden. A few days later, of course, Morris realized the trap he had fallen into, but it was too late, and on 3 September *Adams* was destroyed to avoid capture.

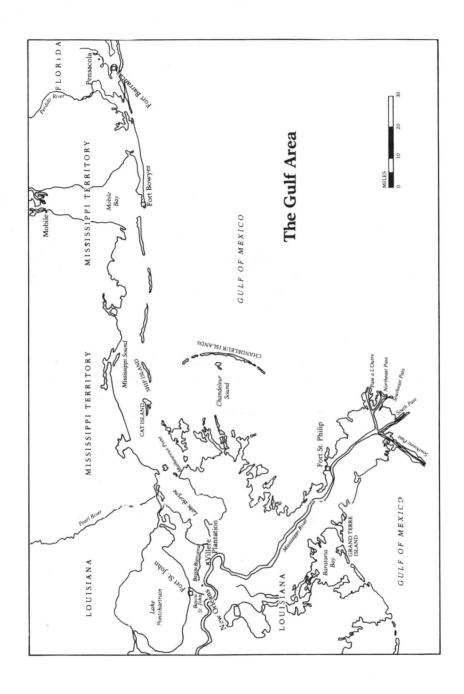

# The Gulf Area

FLORIDA
Pensacola
Fort Barrancas
Perdido River

MISSISSIPPI TERRITORY
Mobile
Mobile Bay
Fort Bowyer

MISSISSIPPI TERRITORY
Mississippi Sound
SHIP ISLAND
CAT ISLAND
Pearl River
Malheureux Point
Lake Borgne

LOUISIANA
Lake Pontchartrain
Fort St. John
Bayou St. John
Bayou Bienvenu
x Villeré Plantation
New Orleans

GULF OF MEXICO

CHANDELEUR ISLANDS
Chandeleur Sound

Fort St. Philip
Mississippi River

Pass a L'Outre
Northeast Pass
Southeast Pass
South Pass
Southwest Pass

Barataria Bay
GRAND TERRE ISLAND

LOUISIANA
GULF OF MEXICO

MILES
0   10   20   30

As a coastal defense force, the American navy had been completely ineffectual. The much vaunted and celebrated gunboat flotillas had proven how useless they were in the face of a determined and well-equipped enemy. With some variation the story was much the same at the other point of major British attack on the coast — New Orleans.

According to their instructions, the British forces moving against New Orleans were "to obtain command of the embouchure of the Mississippi, so as to deprive the back settlements of America of their communication with the sea; and secondly, to occupy some important and valuable possession, by the restoration of which the conditions of peace might be improved, or which we might be entitled to exact the cession of, as the price of peace."[21] With these instructions in hand, the British force, military and naval, rendezvoused at Negril Bay, Jamaica, and then proceeded across the Gulf and were off the Mississippi by 8 December 1814.[22]

After some consultation, the commanders decided to attack the city from the seaward side. Going directly up the river against the currents and wind was not practical. Such a procession would present an ideal target to American batteries; instead, a route intended to bypass the American fortifications was selected, which led across a shallow body of water, Lake Borgne, and then to Bayou des Pêcheurs, only a few miles from the city, where the army would disembark for the attack.

First to oppose the enemy was a small American flotilla under the command of Lieutenant Thomas Ap Catesby Jones, a young officer whose tempestuous career would span several decades. Jones had at his command five gunboats and two or three additional smaller craft. His first position was near the point at which the lake met the Gulf. It was here on 10 December that he saw the British approaching in their barges. Realizing the impossible odds, Jones elected to withdraw in the face of the advance, hoping to find a better position or at the very least by his presence make the British more cautious and slower in their approach. It was a good plan and a classic example of trading space for time. On 14 December strong tides and a contrary breeze made further retreat impossible; Jones drew his vessels into a battle line and watched the enemy draw near. They had nearly fifty boats to Jones's mere half dozen. As the British pulled ahead, cannon fire from Jones's flotilla took its toll and inflicted heavy damage. With their sheer weight of numbers, though, the British closed on the Americans and overwhelmed them. Jones, severely wounded, surrendered, and in less than half an hour the remainder of the flotilla followed suit. With that obstacle cleared, the British were now able to land their forces.

In the ensuing days, more troops were landed and the army began its penetration toward New Orleans. In the meantime the American commanding general, Andrew Jackson, was busily preparing his own special welcome for the British.

On the evening of 23 December, as the British bivouacked along the Bayou Bienvenu, another American navy vessel provided them a surprise. Confident that the surrounding area was well under control, the troops were relaxing when at about seven-thirty they were alerted to something in the bayou. What they heard was Lieutenant John D. Henley calling out, "Give them this for the honor of America!" The next sound to go through the camp was that of cannonballs whistling by and slamming into the soft earth. Henley was in command of *Carolina*, a small schooner that had been on the New Orleans station for a year and a half patrolling against pirates. Indeed, under Henley's command she had recently participated in an attack that destroyed Barataria, the lair of the notorious pirate Jean Lafitte.[23]

Staying just beyond musket range, Henley peppered the camp, sending the troops scurrying for cover. With only two pieces of light artillery available, there was little they could do except keep their heads down. After an hour, more fire could be heard from another direction. It was Jackson's men attacking on the landward side. The night action that followed turned in favor of the Americans, and while by no means decisive, it did at least throw the enemy off balance and inspired the American troops to greater things.

*Carolina* was joined in her efforts the next day by *Louisiana*, under the command of the senior naval officer present, Daniel

T. Patterson. Together, for the following two days, they continued with their harassment. By the 27th the British were able to bring up heavier guns, and on that day they finally blew up *Carolina*. A little luckier, *Louisiana* managed to withdraw closer to the city. Her guns and men were transferred ashore; in the coming days they added measurably to Jackson's defense of the city and his final spectacular victory on 8 January.

## 13

---

# Unfinished Business
# and Peace

Congress one and all ought to be hung, they have destroyed the Nation by delays and folly."[1] Such were the sentiments of Joshua Barney, veteran captain of the Revolutionary navy, French naval officer, privateersman in the War of 1812, commander of the Chesapeake Bay gunboat flotilla, and commodore by courtesy.

As might be expected from a man who had witnessed the debacle at Washington, Barney's opinions were not entirely without bias, but neither were they entirely wrong. Serious mistakes had been committed, many of them in the years before the war. The decision, for example, to build a plethora of gunboats on the assumption that a swarm of gnats could halt the advance of an elephant proved to be ill founded. So too may fault be laid at the other extreme, toward those who urged the construction of large ships of the line — an equal misuse of resources.

The pressures of running both the navy and the treasury had taken their toll, and in December 1814 Jones stepped down as secretary and left the administration to return to private life. Shortly before he departed, he made a report to Congress suggesting methods of reorganizing his department. As the man who had run the navy for most of the war, he had much to say. He began by bemoaning the heavy burdens that fell on the secretary, especially in wartime — duties that, in his words, were "beyond the powers of any individual to discharge."[2] With a degree of modesty unusual for the time, he even admitted to having made some errors, born, he confessed, of his own lack of professional knowledge. To prevent such errors from recurring, Jones put forth the idea that the secretary ought to be assisted and advised by a Board of Inspection made up of professional officers at the rank of captain. Before sending his report to Congress, he had wisely sought the advice of these same officers; needless to say, it won their full support.

Another part of his report, however, was less well received. Jones was several decades ahead of his officers when he recommended the establishment of a naval academy. His model was West Point, the recently established military academy. Charles Stewart summed up the attitude of his brother officers to such a notion when he rather bluntly informed the secretary that "the best school for the instruction of youth in the profession is the deck of a ship . . ."[3]

Jones's final report laid the groundwork for naval policy over the coming years. His successor, the Salem merchant Benjamin Crowninshield, helped to implement many of these suggestions. In retrospect, what seems most remarkable is that the report should have been made at all. At a moment when peace seemed near the secretary might, with equal logic, have submitted a document to Congress detailing a scheme to put the navy back into ordinary, as had been done following the Quasi and Barbary wars. Instead, this time there was no talk of dismemberment, but rather discussion about how much to augment the navy. The signal triumphs of the navy, despite its many losses, had provided moments of glory for a nation hungry for victories. The exploits of naval officers had been romanticized, eulogized, and glorified. It would be hard to argue in any public forum against support for a force that had served the republic so well. Coupled with that was the general upwelling of nationalism accompanying the end of the war. Everywhere, except in New England, the war was celebrated and enthroned as a victory for the American republic and a sign of great times to come. From another point of view, the war had shown with equal clarity the difficulties America faced at sea, and the need to be strong in the maritime world was now readily accepted, even by the Jeffersonians.

As Jones was packing to leave, good news was en route to America from the town of Ghent in Belgium. Since early August, American and British negotiators had been meeting there, trying to work out a peace settlement. They finally signed an agreement on Christmas Eve, which was quickly sent off to Washington and arrived there on 11 February. On 16 February the Senate ratified the treaty by a vote of 35 to 0.

The end of the war with Great Britain did not bring peace everywhere. Taking advantage of America's preoccupation, the dey of Algiers once more let loose his corsairs to molest American ships.

Less than a week after proclaiming peace with Great Britain, President Madison asked Congress to declare war against Algiers. They complied happily, expecting a quick and easy victory. With several ships ordered during the war now ready, and those blockaded finally released, Madison had at his disposal enough vessels for not one but two powerful squadrons. One was put under the command of Commodore Stephen Decatur, and the other under Commodore William Bainbridge, who was to hoist his flag on the new seventy-four-gun *Independence,* the first American ship of the line to get to sea.

Decatur got under way ahead of Bainbridge. His squadron was led by the spanking new frigate *Guerrière* sailing as flagship, accompanied by the frigates *Constellation* and *Macedonian.* Also in formation were the sloops of war *Epervier* and *Ontario;* the brigs *Firefly, Spark,* and *Flambeau;* and the schooners *Torch* and *Spitfire.* With Bainbridge also preparing to sail for the Barbary Coast, clearly Madison meant business.

It was on 17 June off Cape de Gata that the lookout aboard *Constellation* called down to the deck that he saw a large ship in the distance, soon identified as the Algerine frigate *Mashuda,* forty-six guns. Three of the American squadron were able to draw within range and engage: *Constellation, Guerrière,* and *Epervier.* Shortly after their captain was cut in two by a forty-two-pound shot from *Guerrière,* the crew of *Mashuda* hauled

down their flag. *Mashuda*'s capture was the only important battle of this very short war. On 30 June Decatur signed a treaty,
and after a few port visits in the Mediterranean he was back in
New York by early November. Matters had gone so well and so
quickly that Bainbridge's force never had to get involved, much
to his chagrin.

The return to America of Decatur's squadron marked the
end of an era. Since its founding the United States had been
almost constantly embroiled in war, wars that had imperiled the
very existence of the nation. That was now past, independence
was vindicated, and the American republic was firmly established as a national entity with which to be reckoned. For this,
much of the credit must go to the navy of the new republic.

*Appendix*
*Notes*
*Bibliography*
*Index*

# Appendix

## Rules and Regulations for the Government
## of the Navy of the United States

SEC. 1. That, from and after the first day of June next, the following rules
and regulations be adopted and put in force, for the government of the navy
of the United States.

Art. 1. The commanders of all ships and vessels of war belonging to the
navy, are strictly enjoined and required to show in themselves a good example
of virtue, honor, patriotism, and subordination, and be vigilant in inspecting
the conduct of all such as are placed under their command; and to guard
against, and suppress, all dissolute and immoral practices, and to correct all
such as are guilty of them, according to the usage of the sea service.

Art. 2. The commanders of all ships and vessels in the navy, having chaplains on board, shall take care that divine service be performed in a solemn,
orderly, and reverent manner, twice a day, and a sermon preached on Sunday, unless bad weather, or other extraordinary accidents prevent it: and that
they cause all, or as many of the ship's company as can be spared from duty,
to attend at every performance of the worship of Almighty God.

Art. 3. Any officer, or other person, in the navy, who shall be guilty of
oppression, cruelty, fraud, profane swearing, drunkenness, or any other
scandalous conduct, tending to the destruction of good morals, shall, if an
officer, be cashiered, or suffer such other punishment as a court-martial shall
adjudge: if a private, shall be put in irons, or flogged, at the discretion of the
captain, not exceeding twelve lashes; but if the offence require severer punishment, he shall be tried by a court-martial, and suffer such punishment as
said court shall inflict.

Art. 4. Every commander, or other officer, who shall, upon signal for
battle, or on the probability of an engagement, neglect to clear his ship for
action, or shall not use his utmost exertions to bring his ship to battle, or shall
fail to encourage, in his own person, his inferior officers and men to fight
courageously, such offender shall suffer death, or such other punishment as a
court-martial shall adjudge; or any officer neglecting, on sight of any vessel or
vessels of an enemy, to clear his ship for action, shall suffer such punishment
as a court-martial shall adjudge; and if any person in the navy shall treacher-

ously yield, or pusillanimously cry for quarters, he shall suffer death, on conviction thereof, by a general court-martial.

Art. 5. Every officer, or private, who shall not properly observe the orders of his commanding officer, or shall not use his utmost exertions to carry them into execution, when ordered to prepare for, join in, or when actually engaged in, battle; or shall at such time basely desert his duty or station, either then, or while in sight of an enemy, or shall induce others to do so, every person so offending shall, on conviction thereof by a general court-martial, suffer death, or such other punishment as the said court shall adjudge.

Art. 6. Every officer, or private, who shall, through cowardice, negligence, or disaffection, in time of action, withdraw from, or keep out of battle, or shall not do his utmost to take or destroy every vessel which it is his duty to encounter, or shall not do his utmost endeavor to afford relief to ships belonging to the United States, every such offender shall, on conviction thereof by a general court-martial, suffer death, or such other punishment as the said court shall adjudge.

Art. 7. The commanding officer of every ship or vessel in the navy, who shall capture, or seize upon, any vessel as a prize, shall carefully preserve all the papers and writings found on board, and transmit the whole of the originals, unmutilated, to the judge of the district to which such prize is ordered to proceed, and shall transmit to the Navy Department, and to the agent appointed to pay the prize money, complete lists of the officers and men entitled to a share of the capture, inserting therein the quality of every person rating, on pain of forfeiting his whole share of the prize money resulting from such capture, and suffering such further punishment as a court-martial shall adjudge.

Art. 8. No person in the navy shall take out of a prize, or vessel seized as a prize, any money, plate, goods, or any part of her rigging, unless it be for the better preservation thereof, or absolutely necessary for the use of any of the vessels of the United States, before the same shall be adjudged lawful prize by a competent court; but the whole, without fraud, concealment, or embezzlement, shall be brought in, and judgment passed thereon, upon pain that every person offending herein shall forfeit his share of the capture, and suffer such further punishment as a court-martial, or the court of admiralty in which the prize is adjudged, shall impose.

Art. 9. No person in the navy shall strip off their clothes, or pillage, or in any manner maltreat, persons taken on board a prize, on pain of such punishment as a court-martial shall adjudge.

Art. 10. No person in the navy shall give, hold, or entertain any intercourse or intelligence to or with any enemy or rebel, without leave from the President of the United States, the Secretary of the Navy, the commander-in-chief of the fleet, or the commander of a squadron; or, in case of a vessel acting singly, from his commanding officer, on pain of death, or such other punishment as a court-martial shall adjudge.

Art. 11. If any letter or message from an enemy or rebel be conveyed to any officer or private of the navy, and he shall not, within twelve hours, make the same known, having opportunity so to do, to his superior or commanding officer; or if any officer commanding a ship or vessel, being acquainted therewith, shall not, with all convenient speed, reveal the same to the commander-in-chief of the fleet, commander of a squadron, or other proper officer, whose duty it may be to take cognizance thereof, every such offender shall suffer death, or such other punishment as a court-martial shall adjudge.

Art. 12. Spies, and all persons who shall come or be found in the capacity of spies, or who shall bring or deliver any seducing letter or message from an enemy or rebel, or endeavor to corrupt any person in the navy to betray his trust, shall suffer death, or such other punishment as a court-martial shall adjudge.

Art. 13. If any person in the navy shall make, or attempt to make, any mutinous assembly, he shall, on conviction thereof by a court-martial, suffer death; and if any person as aforesaid shall utter any seditious or mutinous words, or shall conceal or connive at any mutinous or seditious practices, or shall treat with contempt his superior, being in the execution of his office; or, being witness to any mutiny or sedition, shall not do his utmost to suppress it, he shall be punished at the discretion of a court-martial.

Art. 14. No officer or private in the navy shall disobey the lawful orders of his superior officer, or strike him, or draw, or offer to draw, or raise, any weapon against him, while in the execution of the duties of his office, on pain of death, or such other punishment as a court-martial shall inflict.

Art. 15. No person in the navy shall quarrel with any other person in the navy, nor use provoking or reproachful words, gestures, or menaces, on pain of such punishment as a court-martial shall adjudge.

Art. 16. If any person in the navy shall desert to an enemy or rebel, he shall suffer death.

Art. 17. If any person in the navy shall desert, or shall entice others to desert, he shall suffer death, or such other punishment as a court-martial shall adjudge; and if any officer, or other person belonging to the navy, shall receive or entertain any deserter from any other vessel of the navy, knowing him to be such, and shall not, with all convenient speed, give notice of such deserter to the commander of the vessel to which he belongs, or to the commander-in-chief, or to the commander of the squadron, he shall, on conviction thereof, be cashiered, or be punished at the discretion of a court-martial. All offences, committed by persons belonging to the navy while on shore, shall be punished in the same manner if they had been committed at sea.

Art. 18. If any person in the navy shall knowingly make or sign, or shall aid, abet, direct, or procure the making or signing, of any false muster, or shall execute, or attempt, or countenance, any fraud against the United States, he shall, on conviction, be cashiered, and rendered forever incapable of any future employment in the service of the United States, and shall forfeit all the pay and subsistence due him, and suffer such other punishment as a court-martial shall inflict.

Art. 19. If any officer, or other person, in the navy, shall, through inattention, negligence, or any other fault, suffer any vessel of the navy to be stranded, or run upon rocks, or shoals, or hazarded, he shall suffer such punishment as a court-martial shall adjudge.

Art. 20. If any person in the navy shall sleep upon his watch, or negligently perform the duty assigned him, or leave his station before regularly relieved, he shall suffer death, or such punishment as a court-martial shall adjudge; or, if the offender be a private, he may, at the discretion of the captain, be put in irons, or flogged not exceeding twelve lashes.

Art. 21. The crime of murder, when committed by any officer, seaman, or marine, belonging to any public ship or vessel of the United States, without the territorial jurisdiction of the same, may be punished with death by the sentence of a court-martial.

Art. 22. The officers and privates of every ship or vessel appointed as convoy to merchant or other vessels, shall diligently and faithfully discharge the duties of their appointment, nor shall they demand or exact any compensation for their services, nor maltreat any of the officers or crews of such merchant or other vessels, on pain of making such reparation as a court of admiralty may award, and of suffering such further punishment as a court-martial shall adjudge.

Art. 23. If any commander or other officer shall receive or permit to be received, on board his vessel, any goods or merchandise, other than for the sole use of his vessel, except gold, silver, or jewels, and except the goods or merchandise of vessels which may be in distress, or shipwrecked, or in imminent danger of being shipwrecked, in order to preserve them for their owner, without orders from the President of the United States or the Navy Department, he shall, on conviction thereof, be cashiered, and be incapacitated forever afterwards for any place or office in the navy.

Art. 24. If any person in the navy shall waste, embezzle, or fraudulently buy, sell, or receive, any ammunition, provisions, or other public stores; or if any officer, or other person, shall, knowingly, permit, through design, negligence, or inattention, any such waste, embezzlement, sale or receipt, every such person shall forfeit all the pay and subsistence then due him, and suffer such further punishment as a court-martial shall direct.

Art. 25. If any person in the navy shall unlawfully set fire to or burn any kind of public property, not then in the possession of an enemy, pirate, or rebel, he shall suffer death: and if any person shall, in any other manner, destroy such property, or shall not use his best exertions to prevent the destruction thereof by others, he shall be punished at the discretion of a court-martial.

Art. 26. Any theft, not exceeding twenty dollars, may be punished at the discretion of the captain, and above that sum, as a court-martial shall direct.

Art. 27. If any person in the navy shall, when on shore, plunder, abuse, or maltreat, any inhabitant, or injure his property in any way, he shall suffer such punishment as a court-martial shall adjudge.

Art. 28. Every person in the navy shall use his utmost exertions to detect, apprehend, and bring to punishment, all offenders, and shall, at all times, aid and assist all persons appointed for this purpose, on pain of such punishment as a court-martial shall adjudge.

Art. 29. Each commanding officer shall, whenever a seaman enters on board, cause an accurate entry to be made in the ship's books of his name, time, and term of his service; and, before sailing, transmit to the Secretary of the Navy a complete list or muster roll of the officers and men under his command, with the date of their entering, time and terms of their service annexed; and shall cause similar lists to be made out on the first day of every second month, to be transmitted to the Secretary of the Navy, as opportunities shall occur; accounting in such lists, or muster rolls, for any casualties which may have taken place since the last list or muster roll. He shall cause to be accurately minuted on the ship's books, the names of, and times at which any death or desertion may occur; and in case of death, shall take care that the purser secure all the property of the deceased for the benefit of his legal representative or representatives. He shall cause frequent inspections to be made into the condition of the provisions, and use every precaution for its preservation. He shall, whenever he orders officers and men to take charge of a prize, and proceed to the United States, and whenever officers or men are sent from his ship for whatever cause, take care that each man be furnished with a complete statement of his account, specifying the date of his enlistment, and the period and terms of his service; which account shall be signed by the commanding officer and purser. He shall cause the rules for the government of the navy to be hung up in some public part of the ship, and read once a month to his ship's company. He shall cause a convenient place to be set apart for sick or disabled men, to which he shall have them removed, with their hammocks and bedding, when the surgeon shall so advise, and shall direct that some of the crew attend them and keep the place clean; and, if necessary, shall direct that cradles, and buckets with covers, be made for their use: and when his crew is finally paid off; he shall attend in person, or appoint a proper officer, to see that justice be done to the men, and to the United States, in the settlement of the accounts. Any commanding officer, offending herein, shall be punished at the discretion of a court-martial.

Art. 30. No commanding officer shall, of his own authority, discharge a commissioned or warrant officer, nor strike, nor punish him otherwise than by suspension or confinement, nor shall he, of his own authority, inflict a punishment on any private beyond twelve lashes, with a cat-of-nine tails, nor shall he suffer any wired, or other than a plain, cat-of-nine tails, to be used on board his ship; nor shall any officer who may command by accident, or in the absence of the commanding officer (except such commander be absent for a time by leave) order or inflict any other punishment than confinement, for which he shall account on the return of such absent commanding officer. Nor shall any commanding officer receive on board any petty officers or men, turned over from any other vessel to him, unless each of such officers and men produce to him an account, signed by the captain and purser of the vessel from which they came, specifying the date of such officer's or man's entry, the period and terms of service, the sums paid and the balance due him, and the quality in which he was rated on board such ship. Nor shall any commanding officer, having received any petty officer or man as aforesaid, rate him in a lower or worse station than that in which he formerly served. Any commanding officer, offending herein, shall be punished at the discretion of a court-martial.

Art. 31. Any master-at-arms, or other person of whom the duty of master-at-arms is required, who shall refuse to receive such prisoners as shall be committed to his charge, or having received them, shall suffer them to escape, or dismiss them without orders from proper authority, shall suffer in such prisoners' stead, or be punished otherwise, at the discretion of a court-martial.

Art. 32. All crimes committed by persons belonging to the navy, which are not specified in the foregoing articles, shall be punished according to the laws and customs in such cases at sea.

Art. 33. All officers, not holding commissions or warrants, or who are not entitled to them, except such as are temporarily appointed to the duties of a commissioned or warrant officer, are deemed petty officers.

Art. 34. Any person entitled to wages or prize money may have the same paid to his assignee, provided the assignment be attested by the captain and purser; and in case of the assignment of wages, the power shall specify the precise time they commence. But the commander of every vessel is required to discourage his crews from selling any part of their wages or prize money, and never to attest any power of attorney, until he is satisfied that the same is not granted in consideration of money given for the purchase of wages or prize money.

### NAVAL GENERAL COURTS-MARTIAL

Art. 35. General courts-martial may be convened as often as the President of the United States, the Secretary of the Navy, or the commander-in-chief of the fleet, or commander of a squadron, while acting out of the United States, shall deem it necessary; *provided,* that no general court-martial shall consist of more than thirteen, nor less than five, members, and as many officers shall be summoned on every such court as can be convened without injury to the service, so as not to exceed thirteen, and the senior officer shall always preside, the others ranking agreeably to the date of their commissions; and in no case, where it can be avoided without injury to the service, shall more than one-half the members, exclusive of the president, be junior to the officer to be tried.

Art. 36. Each member of the court, before proceeding to trial, shall take the following oath or affirmation, which the judge advocate, or person officiating as such, is hereby authorized to administer.

"I, A.B. do swear [or affirm] that I will truly try, without prejudice or partiality, the case now depending, according to the evidence which shall come before the court, the rules for the government of the navy, and my own conscience; and that I will not by any means divulge or disclose the sentence of the court, until it shall have been approved by the proper authority, nor will I at any time divulge or disclose the vote or opinion of any particular member of the court, unless required so to do before a court of justice in due course of law."

This oath or affirmation being duly administered, the President is authorized and required to administer the following oath or affirmation to the judge advocate, or person officiating as such.

"I, A.B. do swear [or affirm] that I will keep a true record of the evidence given to, and the proceedings of, this court; nor will I divulge, or by any means disclose, the sentence of the court until it shall have been approved by the proper authority; nor will I at any time divulge or disclose the vote or opinion of any particular member of the court, unless required so to do before a court of justice in due course of law."

Art. 37. All testimony given to a general court-martial shall be on oath or affirmation, which the president of the court is hereby authorized to administer, and if any person shall refuse to give his evidence as aforesaid, or shall prevaricate, or shall behave with contempt to the court, it shall and may be lawful for the court to imprison such offender at their discretion; *provided,* that the imprisonment in no case shall exceed two months: And every person who shall commit wilful perjury on examination on oath or affirmation before such court, or who shall corruptly procure, or suborn, any person to commit such wilful perjury, shall and may be prosecuted by indictment or information in any court of justice of the United States, and shall suffer such penalties as are authorized by the laws of the United States in cases of perjury, or the subornation thereof. And in every prosecution for perjury, or the subornation thereof, under this act, it shall be sufficient to set forth the offence charged on the defendant, without setting forth the authority by which the court was held, or the particular matters brought, or intended to be brought, before the said court.

Art. 38. All charges, on which an application for a general court-martial is founded, shall be exhibited in writing to the proper officer, and the person demanding the court shall take care that the person accused be furnished with a true copy of the charges, with the specifications, at the time he is put under arrest, nor shall any other charge or charges, than those so exhibited, be urged against the person to be tried before the court, unless it appear to the court that intelligence of such charge had not reached the person demanding the court, when the person so to be tried was put under arrest, or that some witness material to the support of such charge, who was at that time absent, can be produced; in which case, reasonable time shall be given to the person to be tried to make his defence against such new charge. Every officer so arrested is to deliver up his sword to his commanding officer, and to confine himself to the limits assigned him, under pain of dismission from service.

Art. 39. When the proceedings of any general court-martial shall have commenced, they shall not be suspended or delayed on account of the absence of any of the members, provided five or more be assembled; but the court is enjoined to sit from day to day, Sundays excepted, until sentence be given: And no member of said court shall, after the proceedings are begun, absent himself therefrom, unless in case of sickness, or orders to go on duty from a superior officer, on pain of being cashiered.

Art. 40. Whenever a court-martial shall sentence any officer to be suspended, the court shall have power to suspend his pay and emoluments for the whole, or any part, of the time of his suspension.

Art. 41. All sentences of courts-martial, which shall extend to the loss of life, shall require the concurrence of two-thirds of the members present; and no such sentence shall be carried into execution, until confirmed by the President of the United States; or, if the trial take place out of the United States, until it be confirmed by the commander of the fleet or squadron: All other sentences may be determined by a majority of votes, and carried into execution on confirmation of the commander of the fleet, or officer ordering the court, except such as go to the dismission of a commissioned or warrant officer, which are first to be approved by the President of the United States.

A court-martial shall not, for any one offence not capital, inflict a punishment beyond one hundred lashes.

Art. 42. The President of the United States, or, when the trial takes place out of the United States, the commander of the fleet or squadron, shall possess full power to pardon any offence committed against these articles, after conviction, or to mitigate the punishment decreed by a court-martial.

SEC. 2. Art. 1. That courts of inquiry may be ordered by the President of the United States, the Secretary of the Navy, or the commander of a fleet or squadron, provided such court shall not consist of more than three members, who shall be commissioned officers, and a judge advocate, or person to do duty as such; and such courts shall have power to summon witnesses, administer oaths, and punish contempt in the same manner as courts-martial. But such court shall merely state facts, and not give their opinion, unless expressly required so to do in the order for convening; and the party, whose conduct shall be the subject of inquiry, shall have permission to cross-examine all the witnesses.

Art. 2. The proceedings of courts of inquiry shall be authenticated by the signature of the president of the court and judge advocate, and shall, in all cases not capital, or extending to the dismission of a commissioned or warrant officer, be evidence before a court-martial, provided oral testimony cannot be obtained.

Art. 3. The judge advocate, or person officiating as such, shall administer to the members the following oath or affirmation:

"You do swear [or affirm] well and truly to examine and inquire, according to the evidence, into the matter now before you, without partiality or prejudice."

After which, the president shall administer to the judge advocate, or person officiating as such, the following oath or affirmation:

"You do swear [or affirm] truly to record the proceedings of this court, and the evidence to be given in the case in hearing."

SEC. 3. That in all cases, where the crews of the ships or vessels of the United States shall be separated from their vessels, by the latter being wrecked, lost, or destroyed, all the command, power, and authority, given to the officers of such ships or vessels, shall remain and be in full force as effectually as if such ship or vessel were not so wrecked, lost, or destroyed, until such ship's company be regularly discharged from, or ordered again into, the service, or until a court-martial shall be held to inquire into the loss of such ship or vessel; and if, by the sentence of such court, or other satisfactory evidence, it shall appear that all or any of the officers and men of such ship's company did their utmost to preserve her, and after the loss thereof behaved themselves agreeably to the discipline of the navy, then the pay and emoluments of such officers and men, or such of them as shall have done their duty as aforesaid, shall go on until their discharge or death; and every officer or private who shall, after the loss of such vessel, act contrary to the discipline of the navy, shall be punished at the discretion of a court-martial, in the same manner as if such vessel had not been so lost.

SEC. 4. That all the pay and emoluments of such officers and men, of any of the ships or vessels of the United States taken by an enemy, who shall appear, by the sentence of a court-martial, or otherwise, to have done their utmost to preserve and defend their ship or vessel, and, after the taking thereof, have behaved themselves obediently to their superiors, agreeably to the discipline of the navy, shall go on, and be paid them until their death, exchange, or discharge.

SEC. 5. That the proceeds of all ships and vessels, and the goods taken on board of them, which shall be adjudged good prize, shall, when of equal or superior force to the vessel or vessels making the capture, be the sole property of the captors; and when of inferior force, shall be divided equally between the United States and the officers and men making the capture.

SEC. 6. That the prize money, belonging to the officers and men, shall be distributed in the following manner:

1. To the commanding officers of fleets, squadrons, or single ships, three-twentieths, of which the commanding officer of the fleet or squadron shall have one-twentieth, if the prize be taken by a ship or vessel acting under his

command, and the commander of single ships two-twentieths; but where the prize is taken by a ship acting independently of such superior officer, the three-twentieths shall belong to her commander.

2. To sea lieutenants, captains of marines, and sailing masters, two-twentieths; but where there is a captain, without a lieutenant of marines, these officers shall be entitled to two-twentieths and one-third of a twentieth, which third, in such case, shall be deducted from the share of the officers mentioned in article No. 3, of this section.

3. To chaplains, lieutenants of marines, surgeons, pursers, boatswains, gunners, carpenters, and master's mates, two-twentieths.

4. To midshipmen, surgeon's mates, captain's clerks, schoolmasters, boatswain's mates, gunner's mates, carpenter's mates, ship's stewards, sailmakers, masters-at-arms, armorers, cockswains, and coopers, three-twentieths and an half.

5. To gunner's yeomen, boatswain's yeomen, quarter-masters, quarter gunners, sailmaker's mates, sergeants and corporals of marines, drummers, fifers, and extra petty officers, two-twentieths and an half.

6. To seamen, ordinary seamen, marines, and all other persons doing duty on board, seven-twentieths.

7. Whenever one or more public ships or vessels are in sight at the time any one or more ships are taking a prize or prizes, they shall all share equally in the prize or prizes, according to the number of men and guns on board each ship in sight.

No commander of a fleet or squadron shall be entitled to receive any share of prizes taken by vessels not under his immediate command; nor of such prizes as may have been taken by ships or vessels intended to be placed under his command, before they have acted under his immediate orders; nor shall a commander of a fleet or squadron, leaving the station where he had the command, have any share in the prizes taken by ships left on such station, after he has gone out of the limits of his said command.

SEC. 7. That a bounty shall be paid by the United States, of twenty dollars, for each person on board any ship of an enemy of the commencement of an engagement, which shall be sunk or destroyed by any ship or vessel belonging to the United States of equal or inferior force, the same to be divided among the officers and crew in the same manner as prize money.

SEC. 8. That every officer, seaman, or marine, disabled in the line of his duty, shall be entitled to receive for life, or during his disability, a pension from the United States, according to the nature and degree of his disability, not exceeding one-half his monthly pay.

SEC. 9. That all money accruing, or which has already accrued, to the United States from the sale of prizes, shall be, and remain forever, a fund for the payment of pensions and half pay, should the same be hereafter granted, to the officers and seamen who may be entitled to receive the same; and if the said fund shall be insufficient for the purpose, the public faith is hereby pledged to make up the deficiency; but if it should be more than sufficient, the surplus shall be applied to the making of further provision for the comfort of the disabled officers, seamen, marines, and for such as, though not disabled, may merit, by their bravery, or long and faithful services, the gratitude of their country.

SEC. 10. That the said fund shall be under the management and direction of the Secretary of the Navy, the Secretary of the Treasury, and the Secretary of War, for the time being, who are hereby authorized to receive any sums to which the United States may be entitled from the sale of prizes, and employ and invest the same, and the interest arising therefrom, in any manner which a majority of them may deem most advantageous: And it shall be the duty of the said commissioners to lay before Congress, annually, in the first week of their session, a minute statement of their proceedings relative to the management of said fund.

SEC. 11. That the act passed the second day of March, in the year one thousand seven hundred and ninety-nine, entitled "An act for the government of the navy of the United States," from and after the first day of June next, shall be, and is hereby, repealed.

*Approved, April 23, 1800.*

# Notes

## Abbreviations

ASP  *American State Papers, Documents, Legislative and Executive of the*
ASPFR  *Congress of the United States: Foreign Relations [FR], Naval Affairs*
ASPNA  *[NA], and Finance [F]* (Washington: Gales and Seaton, 1832–61)
ASPF

DANFS  *Dictionary of American Naval Fighting Ships*, 8 vols. (Washington: United States Government Printing Office, 1959–81)

DBW  Dudley Knox, ed., *Naval Documents Related to the United States Wars with the Barbary Powers*, 6 vols. (Washington: United States Government Printing Office, 1939–44)

DQW  Dudley Knox, ed., *Naval Documents Related to the Quasi War Between the United States and France*, 7 vols. (Washington: United States Government Printing Office, 1935–38)

AF  Area File of the Naval Records Collection, 1775–1910. National Archives Microfilm, M 625

LRSC  Letters Received by the Secretary of the Navy: Captain's Letters, 1805–61, 1866–85. National Archives Microfilm, M 125

LRSCM  Letters Received by the Secretary of the Navy from Commanders, 1804–86. National Archives Microfilm, M 147

LSSO  Letters Sent by the Secretary of the Navy to Officers, 1798–1868. National Archives Microfilm, M 149

LSSM  Miscellaneous Letters Sent by the Secretary of the Navy, 1798–1886. National Archives Microfilm, M 209

PMHB  *Pennsylvania Magazine of History and Biography*

PRO  Public Record Office, London

Chapter One
Troubles Abroad
(pages 1–16)

1. John Adams to the President of Congress, 6 July 1780, in Francis Wharton (ed.), *The Revolutionary Diplomatic Correspondence of the United States*, 6 vols. (Washington, 1889), 3:833.

2. Robert Morris to the President of Congress, 19 March 1784, Item 137, Papers of the Continental Congress, National Archives.

3. James Madison to Edmund Randolph, 17 June 1783, Edmund C. Burnett (ed.), *Letters of Members of the Continental Congress*, 8 vols. (Washington, 1921–38), 7:190; Louis H. Bolander, "The Frigate *Alliance*, the Favorite Ship of the American Revolution," United States Naval Institute *Proceedings* 63: 1258; Robert Neeser, "Historic Ships of the Navy," *Proceedings*, 54:291.

4. W. C. Ford (ed.), *Journals of the Continental Congress, 1774–1789*, 34 vols. (Washington, 1904–12), 5:431.

5. H. G. Barnby, *The Prisoners of Algiers* (New York, 1966), 11–25; G. Fisher, *The Barbary Legend* (Oxford, 1957); J. Soames, *The Coast of Barbary* (London, 1938); Glenn Tucker, *Dawn Like Thunder* (New York, 1963), 43–56.

6. Ray W. Irwin, *The Diplomatic Relations of the United States with the Barbary Powers* (Chapel Hill, 1931), 25–34; *Journals of the Continental Congress*, 32:362; C. R. King (ed.), *Life and Correspondence of Rufus King*, 6 vols. (New York, 1894–1900), 1:101.

7. William Carmichael to Thomas Jefferson, 4 April 1785, Julian P. Boyd (ed.), *The Papers of Thomas Jefferson*, 20 vols. to date (Princeton, 1950–present), 8:69.

8. Thomas Jefferson to James Monroe, 6 February 1785, *Papers of Jefferson*, 7:639.

9. John Adams to Elbridge Gerry, 12 December 1784, Adams Papers, Massachusetts Historical Society.

10. James Cathcart described the capture in *The Captives* (LaPorte, Indiana, 1899), 5–6.

11. *Pennsylvania Packet*, 22 October 1785; *Massachusetts Centinel*, 5 October 1785, 12 October 1785.

12. *Massachusetts Centinel*, 16 November 1785.

13. Report from Secretary for Foreign Affairs (John Jay), 20 October 1785, *Journals of the Continental Congress*, 29:843.

14. Thomas Jefferson to Nathaniel Greene, 12 January 1786, *Papers of Thomas Jefferson*, 9:168.

15. *Journals of the Continental Congress*, 31:618.

16. Cecelia M. Kenyon, *The Antifederalists* (New York, 1966), 295.

17. Jonathan Elliot (ed.), *Debates in the Several State Conventions on the Adoption of the Federal Constitution*, 5 vols. (Washington, 1861–63), 3:309.

18. *The Federalist*, Modern Library edition (New York, 1937), 67.

19. E. S. Maclay (ed.), *William Maclay Journal* (New York, 1890), 76.

20. Richard Kohn, *Eagle and Sword* (New York, 1975), 170–173.

21. Proposed Address to Congress, April(?) 1789, John C. Fitzpatrick (ed.), *The Writings of George Washington*, 39 vols. (Washington, 1939), 30:302.

22. *DBW*, 1:36.

23. James Fenimore Cooper, *History of the Navy of the United States of America*, 2 vols. (Philadelphia, 1840), 1:235.

24. Quoted in Marshall Smelser, *Congress Founds the Navy* (Notre Dame, 1959), 51.

Chapter Two
"Congress Founds the Navy"
(pages 17–33)

1. This is an oversimplification. For a more detailed analysis of the Federalist-Republican split see Wilfred E. Binkley, *American Political Parties: Their Natural History* (New York, 1962); Morton Borden, *Parties and Politics in the Early Republic, 1789–1815* (New York, 1967); and Noble E. Cunningham, Jr., *The Jeffersonian Republicans: The Formation of Party Organization, 1789–1801* (Chapel Hill, 1957).

2. James D. Richardson, *A Compilation of the Messages and Papers of the Presidents, 1789–1908*, 10 vols. (Washington, 1908), 1:40, 145–147, 148–149; Marshall Smelser, *The Congress Founds the Navy* (Notre Dame, 1959), 49.

3. J. Gales and W. W. Seaton (eds.), *Annals of the Congress of the United States, 1789–1824*, 42 vols. (Washington, 1834–56). 3 Cong. 1 sess, 154–155. Hereafter cited as *Annals*.

4. Smelser, 53.

5. *ASPNA*, 1:5, *Annals*, 3 Cong. 1 sess., 449.

6. William Ellery to William Whipple, 31 May 1778, Edmund C. Burnett, ed., *Letters of the Members of the Continental Congress*, 8 vols. (Washington, 1921–38), 3:269; Humphreys to Robert Morris, 6 January 1793, quoted in Ira Hollis, *The Frigate Constitution* (Boston, 1931), 35; Howard I. Chapelle, *History of the American Sailing Navy*, 115–134; William M. Fowler, "America's Super-Frigates," *Mariner's Mirror*, 59:51; Craig Symonds, *Navalists and Antinavalists: The Naval Policy Debate in the United States, 1785–1827* (Newark, 1980), 35.

7. Symonds, *Navalists and Antinavalists*, 13.

8. *Annals*, 481; Smelser, 57; Melvin H. Jackson, *Privateers in Charleston, 1783–1796* (Washington, 1969), 31.

9. *Annals*, 497–498; *Statutes at Large of the United States of America, 1789–1873*, 17 vols. (Washington, 1850–73), 1:350–351.

10. *ASPNA*, 1:6.

11. A third man, William Doughty, deserves a measure of credit as well. Chapelle, *American Sailing Navy*; Merle T. Westlake, Jr., "Josiah Fox, Gentleman, Quaker, Shipbuilder," *PMHB*, 88:316–327.

12. *ASPNA*, 1:6; Charles Oscar Paullin, *Paullin's History of Naval Administration, 1775–1911* (Annapolis, 1968), 95–96.

13. Hoysted Hacker to Silas Talbot, 22 January 1794, Talbot Papers, G. W. Blunt White Library, Mystic Seaport; Silas Talbot to George Clinton, 13 June 1794, Talbot Papers.

14. John Barry to George Washington, 19 March 1794, in Martin J. Griffin, "The Story of Commodore John Barry," *The American Catholic Historical Researchers*, 4:165.

15. Secretary of War to Captains Barry, Nicholson, Talbot, Barney, Dale, and Truxtun, 5 June 1794, *DBW*, 1:75; Bernard Mayo, "Joshua Barney and the French Revolution," *Maryland Historical Magazine* 36:357–359; Ralph D. Paine, *Joshua Barney* (New York, 1924), 285–287; Henry R. Tuckerman, *Silas Talbot* (New York, 1850).

16. Stephen Higginson to Secretary of War, 12 June 1798, *DQW*, 1:112.

17. *ASPNA*, 1:17–21.

18. Richard Dale, John Barry, and Thomas Truxtun to Secretary of War, 18 December 1794, *ASPNA*, 1:8.

19. The importance of live oak for American shipbuilding is well documented in Virginia Steele Wood, *Live Oak: Southern Timber for Tall Ships* (Boston, 1981).

20. Barry, Dale, and Truxtun to Secretary of War, 18 December 1794, *ASPNA*, 1:8.

21. *ASPNA*, 1:19.

22. Richardson, 1:82.

23. Hunter Miller, *Treaties and Other International Acts of the United States*, 7 vols. (Washington, 1931), 2:299–312.

24. *Statutes at Large*, 1:453. Both Smelser and Symonds provide good analysis of the activities within Congress.

25. Abigail Adams to Mary Cranch, 16 May 1797, Stewart Mitchell (ed.), *New Letters of Abigail Adams* (Boston, 1947), 89.

26. Thomas Truxtun to Joshua Humphreys, 7 September 1797, *DQW*, 1:17.

27. Hollis, *Frigate Constitution*, 58.

28. Alexander DeConde, *The Quasi-War: The Politics and Diplomacy of the Undeclared War with France, 1797–1801* (New York, 1966), 90.

29. *Statutes at Large*, 1:523; *ASPNA*, 1:29–30.

30. *Statutes at Large,* 1:523; *ASPNA,* 1:59–60.

31. Richardson, 1:232–233.

32. The diplomatic and political events leading to the rupture with France are well described in DeConde, *Quasi-War.* See also: Jackson, *Privateers in Charleston,* 6–8; Edward Channing, *A History of the United States,* 6 vols. (New York, 1932), 4:116–150.

33. *ASPNA,* 2:28–65.

34. Richardson, 1:251.

35. Richardson, 1:264.

36. Quoted in James Morton Smith, *Freedom's Fetters: The Alien and Sedition Laws and American Civil Liberties* (Ithaca, 1956), 15.

37. *Statutes at Large,* 1:552.

38. *Statutes at Large,* 1:553; Paullin, *History of Naval Administration.* 98–104; Robert G. Albion, *Makers of Naval Policy* (Annapolis, 1980), 3.

39. Quoted in Robert G. Albion, "The First Days of the Navy Department," *Military Affairs,* 12:4.

40. Quoted in Albion, "First Days," 5.

Chapter Three
War with an Old Friend
(pages 34–58)

1. Benjamin Stoddert to Jeremiah Yellot, 18 June 1798, LSSM; *DQW,* 1:104.

2. Stoddert's correspondence is laced with anti-Nicholson sentiments. For examples see *DQW,* 1:494, 495.

3. Gardner W. Allen, *Our Naval War with France* (Boston, 1909), 63; Edwin N. McClellan, "The Naval War with France," *Marine Corps Gazette,* 7:341.

4. *DQW,* 1:76. Not everyone agrees that commerce along the south coast was important. See extract from Truxtun's Journal, 24 July 1798, *DQW,* 1:240.

5. *DQW,* 1:159–160; Eugene S. Ferguson, *Truxtun of the Constellation* (Baltimore, 1956), 145–146.

6. *Columbian Centinel,* 14 July 1798 and 8 August 1798; Allen, 64–65. *Retaliation* was the name of the privateer Decatur had commanded during the Revolution. Irwin Anthony, *Decatur* (New York, 1931), 9.

7. *Statutes at Large,* 1:578; 1:594; 1:608.

8. *Statutes at Large,* 1:575.

9. *DQW,* 1:433–434; Allen, 72–73.

10. *DQW,* 1:40–43.

11. *DQW,* 2:26–34; John F. Campbell, "The Havana Incident," *American Neptune,* 22:264–276.

12. Revenue cutters were brought into the naval establishment by an act of

25 February 1799, *Statutes at Large*, 3:621. However, in practice the secretary was already directing the activities of some revenue vessels late in 1798. See also Irving H. King, *George Washington's Coast Guard* (Annapolis, 1978), 144–165.

13. This was certainly Truxtun's view. Extract from Truxtun's Journal, 24 July 1798, *DQW*, 1:240.

14. Insurance Agreement, Fulwar Skipwith Papers Box 1 F11 and Insurance Policies VFM 1373, G. W. Blunt White Library, Mystic Seaport.

15. *DQW*, 2:55–57.

16. *DQW*, 2:70–72.

17. *DQW*, 1:73–74.

18. *DQW*, 2:84–85.

19. *DQW*, 2:77–78.

20. *Statutes at Large*, 1:574.

21. Joseph Parker to House of Representatives, 17 January 1799, *ASPNA*, 1:68–70.

22. Benjamin Stoddert to House Committee on Naval Establishment, 29 December 1799, *ASPNA*, 1:67–68.

23. *DQW*, 2:301.

24. *DQW*, 2:304–305.

25. *DQW*, 2:326–331. Ferguson, *Truxtun*, 161–165; and Allen, *Naval War*, 93–98.

26. *DQW*, 2:352–353; 377–379; 468–471.

27. *DQW*, 3:272–273.

28. Stephen Decatur, Sr., to ( ? ), 5 April 1799, *DQW*, 3:19.

29. *DQW*, 3:49–51.

30. *DQW*, 3:85, 112, 161, 399, 538–539.

31. Allen, 126–127.

32. James D. Richardson, *Messages and Papers of the Presidents 1789–1908*, 10 vols, (Washington, 1908), 1:289–292.

33. *DQW*, 4:304.

34. P. C. F. Smith, *The Frigate Essex Papers* (Salem, 1974).

35. For an account of the voyage see Christopher McKee, *Edward Preble: A Naval Biography* (Annapolis, 1972), 66–81.

36. *DQW*, 5:1–6.

37. Allen, 146–148.

38. *Connecticut Courant*, 2 June 1800; *DQW*, 5:390–391.

39. Richard Dale had for the time being returned to the merchant service.

40. I am indebted to Commander Tyrone G. Martin, U.S.N. ret., for bringing this to my attention.

41. *DQW*, 5:159.

42. *Claypoole's American Daily Advertiser*, 25 March 1800.

43. *DQW*, 5:160.

44. *DQW*, 5:167.

Chapter Four
Dancing and Wenching in the Mediterranean
(pages 59–81)

1. Edward Channing, *A History of the United States*, 6 vols. (New York, 1912–25), 4:239.

2. As a result of this electoral complication, the Twelfth Amendment to the Constitution was prepared and ratified.

3. James D. Richardson, ed., *Messages and Papers of the Presidents 1789–1908*, 10 vols. (Washington, 1908), 1:322.

4. Albert Gallatin, "State of the Finances, 18 December 1801," *ASPF*, 1:701–706; Alexander S. Balinsky, "Albert Gallatin, Naval Foe," *PMBH*, 82:294.

5. Robert Smith reached the secretary's post by a rather circuitous route. The job was originally offered to his brother Samuel. He refused the official appointment but said until someone was found he would run the office without pay. Secretary of War Henry Dearborn was appointed acting secretary of the navy but did none of the work, while Samuel Smith, with no appointment, did it all. As this was going on, two more candidates were asked to serve. Both refused, leaving Robert Smith, with his brother's backing, as the final choice. He accepted.

6. *DBW*, 7:134–138; 1:423–424.

7. In his first budget Jefferson provided slightly under one million dollars for the navy. Thereafter, in his first administration, the figures went up steadily. *DBW*, 6:329.

8. See *DBW*, vol. 1; Glenn Tucker, *Dawn Like Thunder* (Indianapolis, 1963), 11–26.

9. *DBW*, 1:382–384.

10. *DBW*, 1:429; Craig L. Symonds, *Navalists and Antinavalists* (Newark, 1980), 90–91.

11. *DBW*, 1:426–427; Gardner W. Allen, *Our Naval War with France* (Boston, 1909), 257.

12. *DBW*, 1:428–429; Eugene S. Ferguson, *Truxtun of the Constellation* (Baltimore, 1956), 222–225.

13. *DBW*, 1:432.

14. *DBW*, 1:463–465, 473.

15. *DBW*, 1:459.

16. *DBW*, 1:484–485.

17. *DBW*, 1:534–535.

18. *DBW*, 1:538–539. In recognition of the bravery of Sterett and his men, Congress resolved "That the President of the United States be requested to present to Lieutenant Sterett a sword, commemorative of the aforesaid heroic action; and that one month's pay be allowed to all the other officers, seamen and marines, who were on board the Enterprize when the aforesaid action took place." *Statutes*, 2:198; Tucker, *Dawn Like Thunder*, 141–144.

19. *DBW*, 1:603–605.

20. *DBW*, 1:628, 633–637.

21. *DBW*, 1:553.

22. Richardson, 1:326, 329–330.

23. *DBW*, 2:19, 76.

24. *DBW*, 2:76; Ferguson, *Truxtun of the Constellation*, 222–224.

25. *DBW*, 2:82.

26. Morris recounted and defended his conduct in Richard Valentine Morris, *Defense of the Conduct of Commodore Morris During His Command in the Mediterranean: With Strictures on the Report of the Court of Inquiry Held at Washington* (New York, 1804).

27. *DBW*, 2:122, 123.

28. *DBW*, 2:180, 273–274, 126–128.

29. *DBW*, 2:176–178, 216.

30. William Eaton to James Cathcart, 4 August 1802, AF.

31. *DBW*, 2:350–355.

32. Quoted in Samuel Edwards, *Barbary General, the Life of William H. Eaton* (Englewood Cliffs, 1968), 123.

33. *DBW*, 2:403–404.

34. *DBW*, 2:408.

35. *DBW*, 2:430, 435–436; Tucker, *Dawn Like Thunder*, 172–178.

36. *DBW*, 2:459–460.

37. *DBW*, 2:457–458.

Chapter Five
Preble Takes Charge
(pages 82–105)

1. The best biography of Preble is Christopher McKee, *Edward Preble* (Annapolis, 1972). For a history of the building of the *Essex*, see P. C. F. Smith, *The Frigate Essex Papers* (Salem, 1974).

2. McKee, 84; *DBW*, 1:425, 437; 2:101, 122.

3. *DBW*, 2:337.

4. *DBW*, 2:405–406.

5. Tyrone G. Martin, *A Most Fortunate Ship* (Chester, 1980), 45–46; *DBW*, 2:427, 428, 429–430, 434, 440, 445, 447–448, 450, 452, 454, 455–456, 459, 460, 462–463.

6. While Preble might not have been aware of it, the composition of his force was in part determined by politics. In the views of Jefferson and Gallatin, it would be enough simply to blockade the Tripolitans to persuade them to be reasonable. Secretary Smith, on the other hand, like Preble, was more inclined to seek greater results, such as cowing all the Barbary States. The former was a cheaper course and could be accomplished with smaller vessels. Hence it was adopted. McKee, 128.

7. *DBW*, 2:488.

8. *DBW*, 2:474–477.

9. *DBW*, 3:1–3.

10. The account given here is taken from McKee, 141. See also Glenn Tucker, *Dawn Like Thunder* (Indianapolis, 1963), 192–193.

11. *DBW*, 3:46–47; Charles O. Paullin, *Commodore John Rodgers* . . . (Cleveland, 1910), 111–112; McKee, 147–148.

12. *DBW*, 3:70.

13. *DBW*, 3:133–134; 143–144; 154–159; McKee, 173–175.

14. The *Philadelphia* story has been told and retold. See *DBW*, 3 for the most important documents.

15. This description of the harbor at Tripoli is taken from a chart in *DBW*, 3:174. See also James Fenimore Cooper, *Lives of Distinguished American Naval Officers*, 2 vols. in 1 (Philadelphia, 1846), 89, 43; Martin, *A Most Fortunate Ship*, 53–55.

16. *DBW*, 3:172. Bainbridge might have tried kedging; that is, carrying the anchor off in a small boat, dropping it, and then hauling in. However, this procedure was not possible, since Bainbridge apparently did not have a boat aboard large enough to accommodate the anchor. Cooper, *Lives* . . . , 46.

17. *DBW*, 3:174.

18. *DBW*, 3:347.

19. *DBW*, 6:415.

20. *DBW*, 3:311–312.

21. *DBW*, 3:417. See also *DBW*, 3:414–427.

22. Quoted in Martin, *A Most Fortunate Ship*, 58.

23. *DBW*, 3:486.

24. *DBW*, 4:90–91, 97–98.

25. *DBW*, 4:267–268.


Chapter Six
"To the Shores of Tripoli"
(pages 106–125)

1. *DBW*, 4:294.

2. Various descriptions of the battle can be found in *DBW*, 4: See also Christopher McKee, *Edward Preble, A Naval Biography* (Annapolis, 1972), 251–267; Irving Anthony, *Decatur* (New York, 1931), 141–146; and Tyrone G. Martin, *A Most Fortunate Ship* (Chester, 1980), 64–68.

3. Joshua Blake's conduct came under heavy criticism. A transcript of the court of inquiry called to inquire into his conduct can be found in Linda and Christopher McKee, eds., "An Inquiry into the Conduct of Joshua Blake," *The American Neptune*, 21:130–141.

4. Some historians have erroneously ascribed this brave action to a seaman named Reuben James.

5. Preble's dissatisfaction with the action is attested to by his reaction when Decatur returned after the battle with three prizes. According to Anthony, *Decatur*, p. 146, the encounter went as follows:

"Well, Commodore, I have brought you out three of the gunboats," said Decatur, proud of his success.

Preble was a madman. He turned upon the words, seized Decatur by the collar and shook him. Red eyed, his face a mask of rage, he shrieked: "Aye sir, why did you not bring me out more?"

6. *DBW*, 4:377.
7. *DBW*, 5:59.
8. Numerous references to *Intrepid* and her ill-fated mission can be found in *DBW*, 4. See also Anthony, *Decatur*, 150–151, and McKee, *Preble*, 303–306.
9. *DBW*, 5:20.
10. *DBW*, 5:139.
11. McKee, *Preble*, 309–310.
12. The exchange can be found in *DBW*, 5.
13. *DBW*, 5:137.
14. *DBW*, 5:164.
15. The confused diplomatic and military situation in the Mediterranean is described well by Piers Mackesy, *The War in the Mediterranean, 1803–1810* (Cambridge, 1957).
16. *DBW*, 5:167.
17. *DBW*, 5:362.
18. *DBW*, 5:362.
19. *DBW*, 5:542.
20. *DBW*, 5:548.
21. *DBW*, 5:556.
22. *DBW*, 6:22.
23. Jefferson submitted the treaty to the Senate on 11 December 1805. It was ratified 17 April 1806. James D. Richardson, *A Compilation of the Messages and Papers of the Presidents, 1789–1908*, 10 vols. (Washington, 1908), 1:390.
24. *DBW*, 6:144.
25. The ambassador Sidi Suliman Mellimelli did in fact go to Washington and made quite an impression on the capital.
26. *DBW*, 6:290.
27. *DBW*, 6:329.
28. C. A. Wright, "The Tripoli Monument," United States Naval Institute *Proceedings*, 58:1930–1941.

Chapter Seven
Men at Sea
(pages 126–140)

1. Herman Melville, *White Jacket or The World in a Man-of-War* (New York, 1963), 94.

2. *Historical Statistics of the United States, Colonial Times to 1970*, Part 2 (Washington, 1975), 1140.

3. *DQW*, 1:43.

4. *DBW*, 2:52.

5. *DBW*, 2:443.

6. Ira Dye, "Early American Merchant Seafarers," *Proceedings* of the American Antiquarian Society, 120:331–360.

7. *DBW*, 2:479.

8. *DQW*, 3:207.

9. *DBW*, 2:494.

10. Technically, midshipmen were appointed by warrant, but since they were expected to climb into the commissioned ranks, they are treated here with that group.

11. *DQW*, 1:13–14.

12. Quoted in Eugene S. Ferguson, *The Life of Commodore Thomas Truxtun, U.S. Navy, 1755–1822* (Baltimore, 1956), 147.

13. "Naval Medicine in the Early Nineteenth Century," pamphlet published by the U.S.S. Constitution Museum (Boston, 1981). The chart on page 134 is published by the kind permission of the Museum; see also J. Worth Estes, "Naval Medicine in the Age of Sail: The Voyage of the *New York*, 1802–1803," *Bulletin of the History of Medicine*, 56:238–253.

14. *Naval Regulations Issued by Command of the President of the United States of America*, January 25, 1802 (reprinted United States Naval Institute, 1970), 18.

15. *DQW*, 4:91.

16. *DBW*, 1:556–558.

17. *Statutes at Large*, 1:523.

18. James E. Valle, *Rocks and Shoals: Order and Discipline in the Old Navy, 1800–1861* (Annapolis, 1980), 48.

19. Thomas Truxtun, *Remarks, Instructions* . . . (Philadelphia, 1794), Appendix, xvii.

Chapter Eight
Toward War
(pages 141–161)

1. Remarks at a dinner honoring Nobel Prize winners of the Western Hemisphere, April 29, 1962. *Public Papers of the Presidents of the United States: John F. Kennedy*, 3 vols. (Washington, 1963), 2:347.

2. *DBW*, 2:309; Eugene S. Ferguson, "Mr. Jefferson's Dry Docks," *American Neptune*, 11:109–114.

3. *DBW*, 6:358.

4. Quoted in Irving Anthony, *Decatur* (New York, 1931), 162; *Statutes at Large*, 2:390.

5. *Statutes at Large*, 2:402.

6. *Statutes at Large*, 2:205.

7. *DBW*, 3:282.

8. *DBW*, 3:430–441.

9. Dean R. Mayhew, "Jeffersonian Gunboats in the War of 1812," *American Neptune*, 42:102.

10. The best discussion of gunboat design, including Edward Preble's involvement, can be found in Christopher McKee, *Edward Preble* (Annapolis, 1972), 316–328. See also numerous references in *DBW*.

11. Robert Smith to Thomas Jefferson, 16 September 1805. Smith Papers, Maryland Historical Society.

12. Quoted in McKee, *Preble*, 318–319.

13. Dumas Malone, *Jefferson the President*, vol. 5 of *Jefferson and His Time*, 6 vols. (Boston: 1948–77), 5:xx.

14. Anthony Steel, "Anthony Merry and the Anglo-American Dispute About Impressment, 1803–06," *Cambridge Historical Journal*, 9:336–337; J. F. Zimmerman, *Impressment of American Seamen* (New York, 1925), 260, 267; McKee, 367, note 2, chapter 10.

15. Julius W. Pratt, *Expansionists of 1812* (New York, 1925), 17–59.

16. *DBW*, 6:112–114.

17. *DBW*, 6:114–115.

18. *DBW*, 6:530; Charles Oscar Paullin, *Commodore John Rodgers* (Annapolis, 1967), 183–185.

19. *DBW*, 6 contains many documents relative to the incident.

20. *DBW*, 6:566.

21. James D. Richardson, ed., *A Compilation of the Messages and Papers of the Presidents*, 10 vols. (Washington, 1908), 1:422–424.

22. Burton Spivak, *Jefferson's English Crisis* (Charlottesville, 1979), 72.

23. Records of the court may be found in *DBW*, 6:561–570.

24. *ASPFR*, 3:259.

25. Commodore John Rodgers to Captain Isaac Hull, 19 June 1810, AF.

26. *Lille Belt* is often referred to as *Little Belt;* the following account is taken primarily from the reports later submitted by the American and British commanders. Bingham's account may be found in *London Gazette*, 3 August 1811, 291–295; for Rodgers' see Commodore John Rodgers to Secretary Paul Hamilton, 23 May 1811, LRSC. Diplomatic correspondence may be found in *ASPFR*, 3:476–500.

## Chapter Nine
### 1812 — A Year of Great Victories
### (pages 162–184)

1. I am indebted to William Dudley of the Historical Research Branch, United States Naval Historical Division, for allowing me to examine portions of his forthcoming documentary history of the War of 1812.

2. Alexander Slidell Mackenzie, *Life of Stephen Decatur, A Commodore in the Navy of the United States* (Boston, 1846), 165; Howard I. Chapelle, "The Ships

of the American Navy in the War of 1812," *Mariner's Mirror*, 12:287; for examples of the problems facing the navy, see John Dent to SecNav, 27 April 1812, LRSC; Thomas N. Gautier to John Dent, 22 April 1812, LRSC; Samuel Evans to SecNav, 5 May 1812, LRSCM.

3. Thomas Harris, *The Life and Services of William Bainbridge, U.S.N.* (Philadelphia, 1837), 134; SecNav to John Rodgers, 21 May 1812, LSSO.

4. John Rodgers to SecNav, 3 June 1812, LRSC.

5. Stephen Decatur to SecNav, 8 June 1812, LRSC.

6. Barry J. Lohnes, "British Naval Problems at Halifax, During the War of 1812," *Mariner's Mirror*, 59:317–322; Alfred Thayer Mahan, *Sea Power In Its Relations to the War of 1812*, 2 vols. (New York, 1968 repr.), 1:298–299; Steele's List, October 1813, G. W. Blunt White Library, Mystic Seaport, HFM 57.

7. John Rodgers to SecNav, 1 September 1812, LRSC; Charles Oscar Paullin, *Commodore John Rodgers* (Annapolis, 1967 repr.), 250–256.

8. *Guerrière* was not part of the original squadron. She was bound to Halifax for repairs but joined the squadron temporarily to assist in the search. *Nautilus* had sailed originally as a schooner but was converted to a brig in 1811, *DANFS*, 5:26; "Capture of U.S. Brig Nautilus by HMS Shannon," *Naval Chronicle*, 28:253.

9. The events of the chase are well chronicled. Isaac Hull to SecNav, 21 July 1812, LRSC; Charles Morris, *Autobiography of Commodore Morris*, 51–55; Abel Bowen, *The Naval Monument* . . . (Boston, 1816), 8–9; Ira Hollis, *The Frigate Constitution* (Boston, 1900), 141–155; Tyrone G. Martin, *A Most Fortunate Ship* (Chester, Conn., 1980), 104–111.

10. *The Naval Temple* (Boston, 1816), 56–59; David Long, *Nothing Too Daring: A Biography of David Porter, 1780–1843* (Annapolis, 1970), 64–69.

11. H. Garbett, "The Shannon and the Chesapeake," Royal United Service Institute for Defense Studies *Journal*, 57:797.

12. Because of New England's well-known dissatisfaction for the war, the British tried to court the Yankees by refraining from a full economic blockade north of Cape Cod. The policy did not work, and in the spring of 1814 the Royal Navy finally imposed a complete blockade. Between the opening of the war and the spring of 1814, New Englanders carried on a brisk, albeit illegal, trade with the British. *Niles Weekly Register*, 7:195; Mahan, 1:296–297.

13. For the events of this cruise see: Isaac Hull to SecNav, 21 July 1812, LRSC; James Dacres to Vice Admiral Herbert Sawyer, 7 September 1812, PRO Adm 1/502 541; Record of Court Martial of James Dacres, 2 October 1812, PRO Adm 1/5431; Hollis, *Frigate Constitution*, 156–176; Martin, *A Most Fortunate Ship*, 112–125; Gardner W. Allen, *Papers of Isaac Hull* (Boston, 1929), 26–29.

14. Dacres Court Martial, PRO Adm 1/5431.

15. Abel Brown, ed., *Naval Monument*, 16.

16. Paullin, *John Rodgers*, 260.

17. The battle is described in Stephen Decatur to SecNav, 30 October 1812, LRSC; Alexander Slidell Mackenzie, *Decatur*, 171.

18. Oliver Hazard Perry to SecNav, 6 December 1812, LRSC.

19. Mackenzie, *Decatur*, 171.

20. David Porter, *Journal of a Cruise Made to the Pacific Ocean in the United States Frigate in the Years 1812, 1813, and 1814* (New York, 1822, second edition), 36. This *Journal* and David Long, *Porter*, are the best sources of information concerning the cruise of the *Essex*.

21. *Bonne Citoyenne* had £350,000 on board. Frederick Lindeman to Charles Stewart PRO Adm 1/503.

22. Albert Gleaves, *James Lawrence, Captain United States Navy* (New York, 1904), 115–116; Martin, *A Most Fortunate Ship*, 131.

23. William Bainbridge to SecNav, 3 January 1813, AF; Extracts from Commodore William Bainbridge's Journal Relative to the Action Between the *Java* and *Constitution*, AF; *Naval Temple*, 70–76; Martin, *A Most Fortunate Ship*, 132–140.

24. Bainbridge's Journal.

25. London *Times*, 20 March 1813.

26. Vice Admiral John Borlase Warren to Lords Commissioners of the Admiralty, 29 December 1812, PRO Adm 1/503 99.

27. The size differential was considerable. Albert Gleaves, *James Lawrence*, 94, estimated that in size *Constitution* was to the average British frigate 15.3:10.0. In weight of metal the ratio was to the British advantage, since American shot tended to be approximately 7 percent lighter than British shot of the same caliber. American gunners were more accurate. William James, *The Naval History of Great Britain . . .* , 5 vols. (London, 1822–24), 5:373–374.

28. Charles Stewart, Isaac Hull, and Charles Morris to SecNav, 12 November 1812, *ASPNA* 14:278.

29. Committee Report to House, 27 November 1812, *ASPNA* 14:275–276.

Chapter Ten
1813 — A More Sober Time
(pages 185–209)

1. Frank L. Owsley, Jr., "Paul Hamilton," in Paolo E. Coletta, ed., *American Secretaries of the Navy*, 2 vols. (Annapolis, 1980), 1:93–98; Charles O. Paullin, *History of Naval Administration, 1775–1911* (Annapolis, 1968), 138; Craig L. Symonds, *Navalists and Antinavalists* (Newark, 1980), 174–185.

2. Irving Brant, *James Madison*, 6 vols. (Indianapolis, 1941–1961), 6:126.

3. Frank L. Owsley, Jr., "William Jones," 1:101–109; Edward K. Eckert, *The Navy Department in the War of 1812* (Gainesville, 1973).

4. *ASPNA*, 14:285–286; *Statutes at Large*, 2:821.

5. John Philips Cranwell and William Bowers Crane, *Men of Marque: A A History of Private Armed Vessels out of Baltimore During the War of 1812* (New

York, 1940), 25–26; Charles Stewart to SecNav, 10 February 1813, LRSC; *Charles Gordon to SecNav,* 16 February 1813, LRSCM.

6. Joshua Keene's Notebook, HM 593, Henry Huntington Library; Albert Gleaves, *Captain James Lawrence, U.S. Navy: Commander of the Chesapeake* (New York, 1904), 126–132.

7. David Porter, *Journal of a Cruise Made to the Pacific Ocean in the United States Frigate Essex . . . ,* 2 vols. in 1 (New York, 1822, 2nd ed.), 69. The best secondary account of the voyage is David Long, *Nothing Too Daring . . .* (Annapolis, 1970), 71–174.

8. *Journal,* 1:70.

9. The nine major islands of the Galápagos have both Spanish and English names. Porter used their English names: Abington (Pinta); Bindloe (Marchena); Narborough (Fernandina); Albemarle (Isabella); James (San Salvador); Indefatigable (Santa Cruz); Charles (Santa Maria); Chatham (San Cristobal); and Hood (Española).

10. *Journal,* 1:127, 130, 136.

11. *Journal,* 1:237.

12. Long, *Nothing Too Daring,* 109–110.

13. *Journal,* 2:59–60, 61.

14. *Journal,* 2:137.

15. Tobias Lear to Charles D. Coxe, 6 May 1807, *DBW,* 6:520; *Journal,* 2:44.

16. *Journal,* 2:167.

17. SecNav to Nicholas Fisk, 15 May 1813, LSSM.

18. William B. Gaines, "Craney Island: or Norfolk Delivered," *Virginia Cavalcade,* 1 (1951):32.

19. John Rodgers to SecNav, 3 March 1813, LRSC.

20. John Rodgers to SecNav, 22 April 1813, LRSC.

21. James Lawrence to SecNav, 18 May 1813, LRSC.

22. V. Allan, "Duel of the Frigates," *Blackwoods,* 292 (July 1962):42–43.

23. SecNav to Samuel Evans, 6 May 1813, AF.

24. Gleaves, *Captain James Lawrence,* 169.

25. There are numerous accounts of the *Chesapeake-Shannon* duel. See: Gleaves, *Captain James Lawrence,* passim; H. J. P. Garbett, "The Shannon and the Chesapeake," Royal United Service Institute *Journal,* 57 (June 1913):797–802; the first official American report was William Bainbridge to SecNav, 2 June 1813, LRSC.

26. Lawrence was actually buried three times. He was first laid to rest at Halifax. Following that, a group of Salem merchants went to Nova Scotia under a flag of truce and brought the body back to Salem for interment. Lawrence was later moved to his third and final resting place in New York City.

27. Journal of Surgeon James Iderwick kept on board U.S.S. *Argus,* New York Public Library; Wilbur E. Apgar, "The Last Cruise of the U.S. Brig *Argus,*" United States Naval Institute *Proceedings,* 65 (1939):653–660.

28. Fritz H. Jordan, "The *Enterprise* and the *Boxer*," *Collections and Proceedings of the Maine Historical Society*, 1 (April 1890):103–111; Carlos Hanks, "Gun Brigs off Pemaquid," United States Naval Institute *Proceedings*, 62 (1936):371–372; William A. Baker, *Maritime History of Bath, Maine, and the Kennebec Region*, 2 vols. (Bath, 1973), 1:197–198.

## Chapter Eleven
## Perry and Macdonough
## (pages 210–240)

1. A. T. Mahan, *Sea Power in Its Relations to the War of 1812*, 2 vols. (New York, 1968, repr.), 1:29.

2. SecWar to Congress, 23 December 1811, *ASPNA*.

3. Among the officers assigned to Woolsey was a young midshipman, James Fenimore Cooper. James Franklin Beard, ed., *The Letters and Journals of James Fenimore Cooper*, 6 vols. (Cambridge, 1960), 1:14.

4. John K. Mahon, *The War of 1812* (Gainesville, 1972), 43–54. Mahon provides an excellent bibliography for the war, 429–449.

5. Frank H. Severance, "Career of Daniel Dobbins," *Publications of the Buffalo Historical Society*, 8 (1905):262–263; C. W. Goldsborough to Daniel Dobbins, 15 September 1812, LSSM.

6. Isaac Chauncey to SecNav, 3 September 1812, 24 September 1812, and 26 September 1812, LRSC; SecNav to Jesse Elliott, 4 September 1812, LSSO; Jesse Elliott to Isaac Chauncey, 14 September 1812, LRSC; Jesse Elliott to Daniel Dobbins, 2 October 1812, and Dobbins to Elliott, 11 October 1812, both quoted in Clarence S. Metcalf, "Daniel Dobbins, Sailing Master, U.S.N.: Commodore Perry's Right Hand Man," *Inland Seas*, 14 (Summer, Fall, 1958):95.

7. Isaac Chauncey to SecNav, 8 October 1812, LRSC.

8. Jesse Elliott to SccNav, 9 October 1812, LRSC.

9. An excellent secondary source for the events on Lake Ontario is Ernest A. Cruikshank, "The Contest for the Command of Lake Ontario in 1812 and 1813," *Proceedings and Transactions of the Royal Society of Canada*, 3rd series, 10 (Sept. 1917):161–223, and Cruikshank, "The Contest . . . in 1914," *Ontario Historical Society Papers*, 11 (1924):99–159.

10. Isaac Chauncey to SecNav, 13 November 1812 and 17 November 1812, LRSC.

11. SecNav to Isaac Chauncey, 26 January 1813, LSSO.

12. Quoted in Cruikshank, "The Contest for the Command of Lake Ontario in 1812 and 1813," 167.

13. General Order, 22 April 1813, William Wood, ed., *Select British Documents of the Canadian War of 1812*, 3 vols. (Toronto, 1923, repr. 1968), 2:81–84; Commission Appointing Sir J. L. Yeo Commander of the Naval Forces in the Lakes of Canada, 19 March 1813, Wood, 1:77–78.

14. Andrew Gray to Sir Roger Sheaffe, 29 May 1813, Wood, ed., *Select British Documents*, 2:113.

15. Isaac Chauncey to SecNav, 2 June 1813, LRSC.

16. Mahon, *War of 1812*, 149–151.

17. Unlike Yeo, Chauncey had strong support from his superiors. SecNav to Isaac Chauncey, 16 January 1813, LSSO.

18. There are two nearly contemporary biographies of Perry, which need to be read in tandem: James Fenimore Cooper, *Lives of Distinguished American Naval Officers*, 2 vols. (Philadelphia, 1846), vol. 2, and Alexander S. Mackenzie, *Life of Oliver Hazard Perry*, 2 vols. (New York, 1840).

19. Oliver Hazard Perry to SecNav, 29 January 1812, LRSCM; Perry to SecNav, 11 February 1813, LRSCM.

20. "The Remarkable Statement of Noah Brown," *Journal of American History*, 8 (January 1914):103–108.

21. Perry to Chauncey, 27 July 1813, LRSCM; Chauncey to Perry, 30 July 1813, LRSCM. It is estimated that 25 percent of Perry's force was composed of black seamen. Robert J. Dodge, "The Struggle for Control of Lake Erie," *Northwest Ohio Quarterly*, 36 (1964):26.

22. Quoted in Pierre Berton, *Flames Across the Border* (Boston, 1981), 149.

23. Perry to SecNav, 4 August 1813, LRSCM.

24. For the British side concerning affairs on Lake Erie, see Wood, ed., *Select British Documents*, vol. 2.

25. These figures are taken from Theodore Roosevelt, *The Naval War of 1812*, 2 vols. (New York, 1882), 1:309–310. Various sources are likely to give slightly different figures. The Americans used pivot guns, that is, weapons that could be directed to either side.

26. General Orders, 24 November 1813, Wood, ed., *Select British Documents*, 2:296.

27. Elliott's behavior at the battle became the subject for much invective and bitterness in the years following. James Fenimore Cooper became Elliott's chief defender.

28. After Perry's victory, in the summer of 1814, the Americans moved against the British at Michilmackinac. The venture failed and cost the Americans two vessels, *Tigress* and *Scorpion*, both formerly with Perry. W. H. Breithaupt, "Some Facts About the Schooner *Nancy* in the War of 1812," *Ontario Historical Papers*, 23 (1926):5–7.

29. *Hamilton* and *Scourge* went to the bottom virtually intact. One of the survivors, Ned Myers, later told his entire life history to James Fenimore Cooper. From this Cooper wrote *Ned Myers; or a Life Before the Mast* (Philadelphia, 1843), in which there is a vivid account of the sinking.

In 1971 the Royal Ontario Museum at Toronto commissioned a search for the two schooners. With the aid of very sophisticated underwater equipment, the vessels were found. They are in a remarkable state of preservation. See Daniel A. Nelson, "*Hamilton* and *Scourge*: Ghost Ships of the War of 1812," *National Geographic* (March 1983), 289–310.

30. Cruikshank, 209–211.

31. Quoted in Mahan, *War of 1812*, 2:52–53.

32. Mahan, *War of 1812*, 2:52.

33. In the Chesapeake a gunboat flotilla commanded by Captain Joshua Barney was burned on 22 August 1814 to avoid capture. During the New Orleans campaign, American gunboats and other small craft performed valuable service by harassing and delaying the British advance toward the city. In the end they were destroyed.

34. Quoted in Rodney Macdonough, "The Hero of Lake Champlain's Great Naval Battle," *Vermonter*, 2 (April 1897):153.

35. Daniel D. Tompkins to John Bullus, 13 July 1812, AF.

36. Charles G. Muller, "Commodore and Mrs. Thomas Macdonough," *Delaware History*, 9 (1960/61):343.

37. Thomas Everard to George Prevost, 3 August 1813, Wood, ed., *Select British Documents*, 2:234.

38. "Remarkable Statement of Noah Brown," 107.

39. Wood, ed., *Select British Documents*, 1:116.

40. British activity can best be followed in Wood, ed., *Select British Documents*, 3:334–498.

41. Downie to Pring, 10 September 1814, Wood, ed., *Select British Documents*, 1:123–124.

42. For tonnage and crews of both American and British fleets, figures are taken from Roosevelt, *The Naval War of 1812*, 2:116, 119. Armament figures for the American fleet are from Thomas Macdonough to SecNav, 11 September 1814. Those for the British are from Court Martial Proceedings, Lieutenant Robertson's Statement, Wood, ed., *Select British Documents*, 3:476. Columbiads were "cast-metal homogeneous, smoothbore . . . cannon that fired a 50-pound shot about 600 yards." Mark Mayo Boatner, *The Civil War Dictionary* (New York, 1959), q.v.

43. The plans for both sides, as well as the actual combat, can be followed in the numerous firsthand and secondary accounts. The only real controversy arising grew out of the role of Prevost. The documents in Wood, ed., *Select British Documents*, 3:334–498, particularly those relating to the court-martial, are most revealing.

44. Quoted in William R. Folsom, "The Battle of Plattsburg," *Vermont Quarterly*, 20:253.

45. Thomas Macdonough to SecNav, 11 September 1814.

46. Proceedings of Court Martial, 18–21 August 1815, Wood, ed., *Select British Documents*, 3:401–402.

Chapter Twelve
1814 — The War Ends
(pages 241–260)

1. Edward K. Eckert, "Early Reform in the Navy Department," *American Neptune*, 33:233–234; for a brief biography of Jones, see Eckert, "William Jones: Mr. Madison's Secretary of the Navy," *PMHB* (April 1972), 167–182.

2. Gallatin had gone abroad as minister to Russia.

3. *Statutes at Large*, 2:789, 821.

4. John Rodgers to SecNav, 20 February 1814, LRSC; Charles O. Paullin, *Commodore John Rodgers* (Annapolis, 1967), 272–273.

5. Charles Stewart to SecNav, 8 April 1814, LRSC. There are numerous secondary accounts of the cruise. The best is Tyrone G. Martin, *A Most Fortunate Ship* (Chester, 1980), 141–150.

6. Lewis Warrington to SecNav, 12 March 1814, 29 March 1814, 29 April 1814 and 4 May 1814, LRSCM.

7. Warrington to SecNav, 1 June 1814 and 30 October 1814, LRSCM.

8. This of course is the same *Hornet* that captured H.M.S. *Peacock*, for whom the American vessel was named. The best and most recent biography of Biddle is David F. Long, *Sailor Diplomat: A Biography of Commander James Biddle, 1783–1848* (Boston, 1983).

9. The store ship *Macedonian*, not to be confused with the frigate of the same name, is not mentioned again. Her fate is unknown.

10. Quoted in P. S. P. Conner, "The *Hornet*'s Sting and Wing," *New England Magazine*, 28:271.

11. Lewis Warrington to SecNav, 2 November 1815, LRSCM.

12. William Johnson, "Biographical Sketch of Capt. Johnston Blakely," *North Carolina University Magazine*, 3:1–3.

13. Johnston Blakely to SecNav, 8 July 1814, AF.

14. Blakely to SecNav, 11 September 1814, AF; Blakely to Midshipman David Geisinger, 22 September 1814, AF.

15. *Naval Chronicle*, 32:243–245.

16. Even more distressing was the alleged treasonous behavior on the part of some of the New London citizens. In a letter to the secretary, Decatur described the situation: "Some few nights since the weather promised an opportunity for this squadron to get to sea, and it was said on shore that we intended to make the attempt. In the course of the evening, two blue lights were burnt on both points at the harbor's mouth, as signals to the enemy, and there is no doubt but they have, by signals and otherwise, instantaneous information of our movements." Stephen Decatur to SecNav, 20 December 1813.

17. Minutes of the Action Between the U.S. Frigate *Constitution* and H.M. Ships *Cyane* and *Levant* . . . AF.

18. Ralph D. Paine, *Joshua Barney: A Forgotten War Hero of Blue Water* (New York, 1924), 345–367; for an analysis of the role of gunboats in the War of 1812, see Dean R. Mayhew, "Jeffersonian Gunboats in the War of 1812," *American Neptune*, 42:101–117.

19. Reginald Horsman, "Nantucket's Peace Treaty with England in 1814," *New England Quarterly*, 54:180.

20. Quoted in Alfred T. Mahan, *Sea Power in Its Relation to the War of 1812*, 2 vols. (New York, 1968, repr.), 2:353.

21. Mahan, 2:353.

22. "Account of Operations Against New Orleans," *Naval Chronicle*, 33:484–488.

23. Reed McC. B. Adams, "New Orleans and the War of 1812," *Louisiana Historical Quarterly*, 17:349–350.

Chapter Thirteen
Unfinished Business and Peace
(pages 261–264)

1. Joshua Barney to Commodore Jacob Lewis, 23 January 1815, Box 8, Crowninshield Papers, Peabody Museum of Salem.

2. SecNav to Senate, 16 November 1814, *ASPNA*, 14:320.

3. *ASPNA*, 14:354.

# Bibliography

Naval scholars are blessed (or cursed?) with a wealth of materials. In my own case, the documentation found throughout the text provides the best indication of my bibliographic sources; however, certain materials need special mention.

Before one launches into naval history, seven very important bibliographies ought to be consulted: Robert G. Albion, *Naval and Maritime History, an Annotated Bibliography* (Mystic, 1972); Myron J. Smith, *The American Navy, 1789–1860* (Metuchen, 1974); Robert W. Neeser, *Statistical and Chronological History of the United States Navy, 1775–1907*, 2 vols. (New York, 1974 repr.); John C. Fredriksen, *War of 1812 Resource Guide* (Los Angeles, 1979); Paolo E. Coletta, *A Bibliography of American Naval History* (Annapolis, 1981); published periodically, Charles R. Schultz, compiler, *Bibliography of Maritime and Naval History Periodical Articles Published 1976–1977* (Sea Grant Program, Texas A and M University, 1979); and finally, Naval History Division Department of the Navy, *United States Naval History, A Bibliography* (Washington, 1972).

Luckily for the scholar, the United States Navy both made and kept records. These mounds of documents are now available at the National Archives and can be purchased on microfilm. Collectively, this series is known as Naval Records Collection of the Office of Naval Records and Library, Record Group 45. Altogether, they comprise more than 2,700 rolls of microfilm, covering the years 1790 to 1910.

While the Naval Records provides the main corpus of manuscripts consulted, other, smaller collections were also used. These generally fall into the category of personal papers, such as those located at the Mystic Seaport, the Maryland Historical Society, and the Massachusetts Historical Society.

Published source material for this period abounds. *The American State Papers*, 38 vols. (Washington, 1832–61), publish key documents relating to the First through Twenty-fifth Congresses. Class VI of these papers are naval documents, but pertinent materials may be found among the other series as well. Of considerable use also is James D. Richardson, compiler, *Messages and*

*Papers of the Presidents, 1789–1908*, 10 vols. (Washington, 1908). The published papers of the first four presidents were also consulted.

A valuable source of original documents, particularly for the lake campaigns, is William Wood, ed., *Select British Documents of the Canadian War*, 3 vols. (New York, 1968, repr.). These were originally published by the Champlain Society in 1920.

Those of lesser rank were less likely to write, and often what they did write was not preserved. Aside from the official reports found in Record Group 45, there are a few gems. Chief among these is David Porter's *Journal of a Cruise Made to the Pacific Ocean* (New York, 1822, 2nd ed.). There are literally hundreds of other contemporary accounts, many of them self-serving, written by participants in the various battles. The most valuable source for contemporary British opinion is *The Naval Chronicle*, 40 vols. (London, 1799–1818). Other sources are listed in Smith, *The American Navy*.

There are several general histories of the navy, many of them quite good, which provide an overview of the period. Among these I found most useful Dudley W. Knox, *A History of the United States Navy* (New York, 1948, revised ed.), and Fletcher Pratt, *The Navy: A History* (Garden City, 1941). More specific histories of the navy during this period were also consulted. These included: Marshall Smelser, *The Congress Founds the Navy* (South Bend, 1959); Gardner W. Allen, *Our Naval War with France* (Boston, 1909); Gardner W. Allen, *Our Navy and the Barbary Corsairs* (Boston, 1905); Theodore Roosevelt, *The Naval War of 1812: The History of the United States Navy During the Last War with Great Britain to Which Is Appended an Account of the Battle of New Orleans*, 2 vols. (New York, 1910); Glenn Tucker, *Dawn Like Thunder: The Barbary Wars and the Birth of the U.S. Navy* (Indianapolis, 1963); and Alfred T. Mahan, *Sea Power in Its Relations to the War of 1812*, 2 vols. (New York, 1968, repr.).

In addition to naval histories of the period, several military, diplomatic, and institutional studies are worth knowing about. One of the most recent in the first category is Pierre Berton, *Flames Across the Border: The Canadian-American Tragedy, 1813–14* (Boston, 1981). Another recent book in the same genre is John K. Mahon, *The War of 1812* (Gainesville, 1972).

Good diplomatic studies are not as abundant as military and naval ones. For the Quasi War, the best is Alexander De Conde, *The Quasi-War: The Politics and Diplomacy of the Undeclared War with France, 1797–1801* (New York, 1966). For the events leading to the War of 1812, Bradford Perkins, *Prologue to War: England and the United States, 1805–1812* (Berkeley, 1961), is an excellent source and should be supplemented by Julius W. Pratt, *Expansionists of 1812* (New York, 1925).

Two classic institutional studies of the period, and ones that remain useful, are both by the same author, Leonard D. White, *Federalists: A Study in Administrative History, 1789–1801* (New York, 1948) and *The Jeffersonians: A Study in Administrative History, 1801–1829* (New York, 1951). A particularly able study of naval policy in this era should also be examined: Craig L. Symonds, *Naval-*

*ists and Antinavalists: The Naval Policy Debate in the United States, 1785–1827* (Newark, 1980). In this latter category must also be listed two multivolume histories of this period, general in nature and quite old, but still indispensable: Henry Adams, *History of the United States During the Administrations of Thomas Jefferson and James Madison*, 9 vols. (New York, 1889–1891), and Edward Channing, *A History of the United States*, 6 vols. (New York, 1905–1925).

Last in this very select list, I must mention biographies. These range all the way from the very excellent to the absurd, from hagiography to character assassination. Two current naval scholars have made important contributions to the quality of work in this area. David Long, *Nothing Too Daring: A Biography of Commodore David Porter, 1780–1843* (Annapolis, 1970), and Christopher McKee, *Edward Preble: A Naval Biography* (Annapolis, 1972), are both to be emulated. Many other reasonably good biographies done in this century might also be read to the scholar's benefit. The older the biography, the more suspect; those produced in the nineteenth century have a tendency to be more polemic than history.

# Index

Bainbridge, William—*Continued*
63–64; in Mediterranean
squadron, 66, 67; commands
*Philadelphia*, 86; takes *Mirboka*,
86–87; at Gilbraltar, 89; block-
ades Tripoli, 93–94; surrenders *Philadelphia*, 94–95;
POW, 95; on mission to
Hamet, 114–15; ransomed,
120; calls for court of inquiry,
120–21; squadron under,
176–78; commands *Constitution*, 177; early career of, 177;
cruising Brazil coast, 179–80;
takes *Java*, 180–82; commands
navy yard, 243; and war
against Algiers, 263, 264
Ball, Sir Alexander John, 98
*Ballard*, 236
Baltimore: blockaded, 208; British assault on, 253, 255
*Baltimore*, 37, 41
Barataria, 259
Barbary States, 4–5, 64–81; *see
also specific states, for example:*
Algiers; Morocco; Tunis
*Barclay*, 191, 194
Barclay, Robert Heriot, 217,
219, 220, 223–24; early career
of, 224; campaign at Lake
Erie, 224–28; squadron of,
226, 227; surrenders, 228
Barney, Joshua, 23, 24, 253, 255,
261
Barreault, Citizen, 44
Barron, James, 75, 120
Barron, Samuel, 66, 67, 117; re-
places Preble, 111; joins Preble
off Tripoli, 113; sick, 113,
114; and Eaton campaign,
118, 119; passes command to
Rodgers, 119, 121; and gunboat building, 143; and
*Chesapeake*, 151–55; court
martial, 156

Barry, John, 1, 2, 20, 22–23, 34,
35, 83; appointment, 23–24;
West Indies command, 39, 46,
47
Bavarian Republic, 117
Beaussier, Bonaventure, 102,
110, 149
*Beckwith*, 237
Beckwith, Sir Sidney, 202
*Bellona*, 153
*Belvidera*, 168–69
Berkeley, G. C., 153, 154
Bermuda, 167
*Betsey*, 4–5
Bickerton, Sir Richard, 98
Biddle, James, 246, 248
Bingham, Arthur, 159
Black Rock, 213, 215, 219, 225
Black seamen, 129–30
Blagge, John, 24
Blake, Joshua, 108, 115
Blakely, Johnston: early career
of, 249; commands *Wasp*, 249;
takes *Reindeer*, 249; sinks
*Avon*, 250; takes *Atlanta*, 250;
disappears at sea, 250
Blockade, British, 165, 168, 187,
208–9, 243, 251, 253; *see also*
Coastal defenses
*Blucher*, 237
Blyth, Samuel, 207–8
Board of Inspection, 262
Boatswain's mates, 130
Bomb ketches, 103, 104, 107
*Bonhomme Richard*, 23
*Bonne Citoyenne*, 179–80
*Borer*, 236
Boston, 165, 175, 203
*Boston*, 50, 70
*Boxer*, 207–8, 249
Brazil, 178–80
Breakfast on ships, 136
*Broke*, 232
Broke, Philip Vere, 169, 204–6
Brown, Adam, 222, 234

|  | DATE DUE |  |
|---|---|---|
| NOV 18 '91 |  |  |
| DEC 18 '91 |  |  |
| JAN 27 '92 |  |  |
| JUN 03 |  |  |
| AG |  |  |
|  |  |  |
|  |  |  |
|  |  |  |
|  |  |  |
|  |  |  |